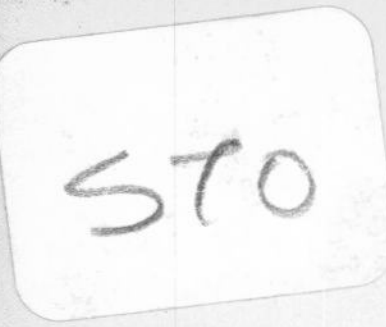
STO

2-19-64

THE POLITICS AND ECONOMICS OF EUROPEAN INTEGRATION

THE POLITICS AND ECONOMICS OF EUROPEAN INTEGRATION

BRITAIN, EUROPE, AND THE UNITED STATES

U. W. KITZINGER

FREDERICK A. PRAEGER, *Publisher*
New York • London

FOR L. K.

"Working at the edge of the development of human society is to work on the brink of the unknown."

DAG HAMMARSKJÖLD

FREDERICK A. PRAEGER, PUBLISHER
64 UNIVERSITY PLACE, NEW YORK 3, N.Y., U.S.A.
77–79 CHARLOTTE STREET, LONDON W. 1, ENGLAND

Published in the United States of America in 1963
by Frederick A. Praeger, Inc., Publisher

Library of Congress Catalog Card Number: 63:9811

THE POLITICS AND ECONOMICS OF EUROPEAN INTEGRATION is an extensively revised and expanded edition of a book previously published in Great Britain by Basil Blackwell under the title THE CHALLENGE OF THE COMMON MARKET.

Printed in the United States of America

Preface

This book is concerned with the transcendence of power politics in international life. It explores one attempt at regulating international affairs by common rules made together in the common interest—indeed the most notable attempt of this kind since the United Nations itself.

This book tries to analyze the peculiar features of the European Community and to speculate on its potential lines of further development; but it also seeks to distill from this European experience lessons for international relations as a whole. President De Gaulle's challenge may for the moment have arrested both President Kennedy's Grand Design and the European Community on which it was so largely based; but this only means we may have to envisage (as is done in the last chapter) a less intensive but far more extensive application of the Community technique. Indeed, the signing of the test-ban agreement in July, 1963, may in due course open up prospects for functional cooperation even far beyond the area most of us would have thought possible some years ago.

Such developments cannot be confidently expected, but they can be realistically worked for step by step: optimism may be unjustified, but idealism never. This book began not as a work of prophecy, but as a pamphlet for action, and if the fulfillment of its aims is delayed, that only reinforces the urgency of its theme.

U. W. K.

The Toby House
Freeland, Oxfordshire
August, 1963

CONTENTS

I

Mainsprings of the European Movement 1945–57

Ideals and Realities

The political impetus for the unification of Europe effectively dates from the closing stages of the war. Those were the years when leading statesmen all over the world, following the principles laid down in the Allies' war aims, sought to create a far stronger League of Nations, a United Nations, even a Federation of the World. Shocked by the legal and illegal crimes against humanity which they had witnessed in the previous decade both in the prewar dictatorships and during the war itself, appalled by the vast problems of hunger and want facing every part of the world at the end of that conflict, the World Federalist movement took as its main aim the abolition of physical force as a method of diplomacy, the abatement or abolition of the national sovereignty without which international war is impossible, and the creation of a body of international law in the full sense of the term, pronounced and sanctioned by a World Federal Authority.

The San Francisco Conference of 1944 did not fulfill these hopes. It produced a United Nations which has certainly shown itself stronger than the old League, but is still not even a confederation of states, let alone a world government. Its General Assembly remains an assembly of governments exercising their sovereignty—not one of representatives of the people deliberating in common for the common good. The final contradiction of the dreams of the war years was to be found in the national right to disobedience of any U.N. majority decision, formally recognized by the right of veto given to the five nations then regarded as big. So the hopes for a world government were dashed to the ground.

By 1947, it was clear that more intensive international cooperation was possible only on a less extensive front. A tighter bond could only be forged between a smaller number of nations. Failing progress on a world scale, the countries of Europe (for which the federalists in Europe felt they had the most immediate responsibility) were to set an example to the world. For some idealists at least, European unity was thus not simply a regionalist approach for its own sake but a pilot project for something to come on a wider scale: Any abdication of sovereignty, even on a regional basis, seemed better than allowing the nation-state to consolidate itself once more after its great moral and material bankruptcy.

It was in Britain in particular that the World Federalist strain was intertwined with the ideal of European federation. The result was not entirely happy. Since federalists were among the most active in postwar relief and in international meetings, Europeans (who cannot always tell an English crank from a normal Englishman) overestimated their strength in Britain. The moral absolutism and salvationist dogma of many of the early postwar federalists stemmed from their belief that federalism was a technical prerequisite for translating the Sermon on the Mount into practice in the twentieth century. But because in their preoccupation with ultimate aims many federalists were classified as starry-eyed, British observers were tempted to write off the federalists on the continent as equally cranky and unrepresentative. For a very long time British policy was affected by this image of federalists as outsiders who were not to be taken quite seriously: All the greater was British surprise when they did succeed in pulling off some of their curious plans.

There was a profound difference in outlook and psychology on the two sides of the Channel. In her finest hour Britain had stood alone. She was undefeated, she escaped occupation, she had not known bitter internal cleavages, she had no feelings of guilt, but came through with greater self-confidence, greater pride in her national virtues and national institutions than she had known for years. The Continent, on the other hand, had just passed through the worst ordeal of its history. Almost every family had experienced the evils of nationalism run riot, almost every country had been subjected first to national defeat and then to enemy occupation. Their national self-confidence, their national institutions had been shattered. Starting from the ruins, it was imperative to develop new conceptions and more grandiose ideas that would make any future civil war between European brother nations impossible. In continental Europe, a federal surrender of sovereignty thus seemed more feasible than in many less disillusioned parts of the globe.

Common opposition to the Hitler regime had brought resistance fighters and exile governments of different nationalities closer together: against Hitler's New Order for a united Europe under Nazi domination, the men from the *maquis* and the underground movements set an alternative ideal. As the European Resistance Movement declared in July, 1944: "Federal Union alone can ensure the preservation of liberty and civilization on the continent of Europe, bring about economic recovery, and enable the German people to play a peaceful role in European affairs." For, if common fear of a third wave of German aggression seemed a bond that could unite many nations for some time, the more far-sighted also knew that it would be impossible to discriminate against Germany forever. Any such attempt would fail and breed just what it was designed to prevent. If German policy was to be subjected to international controls, and if Germany was to be an equal member in the European family of nations, then there was only one way out of the dilemma—other nations must abdicate to supranational bodies the same measure of sovereignty which they intended Germany never to regain.

Indeed, the memories of the last enemy soon became less real than the fear of a new aggressor. Armed Soviet Communism had advanced to the Elbe and beyond, and French and Italian Communism was showing its strength in parliamentary and direct action as far as the Channel and the Pyrenees. The year 1948 saw the Communist *coup* in Prague and the beginning of the Berlin blockade. In the face of this immediate common threat of terrifying proportions, national differences loomed less large, and the unstable politics of certain countries could be buttressed by being contained in a broader-based framework. Only common defense, a common front in foreign policy, and political solidarity at home seemed capable of allowing free Europe to survive the new pressures applied to it from within as well as from without.

To support the common defense effort, and to ward off the threat of subversion from within, it was moreover essential to reconstruct the devastated economies of Europe as quickly and as efficiently as possible, and only common efforts could make the best use of the scant resources available. When the American Secretary of State, George Marshall, offered Europe vast economic aid for a joint recovery program, he was facing the economic side of this challenge. The North Atlantic Treaty of 1949 (setting up NATO) institutionalized a strategic integration which was to become so close-knit with the years that important decisions in this vital field can less and less be taken or implemented by any national government alone without causing severe strains to the whole alliance. The economic and the military spheres were thereafter to be the two in which joint action was regarded as essential by all the West European countries. But in the eyes of many people, such action itself entailed joint political institutions; without such institutions, it was argued, democratically elected parliaments and governments were surrendering their powers and duties only to irresponsible technocrats beyond the electorate's control.

Open Differences and Latent Ambivalence

Here then, the "functionalists," most strongly represented by the British and Scandinavian governments, parted company with the "federalists," who were well represented in the governments of France, Italy, and the Low Countries. It was the hallmark of the federalist that he sought joint action not least as a means for obtaining more effective common political institutions, whereas the functionalist attempted to set up such a minimum of political institutions as might be indispensable to direct the joint action that was most urgently required. While the federalist may be accused of concentrating excessively on legal formalities, the functionalist may have underrated the handicap imposed on effective everyday cooperation by the survival of national vetoes. Federalists and functionalists in the late 1940's failed fully to understand each other, and the federalists—not by accident, but for good historical reasons—were able to sway the policy of six and only six of the countries of Western Europe.

The conflict between federalists and functionalists was thus to mark the whole history of postwar Europe. But there were divergencies even within the federalist camp. The United States' insistence on European cooperation had been one of the conditions of Marshall Aid. The United States was welcomed as an ally by most of those who sought to unite Europe; yet they were far from united on the policy which Europe was to pursue toward the United States once it had been united. The desire for European unity as such was thus, in fact, neutral between two sets of correlative political and economic concepts.

Political unity was advocated as tending to enhance European freedom of movement—whether toward a more equal partnership within a strong Atlantic alliance or whether toward a more independent position in the world as a third force. Whichever way that decision might go, only unity, it was argued, could make it effective.

There was a parallel ambivalence or mixture of economic aims. Economic unity, with its advantages of larger markets and greater specialization of production, was advocated as a means of redressing the balance of dollar payments. But for some the first objective was to form a regional bloc embracing only Europe and the countries associated with it overseas, while others saw the discriminatory removal of economic barriers (between the countries of Europe, but not against the rest of the world) as a tactical move to strengthen the economies of Europe for full convertibility and nondiscriminatory trading relationships with the whole world.

"Third-force" and regionalist concepts in particular were linked closely with a further concern. The rise of the countries of Asia and Africa to a new influence and a new power in world affairs occupied much of federalist thought. Their idealization of European tradition forced many European federalists to take a gloomy view of this imminent shift in the constellation of world power. European political unity would not stem the tide. But some (particularly French circles) hoped it would at least buttress the "civilizing presence" of Europe overseas, while others, faced with the same situation at one remove, felt unity was desperately needed to rehabilitate Europe morally in the eyes of world opinion and to mark the abandonment of the national concept by the very nations that had served as the model for nationalism overseas. Given the rate of expansion of the Afro-Asian countries, economic unity might not keep European resources ahead of the resources available to Afro-Asian countries for very long, but it might produce a margin of economic maneuver that would allow Europe to provide more aid to those countries and thereby cushion and guide even as it accelerated their progress to positions of world power.

The European movement also cut across domestic political fronts. Economic unity was advocated by free-trade liberals who wished to diminish the impact of political boundaries and the influence of national governments on economic life. Yet among its foremost champions there were also those who regarded the national economy as too small an entity for effective planning, and who strove to set up supranational authorities to direct production and trade on a vaster international scale. In the field of industry, the European Communities broadly subscribe to a system of full competition; in the fields of atomic energy and agriculture, on the other hand, planning and the more restrictive agricultural interests seem to have triumphed.

Even the historic cleavage of clericals and anticlericals was bridged by the European idea. Certainly three of the men in the van of the movement were devout Catholics born in Lothair's middle kingdom, an area where the liberal conception of the world and its denizens as naturally divisible into neat nation-states appears unsophisticated in the extreme: Robert Schuman, a German during World War I, Prime Minister of France; Alcide de Gasperi, a Deputy in the Vienna Diet while Austria-Hungary was at war with Italy, Prime Minister of Italy; and Konrad

Adenauer, the noncombatant anti-Prussian mayor of Cologne who flirted with the idea of separating the Rhineland from Prussia after World War I. To them, the restoration of Charlemagne's empire of a thousand years before, with the cultural unity it implied, had an emotional appeal. But the stalwarts of the movement came also from the ranks of the anticlerical Left, organized, in the early postwar years, in the Socialist Movement for a United States of Europe. The Socialist Paul-Henri Spaak, a former Belgian Prime Minister, provided the personal driving force in the drafting of the Rome Treaties, and the French Socialist leader Guy Mollet was Prime Minister during the critical phases of the Common Market negotiations and secured the votes of 100 out of the 101 French Socialist deputies in favor of their ratification.

The European idea was thus originally neutral in foreign policy between a third-force concept and the Atlantic alliance, undecided in trade policy between regionalism and multilateralism, ambivalent in its attitude to the problems of emergent nations in Africa and Asia, silent in cultural and educational matters between Catholicism and anticlericalism, and neutral also in economic policy between *laissez-faire* liberalism and socialist planning. Approached from very diverse points of view, European unity seemed to make sense to Continental leaders, to small but highly articulate pressure groups, and to many of the war and postwar generation: It would give greater scope to Europe for whatever policy aims were envisaged. A sudden realization of Continental federation could have produced sharp conflicts between federalists over the use to which unity was to be put; as it was, the long common struggle and the course of postwar events softened the contrasts of ultimate aim and produced not merely international but also interparty understanding. Only the Communists in every parliament of the Six consistently voted against integration.

The Birth of "The Six": The "Sector Approach"

The year of Prague and of the Berlin blockade saw two beginnings made in the organization of Western Europe: the Convention for European Economic Cooperation, signed in April, 1948, and the Hague Congress in the following month. The first set up the Organization for European Economic Cooperation (OEEC) as a functional, intergovernmental body to assure the distribution of Marshall Aid funds, to coordinate investment programs, and to see that trade started moving again between the countries of Western Europe. The Hague Congress, on the other hand, was the first big demonstration by the federalists and their sympathizers. Men like Churchill, Ramadier, Adenauer, Reynaud, van Zeeland, and Hallstein called for the economic and political integration of Western Europe and for a deliberative assembly of European parliamentarians. As a result of their pressure, they obtained the first official political institution of a united Europe: the Council of Europe, inaugurated in Strasbourg in 1949.

The Council of Europe consists of two political organs: a Committee of Ministers (usually the foreign ministers of the member states), most of whose major decisions require a unanimous vote; and a Consultative Assembly of Representatives (almost always national members of parliament) appointed by the parliament or government of each country, free to harmonize views and frame recommendations on all but defense matters, but without any legislative power and without any executive responsible to it. This Assembly did, however, serve as the great forum in which the future shape of a united Europe was debated, in which leading European parliamentarians could meet with each other, and in which, above all, the federalists could formulate their next tactical aims and exercise pressure to translate them into reality.

Impatient of the purely consultative role of their Assembly, the federalists called for a supranational authority with "limited functions but real powers." Throughout 1949, and above all 1950, the Consultative Assembly pressed for the revision of its own Statute in order to allow for at least a minimal federal authority to be set up in Europe. They failed largely because of the attitude of the United Kingdom. Britain, under the Labour Government, was concerned about the loss of economic sovereignty and the right to plan its economy in a Europe which might be predominantly nonsocialist. Many Continental federalists were deceived by Churchill's oratory, and bitterly disappointed when, after he became Prime Minister again in 1951, Britain would make no further move. Whether under the Labour or the Conservative Government, links with the Commonwealth were regarded as precluding too close links with the countries of Europe. The traditions of British foreign policy—to hold the balance but never to become entirely involved in Europe—as

Table I

MEMBERSHIP OF ORGANIZATIONS

	NATO [1]	OEEC [2]	Council of Europe [3]	European Communities	WEU	EFTA	Population (millions, Jan., 1962)
Austria	—	X	X	—	—	X	7.1
Belgium	X	X	X	X	X	—	9.2
Denmark	X	X	X	—	—	X	4.5
Finland	—	—	—	—	—	—[5]	4.4
France	X	X	X	X	X	—	45.7
Germany	X	X	X	X	X	—	53.8
Greece	X	X	X	—[4]	—	—	8.4
Iceland	X	X	X	—	—	—	0.2
Ireland	—	X	X	—	—	—	2.8
Italy	X	X	X	X	X	—	49.5
Luxembourg	X	X	X	X	X	—	0.3
Netherlands	X	X	X	X	X	—	11.6
Norway	X	X	X	—	—	X	3.6
Portugal	X	X	—	—	—	X	9.2
Spain	—	X	—	—	—	—	30.2
Sweden	—	X	X	—	—	X	7.5
Switzerland	—	X	X	—	—	X	5.4
Turkey	X	X	X	—	—	—	28.2
United Kingdom	X	X	X	—	X	X	52.7

1. Also the U.S. and Canada, from its foundation.

2. In October, 1961, the OEEC was transformed into the Organization for Economic Cooperation and Development (OECD), and the U.S. and Canada became full members. Yugoslavia has an observer in the Organization.

3. Cyprus joined the Council of Europe in May, 1961, and Israel is represented in it by observers.

4. Greece became an Associate of the European Economic Community in November, 1962.

5. Finland became an Associate of EFTA in 1961.

well as the empirical approach, which was thought incompatible with rigid constitution-making, were all invoked against British participation in a European federation, whatever the limits of its competence. The British counterproposal was always for functional cooperation, and where Britain refused to go, the countries of Scandinavia would not go either.

The great divide came in the summer of 1950, when Robert Schuman, the French Minister for Foreign Affairs, proposed "as the first step in the federation of Europe," "to demonstrate that any war between France and Germany becomes, not merely inconceivable, but physically impossible," that "the entire Franco-German production of coal and steel be placed under a common High Authority" open to other European countries. It is not to impugn the purity of French motives to say that they were mixed: that like the whole notion of a European federation itself, the Schuman Plan arose out of a concern over Germany's revival and over economic prosperity no less than over foreign policy at large.

In the early postwar years, France had done what she could to control and limit German industrial activity in order to prevent her political resurgence in Europe. By 1950, the Americans had clearly decided against this policy, and Schuman's plan represented a startling but really quite logical *volte-face*. If the days of the discriminatory Ruhr Authority through which the occupying powers exercised their control looked as though they were numbered, a new egalitarian Community could perhaps achieve the same object on a permanent because nondiscriminatory basis. That way, far from being looked at askance by the Americans for impeding Europe's economic recovery, France would prove the champion of political union. And in giving political expression to the unity of the Pas de Calais–Saar–Ruhr industrial complex "always prescribed by geography, always prevented by history," the problems caused by a likely overproduction of French steel and by the uncertainties in the supply of Ruhr coke to French industry might be brought nearer a solution. Moreover, there was the Franco-German dispute over the Saar, then a unit politically separated from Germany and economically added to France. This was in essence a conflict over coal and steel resources; and by pooling these in any case, the

Coal and Steel Community would facilitate a settlement of this difficulty for Franco-German relations.

Britain, when invited to join the negotiations, refused. It was Mr. Macmillan who said in Strasbourg: "One thing is certain, and we may as well face it. Our people will not hand over to any supranational authority the right to close down our pits or our steelworks." Once again, more intensive progress could be made only on a less extensive front. And so, for the first time, six nations—the Six—met around a conference table: France, Italy, the Federal Republic of Western Germany, Belgium, the Netherlands, and Luxembourg. The Treaty was signed in 1951, it came into force in 1952, and the common markets in coal, iron ore, scrap, and most steels were set up in early 1953. It is worth quoting the preamble to the Treaty, which made it crystal-clear that coal and steel marked but a beginning, made in a chosen key sector. Other sectors were already being considered in intergovernmental discussions and in the Council of Europe: the Pflimlin plan for agriculture, a European transport community, and so forth. The aim of the Six was a full European Economic Community, set up to advance political objectives. The six governments,

> Considering that world peace may be safeguarded only by creative efforts equal to the dangers which menace it;
>
> Convinced that the contribution which an organized and vital Europe can bring to civilization is indispensable to the maintenance of peaceful relations;
>
> Conscious of the fact that Europe can be built only by concrete actions which create a real solidarity and by the establishment of common bases for economic development;
>
> Desirous of assisting through the expansion of their basic production in raising the standard of living and in furthering the works of peace;
>
> Resolved to substitute for historic rivalries a fusion of their essential interests; to establish, by creating an economic community, the foundation of a broad and independent community among peoples long divided by bloody conflicts; and to lay the bases of institutions capable of giving direction to their future common destiny; have decided to create a European Coal and Steel Community.

The institutions for which the Treaty laid the basis were four:

a High Authority of nine members independent of any government and acting in the interests of the Community as a whole; a Common Assembly, modeled on the Council of Europe's Common Assembly, which by a two-thirds vote of censure, could force the High Authority to resign; a Council of Ministers representing the member states; and a Court of Justice to ensure the rule of law in the implementation of the Treaty. We shall meet this basic institutional pattern again in the subsequent Communities. (Compare the chart on p. 66.)

The Supranational Triptych of 1954

The development toward a "Little European" Economic Community thus begun in May, 1950, was lifted sharply out of its natural course by world events and United States pressure. When war broke out in Korea, the United States demanded twelve German divisions for the defense of the European front. The French refused to consent to the re-establishment of a *Wehrmacht* and German membership in NATO. The Germans, if they were to be rearmed, demanded equality of rights. There was but one way of reconciling these three demands: a European army, to which each state would contribute its European forces, all equally under joint European control. This conclusion was embodied in the draft treaty for a European Defense Community (EDC)—and the European movement began a struggle that was to cost it four precious years.

Perhaps there was no alternative once the need for German rearmament was admitted. Certainly the Defense Community was seductive in federalist eyes. It demolished one of the most conspicuous and dangerous elements of national sovereignty: the absolute supremacy over armed military force. Like the European Coal and Steel Community, the European Defense Community was designed as a supranational agency with limited functions but with very real powers; also like ECSC, it was designed as a component to be built into a political framework; more even than ECSC it cried aloud for new European institutions—and indeed it provided for an Assembly directly elected by universal suffrage to wield democratic political control.

In addition to the control envisaged in the EDC treaty itself, more far-reaching political plans were mapped out in detail before the EDC came up for ratification. Within six months of being given the task, an *ad hoc* Assembly (largely identical in membership with the Common Assembly of the Coal and Steel Community) drafted the constitution of a European Political Community based on an indissoluble union of states. A directly elected European People's Chamber and a Senate indirectly elected by the national parliaments were between them to form the European Parliament to which the President of the European Excutive Council and his Cabinet colleagues were to be directly responsible. Both the Coal and Steel and the Defense Communities were to be integrated into this structure: the People's Chamber would control the High Authority of the ECSC and the Commission of the EDC, with a single Council of Ministers and a single Court of Justice acting for all three Communities. From this political structure the Economic Community was to be derived.

The French Assembly was cautious about its approach to the ratification of EDC. Party spokesmen formulated certain conditions without the fulfillment of which, they insisted, Germany could not regain her sovereignty or be rearmed. Two of these were effective political control of the army and a solution of the Saar problem. The *ad hoc* Assembly had with its draft constitution shown the way to the achievement of the first condition, and the plan of the Council of Europe spelled out a "Europeanization" of the Saar. In addition, the French demanded assurances that there would always be sufficient British and United States troops in Europe to calm their fears of German rearmament. France demanded formal legal guarantees of a kind that do not come easily to Anglo-Saxon diplomacy; and although Churchill had, when in opposition, called for a European army in which "we all should bear an honorable part," Britain refused even to give guarantees until it was too late. But this time, at any rate, the blame for the failure of a European scheme could no longer be laid exclusively at Britain's door.

Amid internal dissension of a kind hardly seen since the Dreyfus affair, the country that had originated the project prevented its realization. On the night of August 30, 1954, a coalition of the Communist Left with the Gaullist Right refused to debate ratification when both the Socialists and the Radicals were evenly split on the issue, and only the Christian Democratic MRP, M. Schuman's party, was almost solidly in its favor. What had seemed feasible and almost unavoidable in 1950, while U.N. forces were retreating southward in Korea and the MRP and Socialists were in power, had become unacceptable after Stalin's death, in an atmosphere of relaxing international tension and with both the MRP and Socialists in opposition.

Four arguments above all killed the EDC: It would resurrect the German army; it would destroy the army of France; it would affect French political sovereignty; and it would imply an Economic Community for which the French economy felt unprepared.

That German rearmament was not the one decisive issue was proved to the hilt when, in December, 1954, the National Assembly ratified the Paris treaties. Though these treaties set up a small organization, the Western European Union, to associate Britain with the other Six in the control of German rearmament, they also made Western Germany into a sovereign power, gave her a national army, and made her a member of NATO—the last two the very things which the EDC, to spare French feelings, had been so carefully designed to avoid. Henceforth the movement toward the unity of Europe was freed from the defense issue, and was able—and forced—to return to the task which, in 1950, it had just set itself to begin.

When the Six met again at Messina, in June, 1955, they decided that the next attack could not be too directly political. In effect, if not in form, the draft Political Community had been rejected with the EDC. "The next phase in the building of a united Europe," as the Messina communiqué stated, "must lie in the economic field." It was to the Economic Community foreshadowed in the ECSC treaty that the Six thus returned. Once and for all the economic arguments of French business against any form of political unity had to be cleared out of the way. Explicit safeguards and particular consideration had to be given to the special difficulties that seemed very real to France. Here was the indispensable tactical move without which there could be no further progress toward political integration.

The "Over-all" Economic Approach

At the same time, there were new and important economic reasons for proceeding toward a Common Market in Europe.

For lack of gold and dollars, when raw materials, machinery, and goods of all kinds were in heavy demand, all the countries of Europe had maintained or imposed strict import controls immediately after the war. Trade between them was on the basis of a bilateral bartering of goods for goods, with very little credit granted to allow for temporary disparities between import and export values. In order to overcome the restriction and distortion of trade which this system entailed, the Organization for European Economic Cooperation in 1949 launched its program of trade liberalization: The member countries pledged themselves to abolish quantitative restrictions on a certain percentage of imports from each other, and this "liberalization percentage" was progressively raised. Trade could thus expand and become multilateral on a regional basis.

But to expand and multilateralize trade it was necessary to expand and multilateralize payments. In 1950, therefore, OEEC set up its European Payments Union. This system allowed multilateralized payments by arranging for all intra-European payments, regardless of origin or destination, to be settled not by individual countries with each other, but by a monthly net settlement by each country with the European Payments Union itself. This institution also provided certain very important automatic credit facilities. It served the entire monetary areas of the OEEC members, including the sterling area as a whole.

Six years after OEEC took up its work, intra-European trade had more than doubled in volume. But further progress was proving slow. The intergovernmental structure of OEEC was too loose for its recommendations to be compelling. France, for example, was falling badly short of her liberalization commitments and was counteracting liberalization by imposing a special levy on imports. Other countries also were not fulfilling their obligations, and they, too, pleaded special difficulties as an explanation as to why they could not keep pace. Denmark, Greece, Turkey, and Iceland complained that, while they were attempting to reduce quantitative restrictions on the imports of industrial products, the industrial countries were not reducing their restrictions on the import of agricultural produce and foodstuffs to a corresponding extent. Indeed, in consideration of the special political, social, and economic difficulties caused by shifts of production from agriculture to industry, the liberalization system allowed the industrial countries to maintain higher restrictions on agricultural imports than the agricultural countries were allowed to maintain on industrial goods. Thirdly, the group of Benelux and Scandinavian low-tariff countries complained that, when they liberalized the import of a commodity, this abolished almost all the protection for their producers and their balance of payments: When a high-tariff country liberalized imports, the customs duty still maintained a heavy discrimination against the foreign producer and reduced the impact on its balance of payments.

In spite of the formal symmetry of the liberalization system, it thus lacked an effective material reciprocity between agricultural and industrial and between high-tariff and low-tariff countries; quantitative restrictions in many cases were maintained less to protect the balance of payments than to protect individual producers and industries; and the merely intergovernmental machinery which did not ultimately affect national independence of action still allowed a country to cut its imports from its neighbors when internal adjustments would have seemed preferable from a European point of view.

Where the obvious problem of tariffs was concerned, there were political and historical reasons why OEEC had never made any move. In 1948, to secure imports at all had mattered far more than their price. Quotas could be mutually abolished by swift executive action, while tariff reductions would have involved the agreement of eighteen legislatures. The reduction of tariffs was being investigated on a world basis under the General Agreement on Tariffs and Trade (GATT). Furthermore, it was a principle of GATT that tariffs were not to be lowered on a discriminatory basis. Plainly, Europe had no desire unilaterally to lower her tariffs against the rest of the world at this time; therefore, intra-European tariffs could not be lowered either.

By 1955, at least four of the Six countries were afraid that OEEC's attempts to liberalize trade within Europe were yielding diminishing returns. The Benelux countries had already formed a customs union of their own and were impatient with the slow rate of progress of their neighbors. Holland, in particular, simultaneously an agricultural and a low-tariff country, was anxious to see further advance. Within OEEC, the low-tariff countries requested that the problem of trade barriers be treated as a whole, but little concrete action could then be expected on the level of the eighteen states that made up OEEC.

Three possibilities were open to the OEEC countries as liberalization appeared to grind to a standstill: They could set out on wider progress toward nondiscrimination either on the trade or on the payments side, or on both. But while Britain favored moves toward the convertibility of currencies, others preferred to extend the liberalization of dollar imports. Some countries, like France, were plainly not ready for formal convertibility, and for Britain, Germany, and Benelux to take the plunge might have meant opening a new rift in European economic and thus also political relations.

Such a rift might have been avoided by an alternative plan: the nondiscriminatory but selective reduction of customs duties in unison on only those goods which are traded predominantly between OEEC countries. Formally, this would have been a nondiscriminatory program; effectively, it would have been a regionalist move. But it could hardly have gone very far.

The provisions of GATT did, however, provide one more straightforward way out. Under Article XXIV, tariffs could be reduced on a regional basis provided they were reduced to zero over a reasonable period of time. It was under this article that Benelux had been formed. This article could now be used to solve at the same time the political problem posed by the failure of EDC and the economic problem posed by the slowing down of OEEC progress. Thus, at the Conference of Ministers at Messina, on the proposal of the Netherlands delegation, the economic and the political streams of thought merged once more. The European movement returned to that economic path toward political unity chosen in 1950, which the failure of the Defense

Community had shown to be of vital significance, and which was also thrust into the foreground by the impasse within OEEC.

The Rome Treaties

At the Conference of Messina, in June, 1955, the Foreign Ministers of the Six set up an intergovernmental committee of experts—under the chairmanship of M. Spaak, then Belgian Foreign Minister—which met in Brussels for nine months to explore ways and means of pooling Europe's resources for the development of nuclear energy, and of setting up a Common Market and customs union. The committee's report, presented in April, 1956, prepared the way for the political negotiations.

The Treaties themselves were drafted in some haste to exploit the political constellation of 1955–57, when M. Mollet was French Prime Minister, before Dr. Adenauer had to face his electorate in the autumn of 1957, and while the economies of Europe were experiencing a boom. The negotiations were an intricate mixture of academic exercises in abstruse economic theory and poker games of political skill. To the pure economist without knowledge of the course of the negotiations, the provisions of the Treaty may thus sometimes seem strange. But as its aims are political, so its methods are politically conditioned. Though radical in effect, the transformation will be gradual and gather momentum with time. In three stages, to be completed within twelve (or, exceptionally, up to fifteen) years, the political institutions are to merge the five component national markets into a single Common Market; and in the minds of the draftsmen of the Treaty, their economic task is chiefly valued as a step toward political integration—in the words of the preamble, "an ever closer union."

Agreement was reached and all the drafting completed in less than a year. On March 24, 1957, the Treaty establishing the European Economic Community and the Treaty setting up the European Atomic Energy Community were signed on the Capitoline, in Rome. Ratified by all the member states within a few months, they came into force on January 1, 1958.

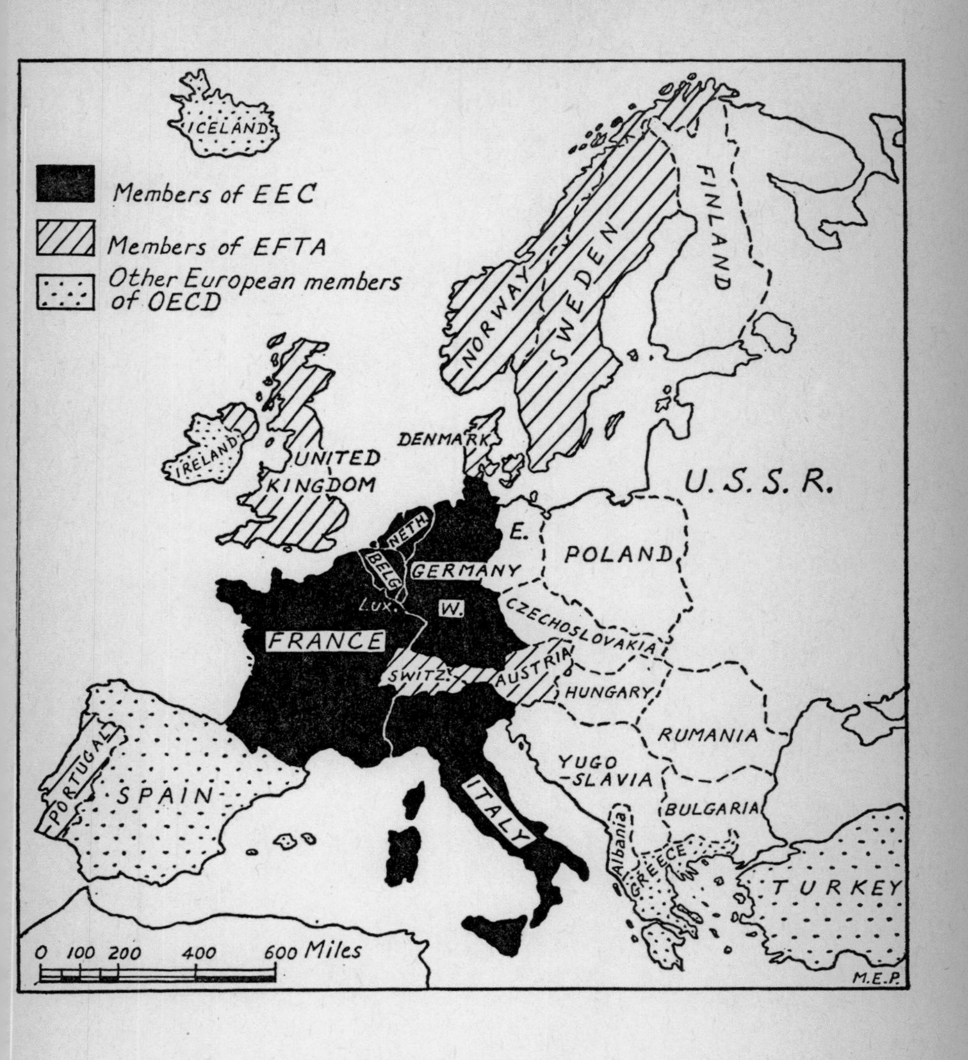
Members of EEC
Members of EFTA
Other European members of OECD
ICELAND
NORWAY
SWEDEN
FINLAND
IRELAND
UNITED KINGDOM
DENMARK
U.S.S.R.
NETH.
BELG.
LUX.
E.
GERMANY
W.
POLAND
CZECHOSLOVAKIA
FRANCE
SWITZ.
AUSTRIA
HUNGARY
RUMANIA
PORTUGAL
SPAIN
ITALY
YUGO SLAVIA
BULGARIA
Albania
GREECE
TURKEY
0 100 200 400 600 Miles
M.E.P.

Table II

RATIFICATION MAJORITIES IN THE LOWER HOUSES OF THE SIX

	ECSC			EEC			Euratom		
	For	Against	Abst.	For	Against	Abst.	For	Against	Abst.
Belgium	165	13	13	174	4	2	174	4	2
France	376	240	11	341	235	—	337	243	—
Germany	232	142	3	Large majorities by show of hands					
Italy	265	98	201	311	144	54	365	144	—
Luxembourg	47	4	1	46	3	—	45	3	—
Netherlands	62	6	32	144	12	—	120	6	—

II

The Economics of the Treaties

The Theory of Integration

Adam Smith laid the systematic foundations of the theory behind free trade. The division of labor, the specialization and optimum combination of factors, the economic benefits of competition, the maximum range of choice for the consumer—all these hackneyed but broadly unrefuted arguments recur throughout the Spaak Report on which the Treaty is based. Such arguments, overriding as they are, need not be restated here.

But most of the Treaty provisions are based on a further, absolutely vital line of thought. Free trade today is not enough: We must go forward to integration. Eighteenth-century theory can be applied in the modern world only if today's very different situation is taken into account.

Three factors are of fundamental importance here. First, the state, which has taken responsibility for the economic fortunes of the nation, is concerned to maintain a high level of effective demand, full employment, and a growing national product: Its business-cycle policy and investment policy set the whole economic climate of the nation. Second, the state has not only itself become the biggest employer and consumer, a large-scale trader, and often a monopolist, but through its taxation and its subsidies, its regulations and controls, it also molds and permeates specific details of every branch of private industry, agriculture, and trade. Faced with different problems, subject to different political pressures, pursuing somewhat different social aims, different states adopt totally different methods of intervention. Third, the associations of producers—cartels and industrial associations, trade unions and farmers' unions—introduce additional rigidities into the economic process and differentiate one country's economy artificially from another.

The whole economic theory of the Community is thus based on recognition of the economic importance of the political frontier, behind which totally different national policies are being pursued. As we shall see in the next chapter, its political theory is based on the obverse of this theorem: the political importance of the economic frontier, now that the right to restrict trade, payments, and labor movement has become a vital aspect of national sovereignty.

In practical terms, the economic argument runs as follows. Merely to open the sluices to the exchange of goods between states whose economies are subject to those different factors will result in distorted patterns of trade and production. It may cause perfectly economic enterprises to close down and uneconomic ones to flourish. Let us take three simple examples: If one country adopts a very deflationary policy, it may well be able to undercut the countries which do not seek to deflate, and will thus put its neighbors out of work and business while its central bank accumulates gold drawn from them. Or if one industry—say, agriculture—is given heavy direct subsidies in one country but is protected by a high tariff in another, then the removal of tariffs will ruin the unsubsidized agriculture of the one, while the other's will mushroom to take over both markets. Or if one country has strict antimonopoly legislation while the other permits monopolies, then the removal of barriers to trade between the two may mean that the monopoly in the one country can by its exports exercise a dominant influence on the hitherto competitive market of the other.

It is thus not only state interventions at the frontier—customs duties and quantitative restrictions—which must be eliminated: *Pari passu* with the opening of frontiers, differences in national policies, laws and regulations, and all forms of discrimination according to nationality behind the frontier must be ironed out insofar as they affect interstate commerce, and instead of the different component areas playing the economic game by totally different sets of rules, there must be a common set of rules for the whole market.

Just how large a part these considerations played in the drafting of the Rome Treaty will become apparent from the two articles which summarize the whole system:

> Article 2:
>
> It shall be the aim of the Community, by establishing a Common Market and progressively approximating the economic policies of member states, to promote throughout the Community a harmonious development of economic activities, a continuous and balanced expansion, an increased stability, an accelerated raising of the standard of living, and closer relations between its member states.
>
> Article 3:
>
> For the purposes set out in the preceding Article, the activities of the Community shall include, under the conditions and in accordance with the timetable envisaged in this Treaty.
>
> (*a*) the elimination, as between member states, of customs duties and of quantitative restrictions in regard to the import and export of goods, as well as of all other measures having equivalent effect;
>
> (*b*) the establishment of a common customs tariff and of a common commercial policy toward third countries;
>
> (*c*) the abolition, as between member states, of obstacles to the free movement of persons, services, and capital;
>
> (*d*) the inauguration of a common policy in the field of agriculture;
>
> (*e*) the inauguration of a common policy in the field of transport;
>
> (*f*) the establishment of a system ensuring that competition in the Common Market is not distorted;
>
> (*g*) the adoption of procedures permitting the coordination of the economic policies of member states and the correction of instability in their balances of payments;
>
> (*h*) the approximation of their respective national laws to the extent required for the Common Market to function in an orderly manner;
>
> (*i*) the creation of a European Social Fund in order to improve the possibilities of employment for workers and to contribute to the raising of their standard of living;
>
> (*j*) the establishment of a European Investment Bank to facilitate the expansion of the Community by opening up fresh resources; and

(*k*) the association of overseas countries and territories with a view to increasing trade and to pursuing jointly the task of economic and social development.

The Common Market as described in Article 3 is to be instituted in three stages of four years each, making a total transition period of twelve years. Within each of these three stages, different types of action are envisaged which, taken together, are each time to result in a balanced step on the path to integration. Institutionally, too, there are important differences between the three stages: In the third stage, in particular, a variety of decisions, which until then can be taken only by unanimity between the six governments as represented in the Council of Ministers, can then be taken by a qualified majority vote (see below, p. 69). Already in the second stage certain decisions pass from the unanimity to the qualified majority rule; but the vital significance of the passage from the first to the second stage lies less in this change of rules on six minor matters of substance than in the rules governing the passage from one stage to another.

The Treaty allowed the first stage to continue for five or for six years if a unanimous decision to pass on to the second stage was not forthcoming from the six governments; only at the end of the sixth year could the second stage be broached as the result of a qualified majority vote. By contrast, the transition from the second to the third stage and the termination of the whole transition period at the end of the third stage are both automatic: Only a unanimous decision of the member governments taken on the recommendation of the Commission could vary the length of these two stages. The transition period, in any case, cannot extend beyond fifteen years. But when the governments on January 14, 1962, finally, after a marathon session, decided to pass on to the second stage—with effect from January 1, 1962—the biggest remaining factor of uncertainty in the development of the Common Market was in fact resolved. It is most unlikely that the Commission would recommend, and the six governments be unanimous in agreeing, that the second or third stage should be prolonged beyond four years each: They are far more likely if anything to reach unanimity on accelerating the Treaty's timetable than they are on slowing it down. We must thus expect the transition period to end and the Common

Market to be fully in operation at the latest by January 1, 1970.

The system which is thus outlined is neither one of centralized public planning nor one of *laissez-faire* competition. It is neither one of nationalization nor one of purely private enterprise. It is the agreed upshot of a much more adaptable, undogmatic approach along different paths to the different problems presented by the economies of the Six in the last half of the twentieth century. For atomic energy, the system contains strong elements of public ownership and public control. For agriculture, it is one of state support and quality control. For underdeveloped regions, it is one of public finance and public encouragement of private capital. For transport, it is one involving central plans and a mixture of European, national, and private enterprise. It provides a harmonized monetary framework and, for most of industry, a system of harmonized rules within which each firm is free to compete, whether it be a private firm like Fiat, a nationalized firm like Renault, or a denationalized one like Volkswagen. The system neither encourages nor prevents nationalization or denationalization. And it is this pragmatic, unideological approach which allowed the Rome Treaties to be ratified by such overwhelming majorities of the Socialists and Liberals, no less than the Christian Democrats, of the member states.

The Common Market Treaty is a long and complicated document taking up, in its unofficial (and very corrupt) English translation, 378 closely printed pages, and the Coal and Steel Community and Euratom Treaties add another 255, just to make things easier. Many of the 572 articles involved lay down only the broad outlines of the policies to be pursued; and although the various annexed lists and protocols sometimes go into extreme detail, a proper understanding of the working of the Communities can only be gained from following through the decisions of the Councils of Ministers made since, and from the various regulations issued by the High Authority and the Commissions.

It goes without saying that only the most rough and ready survey will be possible here. Even so, it may make tedious reading. The noneconomist could in fact be forgiven if, after consulting the section on any aspect in which he is interested and browsing through the other pages simply to gain an impression of the multifarious detailed problems of applying the Treaty, he continued his reading with the Conclusion on p. 58. But the more serious student can hardly be spared this intractable material.

Internal Barriers to Industrial Trade

Articles 13 to 17 lay down the stages by which the customs duties that were applied on January 1, 1957, shall be abolished between the member states over the course of the transition period. On January 1, 1959, every duty was to be lowered by 10 per cent; and this was done. The next reduction, by an average of 10 per cent and a minimum of 5 per cent on every product (10 per cent where the duty would otherwise still be above 30 per cent), took place according to schedule on July 1, 1960. The next reduction was not due until January 1, 1962, but, on the proposal of the Commission, the Council of Ministers decided in May, 1960, that it could do better than that and accelerate the implementation of the Treaty. As a result, the next cut was made a year ahead of schedule, and industrial tariffs within the Community were cut on January 1, 1961, by a further 10 per cent. Moreover, France, by a work of supererogation performed in order to keep French prices down, then went a step ahead of her partners, as she is entitled to do under Article 15: From April 1, 1961, French tariffs on the majority of industrial products were down to 65 per cent, and in the case of some of them, notably in the mechanical and electrical engineering, automobile, textile, and chemical industries, they came down to 60 per cent. The transition to the second stage brought with it automatically yet another reduction with effect from January 1, 1962, and on May 15, the Council unanimously agreed to embark on yet another premature reduction to bring industrial tariffs on trade between member states down to 50 per cent of their basic level by July 1, 1962—only three and a half years after the first cuts were made.

In the case of certain taxes which, though they are not customs duties, tend to have much the same effect, the Commission is to direct the speed at which they are to be abolished. In isolated instances, the member states have not obeyed the Treaty, and five such cases are now being dealt with.

Quotas. The Treaty provides that all quantitative restrictions on trade in industrial goods between the Six shall be abolished by the end of the transitional period; under the acceleration decisions, this aim was almost wholly achieved by the end of 1961—after only four instead of twelve to fifteen years.

Only in a very few cases have countries invoked Article 226 of the Treaty, under which, when serious difficulties are likely to persist in any sector or region as a result of the implementation of the Treaty, the Commission can allow governments to take safeguard measures. Thus the Italian producers of citric acid and calcium citrate, and the penicillin manufacturers of Benelux, have been given a respite during which to put their house in order.

Export Restrictions. The very few remaining export duties between member states were abolished on January 1, 1962, and all quantitative export restrictions between them suppressed shortly afterward.

Intra-Community Trade. It is always difficult to isolate the results of any particular economic measure from all other factors that may have accentuated or counteracted it. Continuing boom conditions, the French devaluation (which was necessitated if by nothing else then by the requirements of the Common Market), investments, and business arrangements across the internal frontiers of the Community and other clauses of the Treaty will have operated together with the reduction in internal tariffs and the expectation of further reductions. At any rate, a 72 per cent rise in intra-Community trade in three years is startling evidence for the swift transformation of the commercial climate in the Community.

External Trade Policy

The General Agreement on Tariffs and Trade stipulates that the common external tariff and other trade barriers of a customs union "shall not, on the whole, be higher or more restrictive than the general incidence of the duties and regulations of commerce applicable in the constituent territories." The draftsmen of the Treaty interpreted this to mean that the duties on any particular product entering the Community should be calculated as the arithmetic mean of the four tariffs levied on that commodity on January 1, 1957, in France, Western Germany, Italy, and Benelux. (For these purposes the customs unions already existing between Belgium, the Netherlands, and Luxembourg was treated as a single unit. There were also various technical complications into which we need not for present purposes enter.) The contracting parties of GATT *de facto* upheld the Six in their interpretation. The common tariff around the Community was thus fixed at a level that was, broadly speaking, higher than the Benelux and German, lower than the French and Italian tariffs.

The Treaty also laid down maximum rates beyond which, in general, the external tariff should not go, whatever the arithmetic mean: 3 per cent for raw materials, 10 per cent or 15 per cent for various types of processed raw materials and semimanufactures, and 15 per cent or 25 per cent for manufactured goods. On the other hand, there were exceptions, notably the famous List G of products, on which no external tariff was negotiated until 1960; though in some of these cases the duties were fixed substantially above the arithmetic mean (often in order to benefit the African associated countries), the average incidence of the duties on List G was lower than that which would have resulted from the arithmetic mean. Only two problems in List G were left unresolved at the end of the first stage: the tariff for manufactured tobacco (which was settled in February, 1962) and that for petroleum products. This last tariff is now to be fixed on the recommendation of the Commission by unanimity: If it is not fixed within the second stage, the Commission can have its proposal adopted by a qualified majority vote.

The pressures for a high external tariff came particularly from France, the country that most feared competition, while the Germans and Dutch, much more heavily dependent on international trade and interested in keeping their costs low, pressed for a lower tariff and a more "outward-looking" Community. Indeed, the Germans unilaterally reduced a whole range of customs duties early in 1957, thus giving their partners in the Community an advance on the internal tariff reductions to be made in due course under the Treaty, and giving the rest of the world a respite from the onset of tariff discrimination on the German market. For a whole range of goods, therefore, it was only after January 1, 1961, that Community goods were given preferences in Germany against goods from the rest of the world.

Stages of Tariff Harmonization. The Treaty foresaw the establishment of the common external tariff in three stages: a first move on January 1, 1962, when all external duties that lay within 15 per cent of the common tariff rate were to be replaced by the common tariff, and when all other duties on goods from outside the Community were to move (whether upward or downward) 30 per cent of the way toward the common tariff. Another 30 per cent of the difference between the pre-existing national tariff and the agreed common tariff was to be eliminated four years later, and the common tariff was to be fully established by the end of the transition period.

Under pressure from the low-tariff countries, the Community decided that the first internal tariff reduction, on January 1, 1959, was to be extended to the outside world, thus avoiding any charges of discrimination from the rest of Europe. Then, two years later, the decision to accelerate brought the Community one year ahead of schedule on most external as well as internal tariffs in the industrial sector. The first moves toward a common tariff were made on January 1, 1961. On the proposal of the Commission, these first alignments (by 30 per cent of the difference between national and common tariff rates) were made not on the basis of the agreed common tariff, but in general on the assumption that this tariff would be 20 per cent lower than agreed. It was hoped that the GATT negotiations of 1960–61 would result in a reciprocal reduction of tariffs on a world basis, and the Community's 20 per cent was meant as a provisional advance given to the rest of the world to encourage a general lowering of customs barriers; as other countries have not fully reciprocated, the lowering of the common tariff may not be fully consolidated. A few goods on List G, some 3 or 4 per cent of Community imports in 1957, were excepted from this 20 per cent abatement. In the case of cocoa and tropical woods, this was once more done to benefit the overseas associated countries by maintaining or extending preferences in their favor as against the rest of the world.

But the first move toward this common tariff, a year ahead of schedule, fell short of the requirements of the Treaty for the end of the fourth year in two respects: It was confined to industrial products, and, in the case of Germany, half the special German tariff reductions made in 1957 could be counted in calculating the difference between the German national and the new common tariff. In accordance with the Treaty, these two defects had to be made good at the end of the fourth year (regardless of whether the second stage began or not): And so, on January 1, 1962, all member states put into force new tariffs —which, incidentally, were then lowered in March, 1962, in accordance with the agreement reached with the U.S. in GATT.

Article 25 of the Treaty provides that where a country cannot cover its demand for certain products within the Community, it may be allowed to continue to import from a traditional third supplier country at a reduced rate of duty or duty-free up to the limit of a certain quota. A few such tariff quotas have been granted, notably for newsprint, to France and Germany. The quotas thus granted in 1961 appear to have covered only about 1.5 per cent of the Community's imports from the rest of the world, and efforts have been made to reduce applications for such quotas for the year 1962. In certain other cases, the common tariff has simply been suspended so as not to disturb existing channels of supply.

Commercial Policy. During the transitional period, the member states must of course coordinate their commercial relations with third countries in order to prepare the way for a single common commercial policy (of which the common external tariff will be a part). Thus, all member states are to insert the so-called "EEC clause" into any commercial agreements they conclude with third countries:

> Should those obligations under the Treaty establishing the European Economic Community which relate to the gradual establishment of a common commercial policy make this necessary, negotiations shall be opened as soon as feasible in order to amend this present agreement as appropriate.

In addition, they are to consult together about any negotiations on commercial agreements in which they are engaged, are to conclude no agreements beyond the end of the transition period, and are to insist that any agreement that does not contain the "EEC clause" can be terminated annually.

After the transitional period, it will be the Commission, and not the member states, that will negotiate trade agreements between the Community and third countries. The Council of Ministers will issue directives to the Commission and provide it with a special consultative committee for the purpose. And the member states will act together in international economic organizations. Indeed, in GATT, it is already the Commission and not the member states that negotiates for the Community as a whole where the common external tariff is at stake.

In the GATT negotiations of September, 1960, to May, 1961, the Community either (in 200 cases) lowered or gave an undertaking not to raise the common external tariff: About 80 per cent of the Community's imports from other GATT countries were covered by these reductions or measures of consolidation, and the contracting parties expressed themselves satisfied that the common external tariff was not more restrictive than the previous tariffs of the component states. Then, at the end of May, 1961, there opened the second, so-called "Dillon round" of negotiations to lower tariffs by 20 per cent, as proposed by the American Under-Secretary of State in 1958. When they were concluded, in March, 1962, the Community had agreed to consolidate most of the linear reduction of 20 per cent, which had been provisionally decided upon in anticipation of a GATT agreement. In return, the U.S. reduced its duties on a wide range of commodities, usually by 20 per cent, but, as the U.S. Administration has no authority for linear reductions, these reductions were made on a product-by-product basis. At the 1958 level, some $1.6 billion worth of trade between the Community and the U.S. is affected by these reductions in the second round, on top of the $1.3 billion worth affected by the reductions and consolidations of the first round. Moreover, since both sides made all their concessions on a most-favored-nation basis, all other members of GATT benefit likewise.

In its chapter (Article 110) on commercial policy, the Treaty declares that:

> By establishing a customs union between themselves the member states aim to contribute, in conformity with the common interest, to the harmonious development of world trade, the progressive abolition of restrictions on international exchanges and the lowering of customs barriers.

This article was greeted with some skepticism when the Treaty was first published, but as we have seen, the Community's record so far is not at all that of a self-sufficient unit cutting itself off from world trade behind high tariff walls. Table III shows that not only has internal trade in the Community leapt up, but that imports from the rest of the world, too, have continued to rise dramatically since the Treaty came into operation.

Table III
IMPORTS OF EEC COUNTRIES
(monthly averages, millions of dollars)

	1961	1962	'58–'62
From each other	976	1,117	+ 97%
From overseas associates	148	160	+ 25%
From EFTA	410	458	+ 52%
From the rest of world	1,147	1,242	+ 36%
All imports	2,681	2,977	+ 56%

SOURCE: *EEC General Statistical Bulletin,* No. 12 (1961), pp.130–34; and *ibid.,* No. 5 (1963), pp. 58–63.

AGRICULTURE

The Treaty lays down that: "The Common Market shall extend to agriculture and trade in agricultural products."

To integrate Europe industrially without any attempt to integrate agriculture would have meant recreating on the level of the Six and in far more acute form the problems of asymmetry between agricultural and industrial countries; and France, Holland, and Italy insisted that if they were to open their markets to industrial goods, the Germans, in particular, must be willing to open theirs to farm produce. But here, plainly, is by far the most difficult sector in which to obtain integration. Technically, economically, and socially, the movement of workers between industries is far easier than the movement of peasants from agriculture into industry—and with something like a quarter of the electorates of the Six composed of peasants and agricultural workers, this was and remains a politically explosive subject. Particularly, German farmers are reluctant to be exposed immediately to the full blast of Dutch and, for certain products, French and Italian competition, so that special safeguard measures were required. Moreover, if there is one sector of the economy which (mainly for political reasons) tends to be artificially buoyed up by the state, shaped and governed by whatever form protection may take, it is agriculture: And since no one is prepared to leave the fate of agriculture to the unrestricted working of the forces of supply and demand, it was not *laissez-faire,* but a common agricultural policy that the Six decided upon.

Such quantitative restrictions on trade within the Community as now remain are chiefly found in the agricultural sector. On January 1, 1961, the import quotas for goods not subject to national marketing organizations were increased by 20 per cent. On produce on which quantitative restrictions remain, the member states also agreed to lower their tariffs ahead of schedule, though only by 5 per cent and not by 10 per cent, as in the case of industrial products. They did not change the tariffs on liberalized imports, which thus remained at 80 per cent of their basic level until the beginning of 1962, when all agricultural tariffs were reduced by a further 10 per cent.

Articles 38–47 of the Treaty lay down the exceptions to the general rules of the Common Market made in favor of agriculture. They also set out the provisions made on top of those rules, especially for agriculture. The objects to be pursued are obvious enough:

> Article 39:
>
> 1. The objectives of the common agricultural policy shall be:
>
> (*a*) to increase agricultural productivity by promoting technical progress and by ensuring the rational development of agricultural production and the optimum utilization of all factors of production, in particular labor;
>
> (*b*) to ensure thereby a fair standard of living for the agricultural community, particularly by increasing the individual earnings of persons engaged in agriculture;
>
> (*c*) to stabilize markets;
>
> (*d*) to guarantee supplies;
>
> (*e*) to ensure the delivery of supplies to consumers at reasonable prices.

But it is the working out of these objectives and the balancing of one against another that matter.

Agricultural policy, in fact, represents the hardest test of all for the strength of the Community vis-à-vis the national governments, who have to take the rap for its consequences from their national electorates. The Treaty recognized this difficulty—and wisely left all the real decisions to be made not before, but after the institution of the Economic Community. Indeed, even then the Treaty is generous in the time it allows for the Community spirit to develop and make a common agricultural policy possible: While it compelled the Commission to submit proposals within two years of the institution of the Community, the implementation of a common policy was to be a less hurried affair: "Member states shall gradually develop the common agricultural policy during the transitional period and shall bring it into force not later than at the end of that period." (Article 40.) The Commission did just comply with their part of the matter, though they substantially revised their proposals of December, 1959, in the first half of 1960: The incredible complexity of the manifold different problems posed by the various products in each country presented a tangle of technical difficulties quite apart from the political ones. But once the Commission's proposals of June, 1960, had been tabled, the issues became increasingly a matter for political decision.

Western Germany went to the polls in September, 1961, and Dr. Adenauer's partners understood the special difficulties this posed. Germany's farming was probably the least efficient of any in the Community, with small peasants operating at high costs, thanks to generous featherbedding; any common market in foodstuffs, any realistic common policy, would therefore mean drastic readjustments for the German farming community, on whom the Christian Democrats relied for many of their marginal votes. Yet, at the same time, France, Holland, and Italy did not feel that they could wait very long. They were being asked to proceed with an accelerated reduction of tariffs on intra-Community trade in industrial goods, from which German exports benefited greatly, and they felt it only fair that in exchange, Germany's frontiers should be opened further to the products in which they excelled: Peasant riots in Brittany and elsewhere in France during the early summer of 1961 equipped the French negotiators with illustrations to their demands for reciprocated sympathy from Dr. Adenauer once his election was over.

It was at this point that the unanimity rule in the Council of Ministers equipped France with a weapon which had just the opposite effect from that which the possibility of veto is traditionally supposed to have: The French declared that they would not regard the first stage of the transition period as completed unless far-reaching concrete decisions on agricultural policy had been taken. So far from retarding integration, the French threat of veto forced the Germans in the last resort to make substantial sacrifices to the Community in the agricultural domain. The negotiations could not be completed on December 30, and continued until 5 A.M. on Sunday morning, January 14, 1962; then, after 140 hours of negotiations, two heart attacks, and one nervous collapse among the participants, agreement was reached on agriculture as on cartels and on equal pay for equal work—and so the French declared themselves satisfied, and agreed to pass on to the second stage.

The agricultural decisions have been called "a second Rome Treaty," and indeed in their bulk and complexity they rival the original document itself. But just as the Rome Treaty had deliberately left many of the more ticklish subjects to further negotiation within the framework of the Community, so these decisions of January 14, too, leave certain vital details (such as the actual price levels) to be determined later, according to rules which were agreed upon. In legal terms, what the Council did was to adopt the substance of eight regulations (now known as Regulations 19–26), four decisions, and two resolutions.* And it is worth noting that, in his determination

* Article 189 of the Treaty defines the different types of pronouncements which the Council of Ministers and the Commission can make: "*Regulations* shall have general application. They shall be binding in every respect and directly applicable in each member state.

Directives shall bind member states to which they are addressed, as to the result to be achieved while leaving to domestic agencies a competence as to form and means.

Decisions shall be binding in every respect upon those to whom they are directed.

Recommendations and *opinions* shall have no binding force." [Author's italics.]

to obtain a common agricultural policy, the French Minister of Agriculture was glad to agree to vital provisions in these regulations which give a far more central role to the Commission than the French President, with his confederal view of European cooperation, would have wished to see on institutional grounds.

The fundamental principles of the common agricultural policy are to be found in treating European agriculture finally as the agriculture of a single Community, inside which no quantitative restrictions, no import duties, and no equivalent barriers to the division of labor are to remain. On the other hand, Community agriculture is to be protected from world competition to a considerable extent, as all the component national agricultures were before. This latter principle could hardly be avoided politically, even had it not been thought socially desirable from the Community's own point of view. The Treaty, after all, demands "a fair standard of living for the agricultural Community," and, given the peasant holdings and traditions of many parts of Europe, farm productivity cannot be drastically raised overnight to the level obtaining in the wide-open spaces overseas.

In the case of such key products as cereals, for example, it was agreed in Regulation 19 that a *target price* should be fixed according to "objective criteria" to be decided by July, 1962. Then the authorities are obliged to buy any domestically produced wheat offered to them at the *intervention price*—not less than 90 per cent of the target price: Here, then, is the guarantee to the producer. Imports pay a levy which is equal to the difference between the landed price (including freight and insurance) from the most economic world supplier, and the *threshold price*—the latter being calculated as the target price minus the cost of bringing the wheat from its point of entry across the frontier to that area in the country which has the greatest grain deficit. Once the transition period is over, on January 1, 1970, there will be a single target price for all the Six, and there will be a single levy system for imports from outside the Community. Until then, the different national target prices are to be brought progressively nearer each other, the levies on imports from outside the Community being approximated *pari passu* with the target prices. During the transition period (beginning in this case on July 31, 1962), all other restrictions within the Community will be replaced by internal levies which will give a certain preference to Community products against the rest of the world, and which will be abolished *pari passu* with the equalization of the target prices.

Regulations 20–22 deal with pig meat (including—of great importance—sausages) with eggs, and with poultry meat. During the transition period, trade in these products will be subject to a levy designed to compensate the difference in the price of forage grains—a levy which will disappear as these are unified within the Community, but will remain on imports from outside. In addition, there will be a fixed charge (normally based, in the case of poultry and eggs, on the present customs duties); this charge will disappear on intra-Community trade by the end of the transition period and be unified for the whole Community on imports from outside it. In addition, there will be a preferential charge, starting at 2 per cent and rising to 7 per cent of an average import offer price, levied on imports from outside the Community. There will in addition be *sluice-gate prices* such that when abnormal supplies from outside the Community threaten to upset the market the levies can be increased.

Fruit and vegetable production will be protected from outside competition by a common tariff from January 1, 1970, with the possibility of safeguards in the case of serious disturbance caused by abnormally cheap supplies from outside the Community. The member states will reduce their mutual tariffs and harmonize their external tariffs during the transition period. Within the Community, the emphasis will be on quality control: Top-quality products may not be subjected to quantitative restrictions or similar measures after July 30, 1962, first-grade products after January 1, 1964, and second-grade products after January 1, 1966 (though here again safeguards against serious disturbance are allowed). The production of quality wines was to be the subject of a regulation by the end of 1962—that of April being mainly concerned with a register of vineyards and the declaration of quantities produced. Germany, France, and Italy, by a Council decision, opened quotas of 1.2 million, 0.8 million and 0.8 million hectoliters (31.7 million, 21.1 million, 21.1 million gallons) of wine respectively for imports from other member states.

These first regulations clearly set certain patterns and principles for the framework of the Community's agricultural policy, even if many vital products—milk products and beef, for example—are not yet covered by them. As to its substance, it will depend on the level of target prices not yet fixed just how self-sufficient or outward-looking the Community's policy is actually to be.

The receipts from all the levies on imports from outside the Community will, naturally, go not to the member state across whose frontier they happen to enter, but to the Community. And since the agricultural policy will be a unified one, it will also be the Community that bears its costs: subsidies on exports to nonmember countries, interventions in the market to buy up produce, and the financing of structural reforms. For the Community will intervene not only on the side of demand, but also on that of supply. The Community is acutely aware of the low level of agricultural productivity in the old world compared with the wide-open spaces overseas, and is determined within the limits of the socially and politically possible to rationalize agricultural production. The Agricultural Fund will make grants and take other measures to encourage the consolidation of small, uneconomic holdings and farm mechanization. In addition, the Community's Investment Bank (described on pp. 50–52 below) will be able to help attract labor off the land in the poorest areas and thus raise output and farm income per head. And by encouraging research, agricultural advisory services, and occupational training, the Community will also seek to improve the often deplorably primitive standards of cultivation.

Free Movement of Persons, Services, and Capital

For economic integration, free trade in goods is not enough; restrictions on the movement of the factors of production must also be abolished. Articles 48–73 are concerned with ensuring the mobility of people and enterprises.

Labor. Workers are to be free to move within the Community not later than at the end of the transitional period, and all discrimination based on nationality is forbidden. Except in the case of public administration, where a state may of course continue to employ only its own nationals, workers coming from any other member state, once offered a job, must be given equal treatment with a state's own nationals where remuneration and other working conditions are concerned. Indeed, in order to foster Community solidarity, the exchange of young workers is to be actively encouraged. Only on grounds of public health, order, or safety are limitations to be allowed of the rights to accept offers of employment anywhere in the Community and, once employed in a country, to stay there to continue in employment. Such freedom, to be effective, obviously involves mutual recognition of rights to social-security benefits of workers who may have started their careers and paid some of their social-security contributions in one country, but may need to draw on their social-security rights in another. These social-security rights have already been granted by an adaptation of the Coal and Steel Community's Convention on the subject: It now covers all Community workers.

The Council's Regulation 15 of August, 1961, envisages three stages for the progressive freeing of labor mobility. It contains detailed provisions for the first stage, which began on September 1, 1961, and which is not to exceed two years, and rather more vague desiderata for consequent action. During the first period there remains a certain priority for workers from the country in which employment is offered: Only if the national labor exchanges have failed to provide a suitable worker within three weeks is the job open to any Community worker and transmitted to the other labor exchanges of the Community. If, however, an employer asks for a worker by name, then the worker must be granted a work permit without reference to the state of the domestic labor market. Moreover, all restrictions on the numbers or percentages of foreign workers who may be employed by firms and industries in regions or a country will become invalid insofar as Community workers are concerned.

Once a foreign—or rather Community—worker has been regularly employed for a year, he is to be entitled to have his work permit renewed automatically for the same occupation; after three years for any occupation for which he is qualified; and after four years no further discrimination may be applied against him on national grounds. Other provisions in Regulation

15 see to it that a worker can bring his wife and any children under twenty-one, and that these are entitled to schooling and job opportunities.

Here in fact is a field in which the citizens of the Six will progressively be treated as if they had not French or Italian, but Community citizenship. This is a distinct increase in their rights.

At the moment, there is an acute shortage of labor almost everywhere in the Community except in Italy. The only substantial movement that has taken place so far, therefore, has been from Italy northward, particularly to West Germany and also to Holland. France and Germany have of course for some years been anxious to recruit Italian labor to ease their manpower shortages, and have been able to do so to some extent quite apart from the Common Market. But family and communal ties, language, food habits, climatic conditions, and similar factors appreciably restrict the economic motives for labor mobility, and the Federal Republic is already forced to look beyond the Community to such countries as Spain and Turkey for further labor. To facilitate mobility in a more active way, the Commission has now, for example, taken responsibility for a quick program of occupational training for 10,000 Italian workers, the bulk of whom found work in the Federal Republic by the end of 1961. But at the present rate of economic progress it seems doubtful whether Italy will have any reservoir of exportable labor for more than another four or five years. Then we may expect such movement as does take place to be a rather selective reciprocal process. (Indeed, by the summer of 1962, Italian employers were advertising jobs in Italian in the Belgian press to attract labor back to northern Italy.)

Services and the Right of Establishment. Where non–wage-earners are concerned, Articles 52–58 provide that these, too, shall by the end of the transitional period have the right to establish themselves, and Community firms to set up branches, agencies, and subsidiaries in any Community country. The same is true under Articles 59–66 for the provision of services; all restrictions on the supply of services in one country of the Community by nationals or firms from another must be abolished by the end of the transitional period. Professional activities, insurance, building contracts, the film industry, and (under Article 79) transport are obvious examples which fall into these categories. In October, 1961, the Council approved a detailed timetable according to which different types of activity are given their rights under the Treaty at different times during the transition period, January 1, 1964, being made a key date in the services sector.

Capital. Articles 67–73 provide that during the transitional period the member states must abolish restrictions on movements within the Community of capital belonging to their nationals "to the extent necessary for the proper functioning of the Common Market," and must end all national discrimination between Community capital. As a result, all the Six have unconditionally liberalized movements of capital connected with movements of persons, the right of establishment, and trade and services: Payments can be freely made at rates which, the member states have promised, will not diverge too far from the official rates. They have also irrevocably lifted all restrictions on payments for securities quoted on stock exchanges, though there the member states, while declaring their intention to avoid notable and lasting divergences between official and free exchange rates, have given no specific undertaking. Where new issues and securities not quoted on any stock exchange are concerned, the Commission's directive allows a country to retain or reimpose restrictions.

Common Transport Policy

In the case of coal and steel, where transport costs are a heavy item of total production costs and account for a large part of the total cost of goods transported, the Coal and Steel Community abolished discrimination according to the national origins of the goods carried and the additional freight charges calculated beyond any real increase in costs to the transporters each time the goods crossed a national frontier. The Economic Community has now abolished all discrimination according to national origins for all Community goods and is submitting proposals for the abolition of all national discrimination between Community transporters.

But the Rome Treaty goes much further than this in its demands: It not merely negatively rules out discrimination, but positively demands a common transport policy. The Commission interprets this to mean that the Community must secure the development of an efficient transport system which can not only satisfy the demands put upon it by the expansion of the economies and the trade of the Community, but which can also itself act as a stimulus to increased trade and expansion and to the development of more backward regions.

The coordination of road, rail, and inland waterways is difficult enough within any national economy. Just how important the last of these is in the heart of Europe's industrial area, everyone who has ever watched the stream of barges up and down the Rhine will understand. The question of pipelines, which is likely to become of major importance as oilpipes link—e.g., Genoa and Munich—is also under study. The fair sharing of infrastructure costs between the governments in whose territories the transport is required and the countries who will chiefly benefit from them obviously adds to the difficulties. Moreover, the different regional economic and social purposes pursued by the different governments through their intervention in the transport sector make the problem of a rationally harmonized transport policy a still thornier one. With some of these problems the Commission is only just coming to grips.

Where rationalization of existing transport facilities may be difficult, the Commission appears to be more successful in ensuring that transport facilities in the Community are expanded. In 1954, the Germans agreed (as part of the Saar settlement) to the old French wish to have the Moselle canalized in order to connect the Lorraine steel industry by waterway with the coal of the Ruhr. (The quality of Moselle wines, the experts assure us, will benefit rather than suffer from the scheme.) The Commission has since published its own program for the modernization of waterways and railways and for the building of trunk roads throughout the Community. Basing itself on the interests of the Community as a whole, and particularly concerned with eliminating the historical distortions caused in transport systems by the existence of national frontiers, the Commission's study has resulted in various important recommendations: to integrate the electrified systems of Holland, Belgium, and Germany, to electrify the Paris-Cologne run, to double the tracks on the Genoa-Chambery line, to build a canal between the Meuse and the Rhine, to deepen stretches of the Rhine, to standardize inland navigation equipment—to mention only a few. And the European Investment Bank can follow up such recommendations, where necessary, with appropriate finance: Thus, it has recently lent $4 million to France and $20 million to Italy for the modernization of the Chambery-Modane and Modane-Genoa runs—one of the axial transport routes of the Community.

Common Rules of Competition

To eliminate the economic impact of national frontiers is not by itself sufficient to produce fair competition: The Treaty goes further and in its Article 85 forbids any agreements between enterprises and concerted practices "which are liable to affect trade between member states and which are designed to prevent, restrict, or distort competition within the Common Market, or which have this effect." Any such limitation of production, discrimination in purchase or selling prices, market sharing, or similar practice is automatically prohibited unless the Commission has expressly declared it to be allowed; this the Commission may do on the grounds that it contributes to technical or economic progress and fulfills certain other conditions. Similarly, under Article 86, "improper exploitation of a dominant position within the Common Market" (such as a monopoly situation) is prohibited insofar as it affects interstate commerce between Community countries.

Although the Treaty allowed the Council of Ministers to adopt implementing regulations in this field by a qualified majority as from January 1, 1961, a unanimous decision could in fact be reached in December, 1961—in spite of governments which had originally wanted to water down the Commission's proposals. Accordingly, Regulation No. 17 came into force in March, 1962, as the first antitrust regulation of the Community.

This regulation affirmed that Articles 85 and 86 apply automatically without any prior decision from the Commission: On the other hand, the Commission can, at the request of the parties, give clearance to an agreement or a concerted practice if it finds that there are no grounds for it to intervene. Existing agreements must be notified to the Commission before November 1, 1962, if they are to obtain approval, though agreements not affecting trade between member countries, and minor forms of restriction such as resale-price maintenance, clauses governing the use of patents and trade-marks, and joint research agreements are exempt from this time limit. The Commission can back-date its approval at its discretion; it cannot impose fines for past breaches of the Treaty, provided these have been notified by November 1; but it can impose fines up to $1 million or even one-tenth of annual turnover where breaches are committed after it has given its ruling, and may do so in respect of the whole period from January 1, 1958, onward in cases where the agreement was not notified by November 1. New agreements (unless they are of the exempt kind described above) must be notified to the Commission, and (unless they are approved) are liable to expose the parties to them to fines for the period from the beginning of the agreement until its notification.

It will be fascinating to watch the Commission exercising these considerable powers and the reactions of business firms of the Six, which, on top of whatever national antitrust regulations there are, will now also be directly subject to the Community regulation.

Article 91 prohibits the dumping of commodities on the markets of other member states of the Community at less than cost price. Quite apart from any other measures, a state may always ship back any commodity to the exporting country free of duty. A number of complaints about dumping have already been successfully dealt with.

Articles 92–94 forbid state aid which threatens to distort competition by favoring certain firms against others in a manner affecting intra-Community trade; state aids are allowed, however, where they are granted to redress some extraordinary calamity, or as a social measure without national discrimination, or to help certain regions, or to develop projects important for the Community as a whole. As a result of these provisions, certain state aids to French textile manufacturers, German synthetic-rubber producers, and Italian motor manufacturers have been stopped. On the other hand, the Commission has allowed the Italian Government to give some aid to the Italian shipbuilding industry to make itself competitive, and has temporarily allowed the French to help producers of paper pulp.

Other articles deal with problems arising from differences in indirect taxes (such as excise duties) and with the harmonization of such laws as distort the conditions of competition. These can be troublesome matters, but they have not so far proved of major economic importance.

Business-Cycle and Balance-of-Payments Problems

If economic integration is to be defined as making political frontiers economically irrelevant, then there is one problem of a particularly pervasive character that must be tackled: How does one overcome not merely the differences among six national legislations, but the difficulty of five different currencies, with six different governments and five central banks pursuing five different fiscal and monetary policies? (Luxembourg is already part of the Belgian monetary area.)

Ideally, a Common Market would have a common currency. Proposals for a merger of currencies among the Six have been made, and probably, in the long run, a single European currency will be established with a single European central bank. But the Treaty does not itself provide for this, and a common currency is more likely to be a consequence than a precondition for a Common Market. The Treaty must therefore recognize the problem of harmonizing the fiscal and monetary or "anticyclical" policies of the five component monetary areas.

In Article 104 each member state thus binds itself "to ensure the equilibrium of its over-all balance of payments and to maintain confidence in its currency, while ensuring a high level of employment and the stability of the price level." We have seen in postwar Britain how difficult it is to steer the course between inflation and recession. Perhaps the problem is not so delicate on the continent, where no country is trying to combine this balancing feat with the further task of running its domestic currency also as a world store of value and standard of exchange. But the difficulties exist, for different national authorities are always liable to be faced with somewhat different problems and subject to rather different pressures.

For a start, the very opening of the sluices between the partner countries is a force making for conformity. Not only does it, by merging markets, confront governments and central banks with situations that will tend to become more similar, but it also raises the automatic pressures on any country which is tempted to break away from the rest. If it inflates too much, its gold loss will be quicker than when it could close its frontiers against its neighbors; if it tries to disinflate too hard, the export demands on its resources will take over at least some of the effective demand which its own nationals are forced to give up.

The Treaty does not, however, leave it all to these automatisms, which might work only after a considerable amount of tension has been generated. It established a Monetary Committee to keep the monetary and financial situation and the balance of payments of all the member states under review and to formulate opinions on the policies they should pursue. In addition, the Council decided in 1960 to set up a Committee on Policy Relating to Economic Trends to watch over the level of economic activity and prices. In fact, very close relationships have been set up between the different ministries of economics, treasuries, and central banks; their actions are more and more being taken after discussion among themselves in cognizance of each other's views and with reference to each other's policies.

When the Treaty was being negotiated, the problems looked even more complicated, for with an overvalued franc, it was feared that the freeing of trade within the Community would quickly put an intolerable strain on French currency reserves. Article 108 then seemed far more topical than it does today, when all the Community countries have very satisfactory reserves of foreign exchange. This article lays down that when a member state is in balance-of-payments difficulties, the Commission shall examine the situation without delay. (Just how unpleasant such an examination can be to the national officials concerned the French realized in 1957, when the OEEC instituted an examination of this kind—and one may expect a Community examination to be even more penetrating and frank.) The Commission then indicates what measures it recommends the state concerned to adopt. If the state takes this action and it proves insufficient, then "the Commission shall, after consulting the Monetary Committee, recommend to the Council the granting of mutual assistance" such as limited credits, special anticipatory reductions in tariffs, or concerted action in other international bodies such as the International Monetary Fund. Only where a balance-of-payments crisis strikes suddenly and the Council does not act immediately may the member state reimpose safeguards against its partners in the Community; and even then the Community can afterward insist on the abolition of these safeguards.

In fact, so far none of these provisions has ever been invoked. France devalued by about 17 per cent in December, 1958—a few days before the first tariff reductions—and has had no difficulties since. Germany, which was persistently running a heavy surplus with the world outside the Community, revalued the Deutschmark upward by 5 per cent in 1961, and the Netherlands followed suit. But no serious disequilibria between the countries have appeared, and, from 1958 to 1961, price levels in every country of the Community except France have remained almost unchanged. A world recession might throw serious strains on the whole somewhat tenuous machinery of harmonized business-cycle policy; but at least until 1962 there was prosperity without inflation—a phenomenon to which the fall of customs barriers was no doubt a useful contributory factor.

Social Policy

The Economic Community is concerned primarily with the enlargement of the Community cake, and broadly speaking leaves it to the member countries to pursue their own policies as to its distribution. Nothing in the Treaty, for example, refers to the height of income tax or the level of pensions and social services. These are matters in which each national electorate maintains its sovereignty. The member states, in Article 117, merely agree upon the need to promote an "improvement in the living and working conditions of workers in order to ensure that they share in the general progress," and the other articles of the Treaty are to be governed by this. The over-all preoccupation with the level of national income is of course in itself as much "social" as "economic"; and in addition the Treaty on various points specifically reflects egalitarian principles. As some of the greatest disparities in Europe today are regional disparities, the Community's long-term strategy of regional development (noted in the next section) is social in character even to the extent of possibly being "uneconomic." And for the short run, Articles 123–28 of the Treaty set up a European Social Fund to improve employment opportunities and in particular to guarantee workers against the loss of their employment owing to the establishment of the Common Market.

This Social Fund under article 125, is to bear 50 per cent of the expenses incurred by any state for:

> (*a*) ensuring productive re-employment of workers by means of:
> occupational retraining,
> resettlement allowances;
> (*b*) granting aid to workers whose employment is reduced or temporarily suspended whether wholly or partly as a result of the conversion of a concern to other production, in order that they may maintain the same wage-level pending their full re-employment.

For the year 1961, the Fund had at its disposal some $20 million, of which it committed $12 million; for the year 1962, its budget consisted of $29 million, and, in addition perhaps, the $8 million unexpended in 1961. But in view of Europe's present boom, the total amount asked for in respect of the four years 1958–61 in fact only came to less than $26 million.

There are also certain quite specific provisions on social matters embodied in the Treaty; these have a curious history. We have already seen that when the Treaty was negotiated, the French felt unable to compete because of the unrealistic exchange rate of the franc. But this was not a ground on which the French negotiators could argue their case. France's partners would simply have suggested a devaluation; yet, given the domestic political situation, the drastic retrenchment at home and in Africa required to stabilize domestic prices was impracticable, and devaluation would have brought no lasting betterment of her competitive position.

The French therefore made their point in a rather different way, and one which was to leave lasting and perhaps on the whole beneficial traces on the Treaty. They argued that their high rate of social-security payments—nearly 50 per cent on top of wages—raised their costs; so did the law on equal pay for women and the paid-holiday schemes. It was one of their conditions for accepting the Treaty, therefore, that the member states must, by the end of the first stage, ensure the principle of equal remuneration for equal work as between men and women workers, and that they express hopes and resolves of a rather less binding kind on the harmonization of social legislation and social-security systems. The other countries have promised France in Article 120 that they will endeavor to maintain the existing equivalence in paid-holiday schemes (i.e., not lower the amount of paid holidays embodied in their regulations), and it is understood that the problem of overtime charges will be gone into in the same spirit.

After the devaluation of 1958, France came to be much less concerned with the problem of social charges as an element in industrial costs. The prosperity of the member countries did not make the harmonization of social systems a particularly urgent task. But at the end of 1961, though equal pay for men and women was not implemented by the end of the first stage, the Council of Ministers did adopt a resolution whereby the member governments undertook to take all appropriate steps completely to eliminate discrimination in pay according to sex by the end of 1964. So the objectives of social harmonization originally set at French insistence remain very much on the governments' agenda.

Here indeed the labor movements of the other countries will thus have an additional handle for further developing the social systems of their countries; and there are certain social advantages which French labor, in its turn, may be able to press for by using the German or other systems as their model. The "productivity pension" introduced in Germany in 1957, for example—which not only automatically raises pension rates for successive vintages of pensioners with every rise in wages, but also passes on to pensioners a share in the general rise in current prosperity—is perhaps the most advanced national pension system in the world.

The European Investment Bank and Regional Policy

Free trade benefits the totality of countries taking part in it. But economic theory also recognizes that when hitherto separate economic areas begin to trade freely with each other, some of the participants may in fact suffer, though they will suffer less than the others gain. The real social costs of setting up a new industry or moving an existing industry into a particular area are not reflected in the cost to the firms involved: housing for workers, extra roads and transport facilities, and social services such as schools and hospitals have to go where the industries move, but the industries concerned bear only a small part of the costs to the community involved.

But even if all the social costs were reflected in the costs to the firm, it might still move toward the areas that are already most heavily industrialized—in Europe in particular to the Rhine Valley and the industrial triangle around it stretching from northern France to northern Germany, where wages may be high, but labor is skilled, and raw materials, transport, and a thickly populated market are all at hand. Even in the latter case, hypothetical though it is, the firm's new location might be economic from the Community viewpoint, but could still be socially and politically undesirable.

For there are other areas suffering from rural underemployment, like parts of central France, or concentrated on declining basic industries, like some of the Belgian coalfields. These, so far from sharing, tend if anything to be deprived of opportunities, at least in the short run: They cannot compete with the most efficient areas for lack of trained manpower, or for lack of basic infrastructure investment in transport and energy, or for lack of private capital, which is attracted to the more prosperous zones. Southern Italy was to some extent a victim of Italian unification: It is not inconceivable that if everything were left to the mechanisms of the market, European unification would once more result in even greater disparities between different regions. This was the major apprehension of the Italian Government when the Treaty was being negotiated.

The Treaty therefore sets up a European Investment Bank specifically to contribute to the balanced development of the Community as a whole. Both by using its own resources and by issuing guarantees to help raise private capital, it helps finance projects for the less developed regions, for the modernization or conversion of enterprises, and for creating new economic activities; it also helps major projects of common interest to several member states. The Bank may guarantee loans up to two and a half times the amount of its subscribed capital, fixed at $1 billion and contributed as follows: France and Germany $300 million each, Italy $240 million, Belgium $86.5 million, the Netherlands $71.5 million, and Luxembourg $2 million. There is also provision for the governments to grant special loans at 4 per cent up to $400 million to the Bank over and above this capital.

The Bank charges rates of interest "adapted to the conditions prevailing in the capital market" and such as to enable it to meet its obligations, cover its expenses, and progressively build up a reserve of 10 per cent of its subscribed capital. Its interest rates cannot therefore be expected to be very low; and it is not allowed to grant reductions, though a member state may arrange for a rebate at its own expense, provided it does not thereby fall foul of the Treaty provisions on state aid.

In the first three years in which it was operating, the Bank approved loans amounting to $160 million, thus helping investment projects which add up to over $1 billion: An integrated iron and steel works in Apulia, a Franco-Italian project to make diesel engines in Campania, and irrigation works in a backward region in the south of France are examples of the projects approved.

All this is of course not enough to bring the underdeveloped regions of Europe up to the level of the more highly industrialized areas, though at least it represents a beginning. But the Commission is actively interested in policies of regional development and is preparing plans for an integrated attack on these regional problems through a wide variety of means. As a series of policies for different regions comes to be formulated, the Bank may thus have the opportunity of becoming far more active. Moreover, an increase in its permitted scale of operations is by no means ruled out.

The Coal and Steel Community

The Coal and Steel Community was the pioneer in the field of integration. Now in its eleventh year of existence, it has never regarded itself as merely charged with the integration of one particular sector of the economy, but as a pathfinding experiment for the Economic Community that was to come. We have seen earlier that coal and steel represented not just one sector among many for which sector integration was planned: It was a particularly vital one, both from the political and from the economic point of view. How far then, looking back over its work, has the Coal and Steel Community succeeded?

Its transitional period ended in February, 1958. For the goods within its purview—coal, coke, iron ore, steel, and scrap—the Community had by that time abolished all customs duties, quantitative restrictions, dual pricing systems discriminating between Community buyers, currency restrictions for payments made in connection with trade, and transport discrimination by nationality and by the number of frontiers crossed as well as certain special transport rates favoring certain regions. This freeing of trade has not resulted in any major change in the flow of coal between Community countries; but intra-Community trade in scrap rose from 0.4 to 3.3 million tons, in steel from 2.1 to 9.5 million tons, and in iron ore from 9.4 to 26.5 million tons between 1952 and 1960. The bulk of this increase took place in the first three years after the institution of the Community, though there was another spectacular rise after 1958, the year, as it happens, in which the Economic Community began its work.

The Coal and Steel Community has a special responsibility not only for trade, but also for problems of production. One of its functions has been to publish general output objectives and to register investment programs in hand. Where this seems useful, it can aid investment. Its credit is good, for not only has it a governmental guarantee fund of $100 million, but it also has the right to levy its own production taxes, which at the moment stand at 0.35 per cent of the value of coal and steel output. It can thus raise loans on favorable terms—in 1954 it borrowed $100 million in the United States—and can relend these to finance investment that would otherwise be more expensive to make. With funds totaling nearly $300 million, it has been able to aid investments of well over $1 billion. Since it was instituted, steel production has risen from 42 million tons to 73 million tons. Moreover, since 1960 there has been a spurt of new investment in steel, with programs registered that year (including two major coastal steel works) totaling over $1.8 billion, twice as large as those of either of the two previous years, and in 1961 the rate was still $1.35 billion.

Matters are very different where coal is concerned. The Treaty was drafted on the assumption that the acute coal shortage of the postwar decade would be with us for a long time to come; the glut of coal that appeared in 1958 (when pithead stocks tripled in the course of twelve months) revealed not only the challenge of imported coal, but above all that of oil, which had conquered a third of the Community's energy market by 1960. As a result, one of the most delicate tasks of the Community will be to lead an orderly retreat of the coal industry, whose production in 1961 was in fact below that of 1952.

It is particularly the uneconomical Belgian mines which need to be shut down as part of a general reorganization of the industry. The Belgian mines were given special help during the transitional period, but failed to make effective use of it. A detailed new scheme of modernization and closure had to be launched in 1959 over which the High Authority has much tighter control.

Certainly this area of declining basic industries, which coincides with the Walloon (and largely anticlerical) half of Belgium, is facing serious problems; and these grievances, based on the facts of geology and economics, exploded at the time of the general strike in 1960–61. Here is one of those areas where Community action can be of direct relevance to national political problems—in this case to ease inevitable structural reforms.

For the social provisions of the Treaty are generous: Miners moving to other employment are paid a tide-over allowance for up to a year which, in the first four months, amounts to 90–100 per cent of their old wage; in their first year in a new job, their pay, if lower than their colliery earnings, is made up to their old wage; training for a new job is free, and removal and similar costs are paid for. Between 1954 and 1960, the Community paid out $42 million for such readaptation schemes, benefiting 115,000 workers: In each case, the national government matched the Community's contribution, so that double that amount of money was in fact used. In 1960, the Treaty was so amended that the social measures for readaptation would be maintained for the whole fifty years for which the Coal and Steel Treaty was concluded.

Other social measures taken by the Community include special allowances to miners affected by short-time working, assistance in the building of 25,000 dwellings for miners and steelworkers, the establishment of a Mines Safety Commission, research into industrial accidents and diseases, and securing the conclusion of the Convention on Social Security for Migrant Workers, which has since been taken over by the Economic Community.

On the other hand, the High Authority has not won all along the line. The governments have since 1958 been less willing to concede to M. Finet and M. Malvestiti what M. Monnet and M. René Mayer—the earlier Presidents, who also had the good fortune to be in charge at more prosperous times—thought was the High Authority's due. The agreement on the mobility of miners and steel workers has come into force, but the governments have handled the matter so gingerly that its practical effects so far are negligible. The High Authority has been unable to obtain the publication of all transport rates and unable to eliminate distortions resulting from differences in the methods of fixing road and water transport rates. These are minor matters compared with the solid achievements of the Community, but more important is the fact that the High Authority, during the coal glut, found that its powers in a time of surplus were not equal to those the Treaty had given it to cope with the scarcity obtaining when it was negotiated, and proved unable to prevent governments from gently influencing prices behind its back.

Today, indeed, the Community's most vital task would seem to be to formulate an over-all energy policy for the long-run future of the Community—a task which it is to undertake in close collaboration with the Economic Community (responsible for oil and natural gas) and Euratom. A meeting of the Ministers of Fuel and Power of the Six, held for the first time in the spring of 1962 in Rome, gave a certain political impetus to this essential planning, and in July, 1962, draft proposals were put before the Ministers by the Joint Energy Committee of the three Communities. This plan aims at securing the cheapest possible supplies of energy, subject only to two provisos: Excessive social dislocation in mining must be avoided, and continuity of supplies must be reasonably assured. By 1970, therefore, coal and oil are to enter the Community free of any duties or quantitative restrictions, to move freely within it at publicly quoted competitive prices, and to be subject only to harmonized fuel taxes. Mining, however, is to be subsidized up to a point, and quotas may be maintained on supplies from the Eastern bloc in order not to allow too large a share of supplies to become politically vulnerable.

Euratom

"None of our countries," so the Spaak Committee reported, "can by itself afford the vast resources needed for the research and basic investment required for the technical revolution of the atomic age." Unwilling to become entirely dependent on the United States for scientific and technical knowledge and for the plant involved in the use of nuclear energy, the Six decided that this was a field of a very special urgency, where a whole new industry must be fostered immediately by their joint efforts. Moreover, the very special, large-scale, and highly state-supervised or state-run character of the industry predestined it for supranational treatment. In fact it seemed to merit an organization quite distinct from that for the Common Market.

The military uses of nuclear energy are excluded from the Euratom Treaty: The French insisted on this, while the Germans, under the Paris Treaty of 1954, renounced the right ever to manufacture atomic weapons, and the remaining four countries have never developed ambitions to do so.

Euratom's task is not only to coordinate national research programs and circulate technical and scientific knowledge, but also to plug gaps in national research by its own work. It had $71 million earmarked for research in 1962, and its main research center, at Ispra on the Lago Maggiore, employed over 1,000 people at the end of March, 1962, while another 200 were employed at Geel in Belgium, Karlsruhe in Germany, and in starting up a fourth Euratom research center at Petten in Holland.

Euratom has given contracts to industrial firms (e.g., for a German research project into ship propulsion) and to the French Atomic Energy Commissariat (for studies of fusion). Some of its research is concentrating particularly on the smaller types of reactor which are expected to become economic in the near future, and it is encouraging the building of reactors that may not yet be economic for the sake of gaining operating experience for the Community.

Euratom has agreements for cooperation with the United States, Canada, Brazil, and the United Kingdom: In Britain, the Dragon project at Winfrith Heath is partly financed by Euratom, and, on the Continent, British technicians are working with Euratom.

In 1960, Euratom set up the Supply Agency called for by Article 52 of the Euratom Treaty. This is responsible for assembling the supply of ores, raw materials, and special fissile materials for all peaceful uses within the Community. In order to give everyone in the Community equal access to such resources and to implement a common supply policy, the Agency in fact has a right of option on all such materials; it retains property rights in special fissile materials and only puts these at the temporary disposal of the users, whether they be states, firms, or individuals. So far, however, the Agency's function has not proved to be of importance.

Euratom has established a common market without internal customs duties or quantitative restrictions in all fissile materials and in equipment used for processing them, and assures freedom of movement for capital and specialists connected with nuclear energy. It is also concerned with drawing up uniform rules for health and safety and ensuring that nuclear materials are used only for the peaceful purposes for which they were supplied.

The sense of urgency at the time Euratom was established is understandable: For most of the postwar period, Europe had been suffering from an acute shortage of energy, coal was scarce even in 1955, and the Suez crisis, coming in the middle of the negotiations and well before the ratification debates, once more highlighted Europe's dependence on outside energy supplies. But as it happened, the special optimism over atomic energy was a little premature. By 1959 there was a coal crisis in the opposite sense, and the nuclear technicians, for their part, have not yet succeeded in bringing the cost of electricity from nuclear plant down to a competitive level, though they expect to do so before 1970.

The Community's total installed capacity of 73 megawatt of nuclear electricity at the end of 1961 will be raised to twenty times as much by 1965 with the power stations now planned or under construction. The guess of the specialists today seems to be that, given the continual rise in the world's energy needs, nuclear energy will in a decade or so have a very important part to play in Europe's energy supplies. It is for this longer-term aim that the Community is now laying the foundations.

Mention must perhaps also be made of the curious but not illogical clause in the Euratom Treaty which, in the chapter headed "Development of Research," states that "an institution at university level shall be set up." The Euratom Commission has interpreted this as a call for a European University in which most of the major traditional faculties shall be represented. It has proposed that this should be located in Florence, and the Italian authorities have bought a site for the purpose at Marignolle, near that city. For some time the creation of this European

University was opposed by France, but at their Bonn meeting in July, 1961, the heads of government agreed on a compromise: Italy (not the Community) should set up a European University, to whose intellectual life and financing all six member states would make their contribution.

Conclusion

The reader who has had the patience to plough his way through this chapter may carry away a bewildering collection of miscellaneous facts. It would have been easy to present the Treaty simply as a blueprint for action, but that has been done often before. The point to be made today, five years after the Treaty first came into operation, is that things have happened. A hive of activity in Brussels and diplomatic agitation between the capitals have begun to make an impact on economic rules and regulations, on business, on public and private decisions. The Brussels Commissions, like the Luxembourg High Authority, have buckled down to work: They are making their impact felt in a whole gamut of ways in a whole welter of different domains. Hitherto the Economic Community's main achievement had been the reduction of barriers to trade. But particularly since late 1961, the Council has been forced to take crucial major decisions of policy harmonization as well. There is perhaps no moment when the subject could be an untidier one to describe than now. But the untidiness is the untidiness of a building site, and what matters is this: The elements are now largely assembled, and the structure is going up fast.

Nor is the flurry of innovation confined to economic life. The Common Market has triggered off all kinds of Community meetings between young people and university teachers, lawyers and designers, civil servants and trade unionists. From the new meetings, new ideas are sprouting up at every turn. There is a general will to reform outdated organizational structures. The establishment of the Community is forcing every member to compare its institutions and development with every other; it is calling old, established habits into question and opening up channels for new—often young—men to take charge of new and formidable tasks. At times it may assume the form of a mystique; but this liberating experience is one that must have been lived through on the spot, shared with Continental friends and colleagues, for its significance to be fully grasped. The spirit of passive resignation has fled from the center of the Continent: An awareness of their great workshop in which new shapes are being forged, a sense of achievement, a sense of their mastery over their destiny, a sense even of world mission has come over the new generation of Frenchmen and Germans, Dutchmen and Italians who operate the system and who are converting old national institutions and founding new industrial enterprises to meet the new challenge. The economic aspects we have outlined in this chapter matter. But what matters far more is the questing spirit that lies behind them, and which in their turn they foment. It is to the political expression of this spirit that we must now turn.

III

Supranationalism and Sovereignty

Federalist Strategy

The previous chapter has shown the host of detailed matters on which the member states have by treaty bound themselves to take certain *measures precisely specified in advance*. This type of surrender of sovereignty is that implied by any classical treaty in which a state undertakes to do or to abstain from any specified course of action. Even the facts that the Rome Treaties are concluded for an unlimited period and that France renounced her demand for the right of unilateral secession do not radically distinguish such abrogation of sovereignty from other perpetual treaties.

The previous chapter has also shown the welter of other decisions which the member states have bound themselves to take in common—not yet knowing what the action required of them will be, but agreeing to follow a decision-making procedure in which they cannot expect to have it all their own way. It is in this second feature of the Treaties—by which a state pledges itself to take *measures as yet unknown* provided they are decided by a certain procedure—that the first elements of something rather more far-reaching are to be found.

The problem is: How shall these decisions be made? And here we must distinguish sharply between intergovernmental and supranational procedures. States may by treaty decide to take action only when they are all agreed: A rule of unanimity such as existed in the Organization for European Economic Cooperation makes common decision-making no legal infringement of sovereignty. Of course the very fact of sitting together in the same committee room, of looking at problems in the light of a joint discussion and perhaps of the same working documents, of wanting to take decisions in common for the natural reasons which prompt men to want to agree may in practice result in modifications of policy. But the final right of the nation-state to go its own way remains unimpaired by any international organization in which it can interpose its veto.

Supranationality only starts to come into play when a state agrees that it is willing to carry out decisions to which it is itself opposed. Most obviously, such a situation arises when it has agreed to be outvoted if necessary by other states—either by a simple or by some weighted or qualified majority. Let us call this governmental supranationality.

But there is a danger in such an abdication of sovereignty: For may not an alliance of other states, simply pursuing their own interest, outvote one's own state and exploit it, flagrantly neglecting its interests in favor of their own? Coalitions of interest within a unit of decision make for bad government. That is why federalist thinking on institutions goes much further than governmental supranationalism.

In the United States, the Senators may come from different states and on "logrolling" or "pork-barrel" issues may indeed stand for the bread-and-butter interest of their own states as against all the rest. But over the whole range of broader issues they regard themselves as trustees for the union as a whole. And the President, as chief executive and effective initiator of most legislation, is elected to represent the union as distinct from, and if need be as opposed to, the particular interests of any of its component states. Similarly, the federalists of Australia established a commonwealth that decides its policy not by coalitions of state interest, but on a commonwealth basis in the interests of all its citizens; and the same preoccupation is at the root of Canadian federal government.

In just the same way, European federalists, too, believe that—at least until a community of economic interests has been achieved, but all the more naturally thereafter—decisions must not be taken by reciprocal bargains between representatives of member states at all. The parallelogram of national forces may in fact let the Community slither into policies which are not in the long-term interest of any of the members. The states may be represented as parts of the whole, just as labor and management —or agriculture and specific branches of industry, or different political parties—may be represented as equally valid other parts of the whole. But only a body which feels itself to be as responsible for the whole as the President of the United States, a body which is not responsible, not beholden, and not partial to any of the constituent parts as against the rest can take supranational (or "objective") decisions for the Community as such—can act, in other words, not simply as a mediator reconciling existing national policies framed, as they often are, largely to bounce the damage off onto the neighbors, but can look afresh at specific problems as they present themselves on a Community scale and can seek solutions for them at the Community level. Governmental supranationality must, therefore, according to the federalist argument, yield to supranationality of the Community type.

Now what is the nature of Community decisions? Some may be technical, but the main lines of Community policy involve far greater considerations. On the Community's agricultural policy will depend the cost of living of 170 million consumers and the prosperity or bankruptcy of millions of peasants; on its energy policy will depend the livelihood of thousands of miners and the prosperity of six industrial economies; and its investment bank can profoundly transform the economic and social life of whole regions. Long-run benefits must be weighed against short-run costs; one man's advantage must be weighed against damage to another. And stated in this way it becomes obvious once more that these—however economic their subject matter—must be political decisions.

These considerations in fact dispose of a question that has frequently been raised in recent discussions: whether the Community is primarily an economic or primarily a political enterprise. The very question is based on a fallacy—on the notion that there are two different species of questions, some called economic, others called political. There are many different problems—economic, social, moral, penal, diplomatic, strategic—and any of these may at a given moment become political. Nationalization, a health service, a Wolfenden Report, hanging, summitry, unilateralism—these problems become political not because of what they are about, but because of how they are treated. Politics is not the name of another subject, but of the arena in which these subjects are thrashed out toward a communal decision. Today economic problems are among the most important of these subjects: And that is why the Economic Community is a political enterprise not least precisely *because* it is economic.

Who then is to take the Community's decisions? And who is to exercise democratic control over them? The ultimate federalist answer is: a college of citizens of the Community who are appointed not by their national governments, but by the elected representatives of the Community's citizens themselves, to whom they must render account and by whom they may be dismissed. But this is a long-term objective, and on the way toward it, embryonic federal institutions are all that can be hoped for—and perhaps all that is necessary at the outset. These will themselves create the need and the demand for more radically federal institutions.

Federalists believe that integration—whether economic or political, and above all a combination of the two—has its own logic and gathers its own impetus. Once the first few steps are taken, the rest will sooner or later, in one way or another, tend to follow. Integration of coal and steel will remove political obstacles to Franco-German friendship and create certain common interests. It will raise problems of transport harmonization and of social policy. It will institute a technocracy which must be controlled by political means. But once the wider economic questions are broached, broader economic policies come to be harmonized, thus easing further integration and calling for further political control; and the more political machinery there is, the more will it make sense to take economic decisions in common. The process snowballs until a single European Political Community results. Whether this theory is infallible does not now matter. What is essential is to realize that this is the federalists' aim openly repeated and insisted upon almost *ad nauseam* —and that the federalists have an important share in taking the Community's decisions.

In the first chapter, we have outlined the structure which the federalists hoped to give to Europe in the period 1950–54. What they were left with in 1955 was the Coal and Steel Community. Instead of being able to set up a defense community parallel with it and a political community to arch over both, by the Rome Treaty they created two further parallel pillars: the Economic Community and Euratom. The two latter share with the Coal and Steel Community the European Court of Justice. The Coal and Steel Community's Common Assembly has been replaced by a European Parliamentary Assembly supervising the work of all three Communities, and their Councils of Ministers are virtually congruent with each other. In addition they share certain consultative bodies. The Chart on p. 66 outlines this institutional structure. It must now be our task to look at each institution in turn, focusing all the time on two questions: How much supranationality have the member states formally accepted; and what constitutional realities lie behind the new structure?

The Executives and Councils in Law

The only one of the three Community Treaties which contains the brave word "supranational" is that setting up the Coal and Steel Community:

> The members of the High Authority shall exercise their functions in complete independence in the general interests of the Community. In the fulfillment of their duties, they shall neither solicit nor accept instructions from any government or any organization. They will abstain from all conduct incompatible with the supranational character of their functions.
>
> Each member state undertakes to respect this supranational character and not to seek to influence the members of the High Authority in the execution of their duties.*

The High Authority consists of nine members chosen for their general competence. They serve for six years. The original High

* Article 9.

Authority consisted of eight members chosen by the member states acting in agreement, and a ninth co-opted by these eight. M. Jean Monnet, the architect of the French Modernization Plan, became the High Authority's first President. In 1958, when the transitional period of the Coal and Steel Community had been left well behind, eight members were again nominated by the governments, but this time five governments were sufficient to ensure a member's election: The ninth member could be co-opted by five votes out of the eight nominees of the governments. The casting of lots decided which three of these nine should serve for two years, which three for four, and which three for six: And now the resulting vacancies (normally three seats every second year) are filled alternately by the nomination of at least five out of the six governments and by co-option by at least five out of the eight sitting members. No nationality may have more than two members, and so far the High Authority has always contained two Frenchmen, two Germans, two Belgians, one Italian, and one each from the two other Benelux states. The High Authority meets in private, like a cabinet, and—deciding if necessary by simple majority—takes collegiate responsibility for its decisions. It seems in fact that it has rarely, if ever, split along national lines. Indeed, as one of its members said after the first crucial two years were nearly over, "I could count on my fingers the number of decisions on which we were not unanimous."

The High Authority cannot be dismissed by the member governments: These can only refuse to reappoint a man after his six years in office, and even then he could be co-opted back by his colleagues. But the High Authority can be forced to resign in a body if the Assembly, with the High Authority's Annual General Report before it, passes a vote of censure by a two-thirds majority. It is thus not to national governments, but to the indirect representatives of the people that the High Authority is responsible.

The High Authority can intervene directly within the member states. Its production levy is the first European tax fixed and directly collected by the High Authority. (The levy may not, however, exceed 1 per cent of production value unless a two-thirds majority of the Council agrees.) Without going through the member governments, the High Authority can impose fines

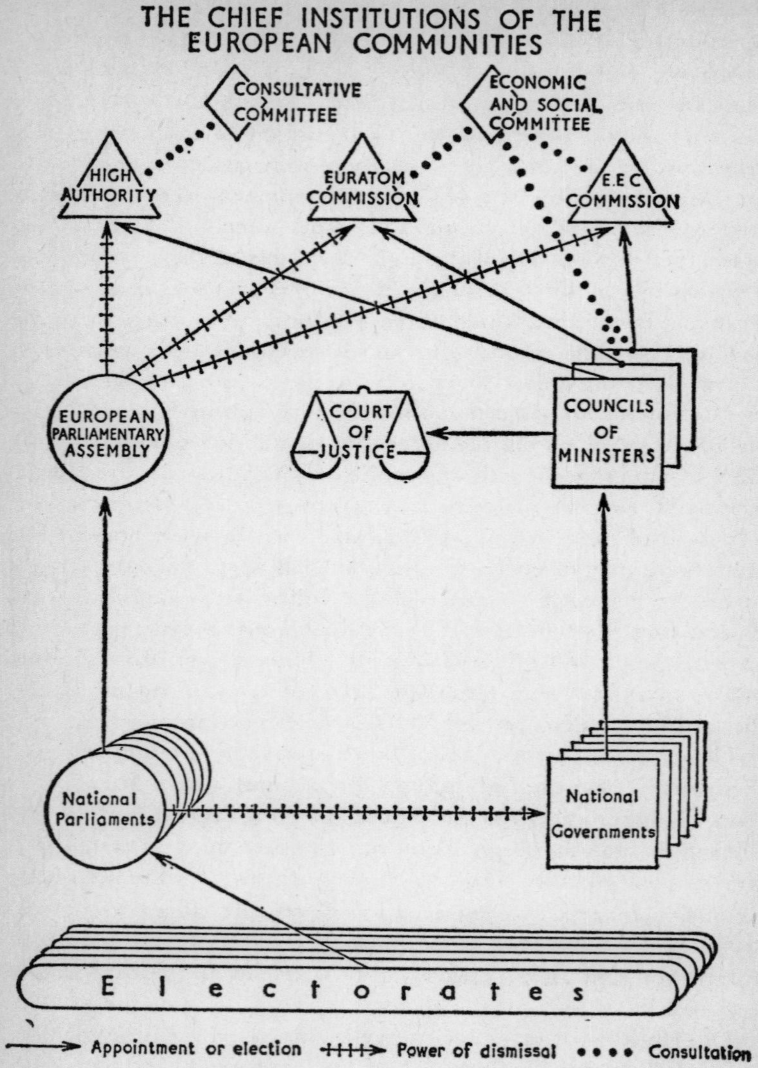

THE CHIEF INSTITUTIONS OF THE EUROPEAN COMMUNITIES

CONSULTATIVE COMMITTEE
ECONOMIC AND SOCIAL COMMITTEE
HIGH AUTHORITY
EURATOM COMMISSION
E.E.C COMMISSION
EUROPEAN PARLIAMENTARY ASSEMBLY
COURT OF JUSTICE
COUNCILS OF MINISTERS
National Parliaments
National Governments
Electorates

Appointment or election ‖ Power of dismissal ‖ Consultation

Strictly speaking, the Commissions and the Court of Justice are appointed by the governments acting in agreement. For the precise method by which members of the High Authority are now appointed, see pp. 64–65.

on enterprises and can declare industrial agreements invalid; its decisions have force of law in all member states unless the Community's Court of Justice, which exercises the judicial control over the High Authority, annuls them.

In the original Schuman Plan, the High Authority was the only executive organ envisaged. But at Belgian and Dutch insistence, a second organ was constructed in the course of the negotiations: the Council of Ministers, representing the national governments, which can in certain fields (notably those marginal to the main purposes of the Treaty) check the actions of the High Authority, though it has no power of initiative of its own. According to the Coal and Steel Treaty, three functions—initiative, decision, and execution—thus in most cases belong to the supranational body of the Community type.

The negotiations setting up the other two Communities were held after the defeat of EDC, and with a rather different alignment of national interests. In the case of the Economic Community (the Treaty which from our present point of view is the most important), there was in fact a curious ambivalence and reversal of motives among the chief negotiating partners. The French had insisted on supranationality of the Community type for coal and steel in 1950, but they found that their own National Assembly rejected it for defense in 1954. For political reasons, they therefore did not wish to give too much power to the Community institutions. Yet, because of French successes with public planning, and because of French preoccupation with their competitive position—which meant in practice with the elimination of disparities, the harmonization of policies, and the public organization of agricultural markets—the French were concerned to give the Community effective powers over the national economies. With the Germans it was just the other way round. For political reasons, Dr. Adenauer was anxious to push on toward strong supranational institutions. But the Germans had built up their "economic miracle" on the basis of a "free market economy" and distrusted *dirigisme* in any form; for economic reasons, therefore, they were anxious to limit the powers of intervention of the Community. The German position was on the whole shared by the Netherlands. Italy, for both political and economic reasons, wanted a strong Community, though she has since not always lived up to that obedience to the Community which such a position would really seem to entail.

The Commission of Euratom consists of five, that of the Economic Community of nine independent members, appointed by mutual agreement among the governments for renewable terms of four years only. The presidents and two vice-presidents are appointed from among the members of each Commission for two years at a time, by agreement among the governments. In the case of Euratom not more than one, in the case of the Economic Community not more than two members may be of the same nationality. The Commissions are responsible collectively, and while the High Authority can be turned out only on consideration of its annual general report, the Commissions can be forced to resign by a vote of censure in the Assembly (which must be carried by a two-thirds majority of those voting and a simple majority of all members) at any time. But the functions of the Commissions are in law circumscribed compared with those of the High Authority. While the latter "shall ensure that the objects of the Treaty are achieved" (Article 8 of the ECSC Treaty), the Commissions, under Articles 155 of the EEC and 124 of the Euratom Treaty, are there merely to:

> Ensure that the provisions of this Treaty and the measures taken by the institutions by virtue of this Treaty are carried out.
>
> Formulate recommendations or give opinions on matters within the scope of this Treaty, if it expressly so provides or if the Commission considers this necessary.
>
> Have power itself to take decisions and in the circumstances provided for in this Treaty participate in the shaping of measures taken by the Council and by the Assembly.
>
> Exercise the powers conferred on it by the Council to ensure effect being given to rules laid down by the latter.

The Rome Treaties thus at first sight mark a retreat from the federalist concept to one of states' rights. Where the High Authority over a whole range of problems frames a policy, decides to implement it, and then goes out to execute it, the Commissions only have the right to frame the policy and to execute it. The decision whether or not a policy is to be adopted is taken by the Council of Ministers, which is thus as it were the legislature of the Community. As a result of this separation of legislative and executive functions, the Assembly, although it is given a closer and more immediate right of control over the Commissions than it has over the High Authority, can control only the body that frames the policy and executes it, but not the legislative organ which decides upon its implementation. In that respect, the unification of legislative and executive functions in the High Authority allowed at least in theory a closer parliamentary control.

The emphasis in the EEC Treaty is thus much more on the Council as the main legislative organ. But this does not make the Economic Community into a merely intergovernmental organization: It simply stresses the governmental type of supranationality as against the Community type when major policy decisions have to be given legal validity. In fact, as we shall see, the bulk of major policy decisions can be taken only on the proposal of the Commission, so that the proposals themselves must come originally from an institution that is supranational in the Community sense. Without such a proposal from the Commission, the Council is hamstrung. With the power of initiative the monopoly of the Community institution, and the power to legislate the monopoly of the governmental institution, the two are effectively interdependent, and policies must be evolved in a dialogue between them.

As for the Council, decision-making of the governmental type may of course be supranational to varying degrees, shading according to the voting procedure from something close to the Community to the merely intergovernmental type. There are in fact five different methods of voting in the Councils, laid down in identical articles in the Rome Treaties (Articles 148 and 149 of the Treaty for the Economic Community, Articles 118 and 119 of the Euratom Treaty). Let us here list them in order of their degree of supranationality:

(*a*) When, in accordance with this Treaty, the Council acts on a proposal of the Commission, it may only adopt amendments to that proposal by a unanimous vote.*

This, in theory, looks like a last federalist hope in the Treaty's decision-making machinery: For it means, in theory, that pro-

* Article 149.

vided the Commission is supported by one country, albeit Luxembourg, then its proposals cannot be amended. (Absence and abstention do not disturb the unanimity required by the Treaty.) Now of course in practice this has proved to be a somewhat unreal legal construction. For instead of trying to amend the Commission's proposals by a unanimous vote, the Council simply refuses to vote on the proposal at all and tells the Commission to go away and think again. Indeed Article 149 goes on expressly to provide for this:

> At any time before the Council reaches a decision, the Commission shall be free to amend its original proposal, especially if the Assembly has been consulted on the proposal in question.

The intergovernmental type of supranationality that comes closest to the Community type, that in which one member state is sufficient to uphold the Commission's proposals, has thus in fact proved impracticable. But if this clause does not enshrine the intergovernmental type of supranationality that comes closest to the Community type, it has nevertheless a vital negative significance: Only if all the states are agreed can they amend the Commission's proposals; and then it would seem fair that they should be able to do so. But unless they are all agreed, the Council of Ministers is unable to amend any proposal from the Commission, so that the Council of Ministers, whenever it has to act on a proposal of the Commission, cannot take any decision except precisely that one which the Commission has put forward. Thus no decisions can be taken that are not approved by the organ which is supranational in the Community sense—a vital safeguard for each state against coalitions of interest being exerted against it, and a safeguard to the Community as a whole which prevents the adoption (by changing majorities) of policies that might be materially incompatible. So much for the possibility of *amendment* of a Commission proposal.

(*b*) Then there are decisions to be taken by a majority vote of the Council's members. In these cases, four of the six member states must be in agreement on a course of action. France and Germany together can thus be outvoted, but only if the rest are all agreed among themselves.

(*c*) The major policy decisions, however, require a qualified majority upon proposal of the Commission. The logic behind this "qualified majority" is fairly straightforward. The fact that a vote can be taken only on a proposal of the Commission is designed to ensure that the proposals to be voted on are made with the interests of the Community as a whole in mind, and cannot result from a mere coalition of national interests. That being the case, no one country should be allowed a veto, for the interests of the Community as a whole are not to be blocked by any one national component of it. Nor should the support of Luxembourg, with its mere 300,000 inhabitants, constitute the justification of a national veto by any of the other states. But if France, Germany, and Italy, with about 50 million inhabitants each, are not to have separate vetoes, then the Benelux countries combined, having a total of less than 22 million inhabitants, must not be allowed a veto either. To satisfy these requirements, France, Germany, and Italy were given four votes each; Belgium and the Netherlands two each; and Luxembourg one; and twelve out of these seventeen votes constitute a qualified majority. This means that Benelux can be overruled only if the big three are agreed with the Commission; if not all of the big three agree with the Commission, then once again at least four member states must agree with the Commission, and even then, any two big states, or any big and any medium state together, can interpose a joint veto.

(*d*) There are a few matters on which the Council can vote without having before it a proposal from the Commission; in such cases, *both* the agreement of four member states *and* twelve votes are required for the qualified majority. Here the Benelux countries, not feeling protected by the Commission, insisted on retaining their joint veto against the big three. This type of qualified majority thus requires either three big states and one from Benelux, or two big states and both Belgium and Holland.

(*e*) Finally, and particularly in the first two stages of the Treaty's implementation, there are decisions that can only be taken unanimously. Here once more, absence or abstention does not invalidate unanimity. This is the situation in which every country, even Luxembourg, has a power of veto, and in which the Council functions in a purely intergovernmental way. Such unanimity is always required for such matters as directives on the movement of capital between member states and third countries, for the harmonization of national fiscal legislation and the approximation of laws in general, for adopting the program for the removal of restrictions on the right to establishment, for determining the provisions for association with the overseas countries, for provisions on the direct election of the Parliamentary Assembly, and for a good many institutional matters.

It would be tedious to list here all the 150 or so types of decisions to be taken under the Rome Treaty and the method of voting laid down for each. But a few figures (which must necessarily disregard the relative importance of different decisions) will give an idea of the division of powers. The Treaty defines only 35 cases where the Commission can act independently of the Council —and these are decisions of a relatively minor executive kind. In 75 further cases, the Council can act only on a proposal of the Commission: Only in 40 cases can the Council proceed autonomously without a Commission proposal before it. Of these 115 decision to be taken by the Council, 55 had to be taken unanimously in the first stage; though now that we are in the second stage, that number has been reduced to 50, while the number of decisions to be taken by a qualified majority has risen from 50 to 55 (and will rise sharply again at the end of the second and third stages). In 10 cases, the Council decides by simple majority.

The details may be left to the experts, but what is essential to note is that as time goes on through the transitional period, the voting system becomes more supranational. For the regulation of cartels and monopolistic practices, the transition from the unanimity to the qualified-majority rule came about as early as January, 1961. In the case of the common agricultural, commercial, and transport policies, to give three vitally important examples, the transition from the unanimity rule to the qualified-majority rule comes at the end of the second stage, though we have seen how the agricultural settlement, unanimously reached in January, 1962, has itself intensified the supranationality of subsequent decisions on agriculture, both by introducing qualified majorities ahead of time and by transferring powers to the Commission. In the Council itself, the qualified majority becomes the broad rule over the whole field of economic substance covered by the Treaty, once the transition period is over. The member states have thus in the Treaty committed themselves not simply to a scale, but to an escalator of supranationality. On the one side, this puts pressure on them to agree more quickly to joint policies; and on the other, it leaves some of the more ticklish majority decisions until a greater sense of community of interest and a more rooted habit of Community action have in the course of time been established.

The Executives and Councils in Practice

So much for the paper dispositions of the Coal and Steel Treaty on the one side, and the Rome Treaties on the other. In practice, there have been fewer differences in the cooperation between Community bodies and governmental bodies than the legal differences in the Treaty provisions might lead one to suppose.

One must here look not only at the procedural, but at the substantive articles of the Treaties. The authors of the Coal and Steel Treaty, restricting themselves to one or two sectors of the economy, facing much more clearly defined problems, set out quite precise solutions in the Treaty itself. In consequence, the "legislative" power of the High Authority is much more a power to issue implementing orders than one of passing genuine new laws. The Euratom Treaty, too, goes into detail on an even more restricted field of application, and leaves the Commission on the whole with less need to ask for decisions from the Council.

The Common Market Treaty, on the other hand, is largely no more than an outline for policy objectives; it leaves the actual policies to be formulated later. The governments have thus simply reserved to themselves the right to fix these policies as they did in the Coal and Steel Treaty—albeit in this case after the signature of the Treaty. Before the treaties were concluded, each government in fact had a veto: It could ultimately refuse to join. When the policies are fixed after ratification of the Treaties, it is natural that the governments try to reserve their powers. And if not each of them separately, but only predetermined combinations of governments retain their veto, this in fact marks a certain degree of real progress toward greater governmental supranationality as compared with the ECSC—a progress made possible because the broad objectives have been fixed, and there is a supranational Commission which the governments trust to see to it that these objectives are respected. Here, in other words, supranationality of the Community type in the executive was required before the governments themselves were willing to accept supranationality of the governmental type for the legislature.

Secondly, there is the way in which executives and councils have in fact behaved. The members of the High Authority have never acted as governmental delegates. But neither have they always been able to maintain Olympian detachment from their own or other national governments; indeed, they have not felt that they should act without close consultation of the national governments. In particular, after the defeat of the EDC, the High Authority decided that it needed not only the support of the Assembly, on which it could always rely if it acted boldly, but also that of the national governments. M. Monnet probably paid the penalty of excessive independence from the French Government when he declined to be a candidate for reappointment in 1955. Then again, when the coal glut of 1958 came, the High Authority found that, in distinction to crises of shortage, it could not even under the Treaty act alone. Under Article 58, it required the agreement of the Council for its measures, and so it found itself no better off than the Common Market Commission even in law. Nevertheless, there are of course many situations in which the High Authority, with its supranational powers of decision in reserve, can press the governments hard, as it has done over a whole range of issues. And if it has not entirely succeeded over cartels, we have seen how much it was able to achieve, particularly once it had the governments on its side.

The Commission of the Economic Community, though it can act by itself only on minor matters, has the sole power of initiative on the real problems of economic substance, and the influence that automatically accrues to any author of the first draft. On the other hand, it is forced throughout to ask itself what kinds of proposals it can expect to get through the Council and what kinds of proposals the Council is likely to throw out. There will be times when the national governments, unable to agree, will ask the Commission to help them out of their disagreement. But there may also be times when members of the Commissions—aware that they depend on the governments for reappointment, and, in distinction to members of the High Authority, have only four years of office—will be unwilling to display excessive independence of spirit. We have seen already how, over the question of agricultural policy, the Commission thought it best to go slowly while it felt that governments would give its proposals a cool reception, and how, by a gentlemen's agreement between governments, the timing of the Community's decisions may be affected by national elections, and their content by regional riots. And M. Étienne Hirsch, the first President of Euratom, was refused a second four-year term by his own French Government, partly perhaps because a post was required for M. Pierre Châtenet, but largely also because of his refusal to follow his government's line in atomic matters.

Thirdly, another factor has come to light more clearly since January, 1962, which once more makes apparent the legal difference between the supranationality of the ECSC Treaty and that of the EEC Treaty. To some extent in the negotiations over restrictive business practices, but far more so in those over the common agricultural policy, the existence of the Commission and the possibility of delegating to it problems which are too delicate to be solved by intergovernmental negotiations allowed the governments to divest themselves of powers and to transfer decisions to an institution that was supranational in the Community sense. In the agricultural sector, for example, the Commission can now make decisions that are not subject to revisions by the Council. It may authorize a member state to reduce its levies on pig meat and it may authorize safeguard measures for "top-quality" fruit and vegetables; and in the agricultural as in the industrial sector, it may decide whether agreements between producers or practices which they follow are incompatible with the Common Market. Even in the lump-sum figure which in fact determines the margin of preference given to Community cereal producers over the rest of the world (and therefore fixes in effect the "inward" or "outward" look of the Community in this sector), the Commission's decisions are immediately applicable, and the Council can vary them only by a qualified majority within a month or less of the Commission's decision. The same procedure has been laid down for levies on eggs and poultry and for the sluice-gate price for pig meat. It is not least due to the agricultural settlement that if, by July, 1962, only eleven out of fifty-seven Community regulations were issued by the Commission acting alone without the Council, fifteen more such regulations would be due by September.

But either way, the national governments must be and are constantly consulted. The Council itself had held sixty-five sessions by April, 1962—an average of fifteen sessions a year, each lasting anywhere between one and four days (though the mammoth session from December 18, 1961, until January 14, 1962, was a notable exception). These meetings, however, are held to take decisions which the ministers alone can take. In order to facilitate consultations, therefore, the governments have sent permanent representatives to Brussels—men of senior status within the rank of ambassador. Long before the Council meets, the permanent representatives have been mulling over the questions on its agenda at their weekly meetings, have all put forth their governments' points of view, and have together sought to harmonize their views with those of the other governments and those of the Commission.

More recently, the constitutional gulf between the Commission and the Council has been bridged by still another link—not only by the permanent representatives, but by special committees in which the Commission's representatives and the representatives of national ministries, under the general supervision of the permanent representatives, hammer out together the problems arising out of a proposal from the Commission. The Rey Committee on Trade (named after the member of the Commission responsible for the subject) and the Special Committee on Agriculture have thus been meeting several times a month, and bilateral talks to facilitate Council decisions are frequent between their meetings.

Once policies have been decided by the Council, the technical problems of their implementation are worked out; while the governmental experts are carefully kept out of the process by which the staff of the Commission prepares the Commission's proposals to the Council, the governmental experts have a major role to play in helping the Commission implement the Council's decisions. Formally, they do not commit their governments when they assist and advise the Commission's staff on matters of technical execution, but if they can agree with the competent department in Brussels and with each other, the Commission can expect a clear run. The dimensions of the work involved can perhaps be gaged by the fact that, in 1961, over a thousand such meetings of experts were convened by the Commission and chaired by its European civil servants; and quite apart from their direct usefulness, these exercises are beginning to spread, within each of the six national administrative machines, a habit of cooperation, of thinking in European terms and bearing each other's problems in mind.

All this procedure is more than purely international negotiation, for the Commission is there in a leading role not just as a broker, but to represent the interests of the whole against the parts. But it is less than Community supranationalism, and on questions on which unanimity is required it is of course less than governmental supranationalism, too. It is in fact a limbo in between all these, in which a highly sophisticated political game is played that involves not only all the pieces on six national chessboards, but also the whole European dimension corresponding to each: European party groups and European pressure groups have formed across national frontiers to organize pressure at the Community level and to match the institutions of the Community as they do those of each nation-state. Decisions in this procedure tend to be not so much taken as evolved.

We must therefore turn to the other official European institutions that have a hand to play in this game. As the Commission represents the interests of the Community as a whole and the Council represents the member states, so the Parliamentary Assembly is designed to represent the parties; the Consultative Committee of ECSC and the Economic and Social Committee of the two other Communities, as "corporate" advisory institutions, give formal representation to the main interest groups; and the Court of Justice is there to uphold the law of the Treaties.

The Common and the Parliamentary Assembly

When M. Schuman first put forward his plan for a High Authority, it was criticized on the grounds that it would set up an international technocracy responsible to no one: If it were independent of governments, who would there be to control it? The Council of Europe here provided a model for a second organ: and so M. Monnet early in the negotiations proposed a Common Assembly consisting of representatives of the parliaments of the member states to exercise democratic control. (This was before the Council of Ministers had been proposed.)

The Coal and Steel Treaty thus laid down that:

> The Assembly shall consist of delegates whom the parliaments of each of the member states shall be called upon to appoint once a year from among its own membership, or who shall be elected by direct universal suffrage, according to a procedure determined by each respective high contracting party.

So far, they have in fact been elected by their national parliaments. The High Authority must submit an annual report to the Assembly, and a vote of censure passed by two-thirds of the votes cast and representing a majority of the total membership forces the High Authority to resign as a body. This is of course an important ultimate sanction, on which the influence of the Assembly is partly based; but it is in a sense so ultimate that it is unlikely to be used. The High Authority is also bound to answer any questions put to it by the Assembly or any of its members and finds itself involved in detailed debates with it.

The Common Assembly met in the Council of Europe's building in Strasbourg several times each year, for a week or so at a time, from 1952 until 1958. It had seventy-eight members, who in 1958 included thirty-seven Christian Democrats, twenty-two Socialists, and seventeen Liberals, with an equal number of substitutes drawn from the same national parties. During and between its meetings, there would be committee meetings, throughout most of the year. Its committees, like those of Continental parliaments in general, were specialized, so as to ensure expert supervision by parliamentarians specialized in a particular field:

social questions, transport, commercial policy, mine safety, and so forth—with a political committee which often almost regarded itself as part of a general staff planning further advances toward political integration.

The Common Assembly, dealing with concrete problems and exercising parliamentary control over the first European supranational authority with limited functions but very real powers, quickly turned into a far more influential body than the Council of Europe's purely consultative Assembly has ever become. It soon developed, too, into something that looked much more like a parliament: It organized itself officially into three party groups, whose budgets were met out of the funds of the Community.

The Socialists were the first to set up a well-organized party group, based on the International, with regular meetings, a permanent secretariat, their own rooms in the Assembly building, and an elected leader who spoke and put questions and proposed motions and amendments on behalf of French and German, Italian and Dutch, Belgian and Luxembourg Socialists combined. What evolved was a Socialist policy for the Community (particularly on social affairs), and the High Authority has had to take this strong group in the Assembly very much into its confidence and adapt its policies to their demands.

The Christian Democrats and particularly the Liberals did not achieve quite the same degree of cohesion, but it is remarkable that Community problems are argued out more and more between party colleagues of different countries rather than between national colleagues of different parties. Where at the beginning the party groups would adjourn to allow the Assembly to meet, the tendency now has become for the Assembly to adjourn in order that the European party groups may define their attitudes. And the voting pattern in the Assembly has crystallized not along national, but along party lines: Belgians of the Christian People's Party find themselves voting on the same side with Italian Christian Democrats far more often than with Belgian Socialists.

On the Assembly side, then, a Community spirit very quickly superceded national preoccupations. The parliamentarians were more acutely conscious of political problems and perhaps also less timid about giving up national sovereignty than the ministers and civil servants whose daily task it was to exercise that sovereignty and to cope with administrative problems in their own accustomed way. It was not surprising that the High Authority found the Assembly more "European" than it was itself.

The Common Assembly was widely reported in the Continental press and acted as a catalyst of public opinion in much the same way as a national parliament. But the intimate cooperation of parliamentarians in Strasbourg in turn had its repercussions on national parliaments. To some extent the parliamentarians who went to Strasbourg asked or were willing to go because they were already interested in Community problems; others, sent to make up the numbers, soon found themselves involved. Both discovered that they were better informed and more enthusiastic about the Community than their party colleagues at home. And back in their national parliaments, many of them naturally formed the nucleus of a group of "Europeans" with a membership that cut across party lines—a European "fifth column," acting on national governments through national parliaments. The parliamentarians were thus a doubly valuable ally to the High Authority. Not only could the High Authority use the Assembly to bring pressure to bear on the Council, but the members of the Assembly could also press the members of the Council: For though the Council was not responsible to the Assembly, its members after all remained responsible to their national Parliaments even for their actions on the Council.

Their simultaneous membership in both the European Assembly and a national assembly (not to mention their party and constituency work), imposed a crushing burden—the study of technical documents, traveling time, and night sittings in smoke-filled rooms—on the parliamentarians concerned. It was very difficult (at least pending direct elections) for the members of the European Assembly really to be effective, unless they were at the same time in national politics. But then the whole European movement, like any other political movement, depended on the concentrated work and sacrifice of time and private life by thousands of people—voluntary organizers in backstairs offices, civil servants of all kinds, and "intellectuals." Many of the parliamentarians (*per diem* allowances or no) felt themselves part of this freemasonry and as such were prepared to jeopardize career chances in domestic politics for their European work.

The Rome Treaties replaced the Common Assembly by what is called simply "the Assembly" to deal with all three Communities: This was called the European Parliamentary Assembly in French and Italian, and the European Parliament in German and Dutch, until the latter title was adopted in all four official languages in March, 1962. The Treaties laid down that on all major Commission proposals, the Assembly has to be consulted before the Council takes its decision, and while the Council is in no way bound by the recommendations of the Assembly, these do in practice carry a certain weight and add a certain degree of moral authority to the arguments of those governments which agree with the Assembly's recommendations. Because of its new, much wider field of competence, the new parliamentary body has had to be enlarged, compared with the old, from 78 to 142 members: France, Germany, and Italy have 36 members each, Belgium and Holland 14, and Luxembourg 6. This enlargement has strengthened its technical competence to deal with the manifold problems of the six economies as a whole: But it has also, very naturally, strengthened the political as against the technical character of its work.

Meeting for the first time in 1958, the Parliamentary Assembly changed from the alphabetical order of seating in the hemicycle to the seating customary in Continental parliaments: The three party blocks as distinct wedges face the President, in this case with a front bench for the Commissions and the High Authority, for party leaders and committee *rapporteurs*. The new Parliamentary Assembly intensified the activity of the Common Assembly: Thus, in the nine months from September, 1961, to June, 1962, it held nine plenary sessions of three or four days each—one session every month. In addition, of course, its committees met between the plenary sessions as well, often grilling the member of the Commission or High Authority responsible for its particular field, and demanding and receiving confidential information to help it define its viewpoint. The Assembly has strengthened its contact with both the executives and the councils, publicly training a battery of written questions particularly on the Commissions, and introducing so-called "colloquia"—joint sessions with the ministers, with the latter taking an active part in the discussion. On the whole, the Assembly has tended to come out strongly on the side of the Commission as against the Council of Ministers, pressing for speedy integration and only chiding the Commission when it showed lack of spirit in dealing with the Council. It has tended even more to debate broad political issues, and has continued to act as a motor for further progress toward political integration. Moreover, it is now planning to transcend itself and become a truer parliament by being directly elected by universal suffrage.

The Consultative and the Economic and Social Committees

Just as national governments have their consultative machinery, by which a formal channel is set up between the groups interested in any set of decisions and the governmental authorities taking the decisions, so it was felt the High Authority, too, must have a Consultative Committee attached to it in an advisory capacity: This consists of "not less than thirty and not more than fifty-one members, and shall include an equal number of producers, workers, and consumers and dealers." The trade unions argued that they should have more than a third of the seats, for they were after all representatives of the domestic consumers; but it was decided that only industrial consumers should share with the dealers the last third of the seats.

At least one member of the High Authority has always been a trade unionist—indeed, its last President, M. Finet, was a life-long trade unionist and was Secretary-General of the Belgian Free Trade Union Federation at the time of his appointment to the High Authority. But the trade unions attach considerable importance to a formal platform giving them access to the High Authority, and therefore make great use of the Consultative Committee.

The employers and the industrial consumers and dealers, on the other hand, after taking the Consultative Committee seriously in the first few years, have since tended to lose interest: They rely more easily on all the informal machinery of pressure groups and on their contact offices in Luxembourg to make their point with the High Authority. The Consultative Committee has thus failed fully to play the part for which it was designed.

When the Rome Treaties were drafted, the governments were not anxious to have any analogous corporate institution to exert pressure on Community policy, but the non-Communist trade unions, both syndicalist and Catholic, were insistent, and the architects of the Treaty, too, also thereby hoped to cement the Community's institutions more firmly into the existing framework of economic associations. They got their way, and a new body was established to serve Euratom and the Economic Community: the Economic and Social Committee, made up of "representatives of producers, farmers, transport operators, workers, merchants, artisans, the professions, and representatives of the general interest." These are appointed by the Council for four years, in the national ratios of 24 each for the big states, 12 each for Belgium and Holland, and 5 for Luxembourg—101 members in all. As between the interests, a tripartite division was agreed upon in practice whereby the trade unions, the employers, and the rest of the community are each assigned a third of seats: Each of these thirds is then split up among different organizations in each sector, after elaborate calculations and consultations. In fact, the interest groups have been taking the Committee so seriously that some three-quarters of its members are the general secretaries or the chairmen of the national trade-union councils, employers' federations, and other professional associations, and even the Communist trade unions, boycotted hitherto by the Council, are now attempting to have representatives appointed to the Committee.

The Rome Treaties frequently stipulate that the Committee must be consulted before a decision is reached—e.g., in the framing of the common agricultural and transport policies, on the freedom of movement of labor, on social policy, and so forth. And after the Committee debated the Commission's proposals for agriculture, its proposed amendments on social aspects were substantially adopted by the Commission and the Council. In fact, the Commission and Council have repeatedly thought it politically advisable to consult the Committee even where the Treaty does not oblige them to do so, as in the case of restrictive business practices and the common commercial policy.

It has indeed been argued that the Economic and Social Committee, representing the interest groups, has a greater influence on the details of economic and social policy than the Parliamentary Assembly, representing political parties, can exert. If this is so, it is due not least to the positions and influence of its members back home and to the expert knowledge which they have or on which they can draw through their organizations. The Economic and Social Committee thus constitutes an institutionalization of the two-way flow of information and views between the Commissions and the interest groups. These groups are in fact more and more forming committees on a European basis, working out their Community policy, opening offices in Brussels (unless, like the free trade unions, they had them there already), and lobbying the Commission as they would a national government. And therein lies a recognition of the impact of the new institutions on the commercial and industrial life of Europe today.

The Court of Justice

The Court of Justice ensures the observance of law in the interpretation and application of all three Community Treaties. It consists of seven clearly independent judges nominated for six-year terms by agreement among the member governments, and is assisted by two advocates-general. It combines the usual written and oral procedures, and there is no provision for dissenting opinions in its decisions.

In the Coal and Steel Treaty, the Court is there chiefly to maintain judicial control over the High Authority. A firm, an industrial association or trade union, a member state, or indeed the Council of Ministers can invoke the Court against the High Authority on any of four grounds: They may claim that a decision or recommendation of the High Authority lacks legal competence, that the High Authority has violated procedural rules or the Treaty itself, or that it has committed a *détournement de pouvoir.* (These four concepts, taken straight from French administrative law, are obviously closely related to the grounds of appeal open in English law: *ultra vires,* the denial of natural justice, and abuse of power.) The High Authority, on the other hand, may appeal to the Court against a resolution of the Assembly or of the Council on procedural grounds or on grounds of lack of competence. The Court can also decide legal disputes between member states arising out of the Treaty or its application. Its competence, in addition, extends to the revision of the Treaty, the use of the veto, matters of discipline, and delictual and contractual liability. It thus exercises many of the functions of a constitutional court, an international court, and an administrative court.

There is no appeal from the Court to any superior instance. It may levy fines on individuals, firms, and associations, and the execution of the Court's judgments is enforceable under the national rules of civil procedure. In the case of the Coal and Steel Community, the Court can impose certain economic sanctions on a member state if it is the state that is the offender. Under all three Treaties, the Court also has the responsibility of determining questions raised before a domestic court or tribunal about the interpretation of the Treaties and the validity of the acts of the Communities' common institutions; without this competence to make preliminary decisions of such a kind, there would have been the danger that six different interpretations of the common rules could come to be enshrined in the domestic jurisprudence of the member states. A court of first instance therefore may, and a national court of last instance must, refer such questions to the Court of the Communities.

In taking its decisions, the Court has had to be guided by legal rather than economic criteria—though under the ECSC Treaty, the Court may review the High Authority's evaluation of a state of economic affairs if the High Authority is alleged to have patently misconstrued a text or committed a *détournement de pouvoir*. (There is no analogous provision in the Rome Treaties.) The sources of law which the Court has used—over and above the Treaties and the texts issued under them—have been mainly national laws, the decisions of national courts, and the textbook authorities: Where necessary, it has sought to distill a common denominator out of the six national systems. International law has rarely been invoked in its jurisprudence.

By now, the Court has decided some hundred cases under the ECSC Treaty, and its jurisprudence has been an unpolitical one. It has been concerned with the interpretation of texts more than with the political factors involved in the cases before them. One of its early decisions inflicted a reverse on the High

Authority when it ruled against the so-called "Monnet margin" (a certain flexibility in steel price quotations), but it upheld the High Authority in its reorganization of the GEORG, the monopolistic Ruhr coal sales organization. Occasionally, governments or producers have tried to influence events by threatening to file suits or by doing so: Thus the Dutch Government filed a suit against the High Authority to goad it to take action against GEORG. The Court has in fact acquired considerable prestige, and no one has yet dared to challenge or obstruct its rulings.

In the Rome Treaties, this Court of Justice of the Coal and Steel Community was taken over and given similar functions in relation to the Economic Community and Euratom. Since the main decisions are under the Rome Treaties taken by the Councils, the Court here exercises judicial control over the Councils just as much as over the Commissions. Moreover the Commissions may sue the member states for not fulfilling their part in the execution of the Treaties. The first two cases of this kind were brought by the Commissions in spring, 1961: The Italian Government had ignored its formal protests against Italy's raising of her customs duties on certain radio electrical equipment and against her suspension of pork imports. In both cases, the Court ruled in favor of the Commission, and the Italian Government then duly complied with the Treaty. (Had the Italian Government not complied, there would—unlike that on coal and steel—have been no means of Court enforcement; but the common institutions would, under the Rome Treaty, be able to take, and to authorize the other member state to take, retaliatory action.

The Civil Service of the Communities

There has been some confusion in recent debates as to the constitutional nature of the Commission, whose members have been described as "European civil servants." But the Commission is not part of any civil service. A civil service is not appointed for four years; a civil service cannot be removed by a parliamentary vote of no "confidence"; a civil service does not have powers of decisions of its own without the need for ratification by a superior political institution; a civil service does not take decisions collectively under a system of cabinet responsibility;

a civil service does not initiate policy autonomously, and no unanimity from anyone is required to amend its proposals. Nor does a civil service make its proposals publicly, or have them publicly debated in the Parliament and the Economic and Social Committee before they go for their final decision. Nor does a civil service constantly appear before the parliamentary body to answer questions and recommend lines of policy. And indeed a look at the personnel of the present EEC Commission reveals that the majority have been national parliamentarians and ministers before they joined the Commission.

The status of the Commission is essentially a new one, which our old national categories do not cover. But the most helpful analogy would be to regard it as the executive cabinet of the Community, with the Council of Ministers as the legislature (somewhat akin in its nature to the American Senate, or even more, to the German Upper House), while the Parliamentary Assembly has the right to dismiss it and, together with the "corporate" Committees, acts as an advisory body.

There is, of course, a European civil service, which takes instructions from its political masters, acts discreetly, is hierarchically organized, prepares the policy decisions, and is involved in their detailed execution. These are the permanent appointees of the two Commissions, of the High Authority, and of the other common institutions. The Economic Commission has a staff of some 2,200—600 of them in the administrative grade. As many as half of them perhaps have been seconded or released from their national civil service; others have come from academic life, from business administration, or from other international organizations—and for some it is a first permanent post. They are organized into nine directorates-general, each headed by a director-general who is the permanent head of department, responsible to the appropriate member of the Commission (to Professor Hallstein in the case of external affairs, to M. Henri Rochereau in the case of associated overseas countries, to M. Sicco Mansholt in the case of agriculture, to M. Lionello Levi Sandri for social affairs, etc. In addition, an Executive Secretariat is responsible for coordination, and a Spokesman's Group for public relations.

Euratom has a staff of another 2,100, of whom 600 are concerned with the administration, while 1,500—largely nuclear physicists and their assistants—are paid out of the research budget. The High Authority of ECSC has a staff of 900, while the three executives share common legal, statistical, and information services with a staff of about 350. In addition, of course, there are the staffs of the European Parliamentary Assembly, the Economic and Social Committee, and the Court, thus bringing the over-all total of employees of the three Communities up to about 6,500—porters, drivers, and mimeograph operators included.

Measured against the standards of national administrations, this may seem a small staff—particularly in view of all the complications introduced by four official languages. Even so, there has been criticism that too much staff was recruited in a hurry at the beginning, for budgetary reasons. The best men in Brussels easily measure up to the best that any of the national civil services can offer—the French in particular have a galaxy of talent in the European institutions—but it is also inevitable in any international organization that those who have not made a success of their national career are more attracted by the opportunities of new tasks in the international sphere, and are perhaps less repelled by the personal and family sacrifices involved in expatriation. As a result, all international civil services tend to be uneven. And since promotion no less than the allocation of jobs has for the moment partly to be governed by national and political considerations no less than personal merit, the people who really make such organizations "tick" tend to be scattered about various ranks and various departments. These form a cameraderie of their own, and find that they are sometimes serving the organization most effectively when they supplement official channels by less formal direct contacts among those in the "mafia" of those who really get things done.

Plans for Institutional Development

To measure the institutions we have just described against the federal ideal is to realize how far short of Community supranationality they still fall. The Parliamentary Assembly remains indirectly elected; supranationality is not applied to more than a part of Community decisions even in its governmental, let alone in its Community form; the organs which take the real decisions are not yet immediately subject to the Assembly's control. Three different executives divide among themselves the responsibility for the main sources of Europe's future energy supplies. And—perhaps symbolically the most embarassing defect—the governments who have been willing to merge their policies in vast domains have not yet been able to agree on a European capital: The Assembly meets in Strasbourg, its secretariat works in Luxembourg and drives up to Strasbourg for its sessions with vanloads of office machinery, documents, and typists. The Court, like the High Authority, stays in Luxembourg, while the Commissions sit in various buildings dotted through Brussels. On the institutional as on the economic side, things are still in untidy transition.

Where, ask the federalists, do we go from here? We have three Communities. How can we get real political integration?

Now that the Economic Community is well on its way—"a ship whose speed and course have been set," in Professor Hallstein's words—there is a strong feeling, expressed above all in Assembly debates, that as Europe was relaunched economically in 1955, so she must be relaunched politically today. The Messina operation has been successful. It is time for a new offensive.

The Assembly favors two particular schemes. The Rome Treaties insisted that the Assembly shall itself draw up proposals for elections by direct universal suffrage, and that the Council shall by a unanimous vote recommend that the Member States adopt the necessary measures in accordance with their respective constitutional rules. In 1960, the Assembly agreed upon a draft text for such a Convention.

This provides for a tripling of the size of the Assembly, to 426 members. Two-thirds of these would be immediately elected by universal suffrage. All Community citizens over the age of twenty-one would be entitled to vote. For the moment, the constituencies would be drawn and the electoral methods fixed by the member states themselves. The other third would for the moment be elected indirectly by the national parliaments—would, in fact, in numbers as in method of election be very similar to the present Assembly. Not later than the end of the transitional period, the whole Assembly would be due for direct election. At the present rate of acceleration, this could be well before the end of the 1960's. Whether Assembly members can still remain national parliamentarians after that point would be decided by the Assembly itself.

Once given such a popular "mandate," the Europeans hope to strengthen the Assembly's hand above all for three demands: If obtained, these would make it more of a real federal parliament. Firstly, the Assembly demands the rights to exercise budgetary control over the three Communities; secondly, it demands the right not merely to dismiss the executives in a body, but to have a say in appointing their individual members; and thirdly, it demands the right to introduce legislation itself. Whether or when a directly elected Assembly would obtain these rights it would be difficult to say. But provided the electorate turned out in force—and there is every reason to believe that it would—direct elections could give the Assembly a tremendous access of strength. The House of Commons, too, did not start life with the powers it has today, and it is difficult to imagine that, once organized, 400-odd politicians, ex-ministers and future ministers, will fail to make an impression on Europe's political life.

The second proposal—supported by the presidents of all three executives—is the fusion of the High Authority with the two Commissions. This would result in a single Community executive which, with the prestige and the public support it could command, would gain in weight vis-à-vis the national governments. In it, some would see an embryonic federal cabinet embodying the principle of supranationality of the Community type.

Against these federalist aspirations, President de Gaulle in early summer, 1960, put forward a rather different line of advance: the ideal of a "mighty confederation," a "Europe of states." Where the federalists see the deepening and intensification of the existing Community as their first task, President de Gaulle wishes to extend the scope of European institutions to other domains, notably foreign affairs, here and now. The federalists, too, want to bring at least foreign affairs within the scope of European integration, but at a later date, when a community of interests has had more time to consolidate, so that stronger institutions can be set up.

For, while President de Gaulle wants to extend the scope of institutionalized European cooperation, the new institutions he proposes to set up are weak intergovernmental organs only. For the federalist, the ultimate reality is the individual, and individuals should be free to distribute functions between the existing or newly to-be-created institutions—local, national, regional, or world institutions—that are best fitted to carry out different specific tasks. In President de Gaulle's thinking, on the other hand, the nation-state retains a peculiar significance (and there are times when he speaks as if he were the embodiment of one of them); it is the national governments that must ultimately carry responsibility for the general welfare, and thus only a council of national governments, and not some directly elected assembly bypassing the national framework, can be given any real power. Instead of direct elections, President de Gaulle therefore suggested a referendum—a form of popular consultation in which he has scored some success; and rather than merge the executives of the three existing Communities, he proposed regular meetings of the heads of state or of government, assisted by a political secretariat, to deal (as the existing Communities do) with economics, but also with foreign affairs, culture, and defense. And in his conception, even if five governments were agreed, any sixth should be able to veto joint action.

From the summer of 1960 onward, these two rival concepts—the federalist and the confederalist, or perhaps more accurately the Community and the Gaullist concepts—clashed to the point of almost neutralizing each other. In the summer of 1961, however, the demand for further institutional advance had made itself heard so strongly that the heads of state or of government, meeting at the "second Community summit" in Bonn, felt that the matter had to be faced squarely and properly thrashed out. On July 15, they therefore solemnly decided "to instruct their committee to submit to them proposals on the means which will enable a statutory character to be given to the union of their peoples as soon as possible."

The working committee of the Six referred to in this Bonn declaration was that presided over by M. Christian Fouchet, a former Gaullist deputy, then French Ambassador in Copenhagen. This committee soon found that there was such a welter of different proposals for giving "a statutory character . . . to the union of their peoples" that progress was difficult. Already, in February, 1961, when the committee was originally appointed, Mr. Joseph Luns, the Dutch Foreign Minister, had posed a dilemma: Either the Six would proceed without Britain, in which case De Gaulle's confederal ideas were quite inadequate and far more radical schemes of federalist integration were required; or, if De Gaulle's confederal ideas were to be accepted, there was no reason for Britain not to join in the looser political association, even if she did not enter the Common Market. Britain's application to join the Common Market, announced at the end of July, exacerbated this problem, and the committee seemed to be floundering in the doldrums.

It was at this point that the Quai d'Orsay, in a spirit of helpfulness, submitted to the Fouchet committee a paper which was in fact a refurbished version of the old confederal scheme of a political secretariat that President de Gaulle had already put forward in 1960. This draft treaty for an "indissoluble union" hardly went very far. The heads of state or government were to gather in council every four months; they were to attempt to harmonize foreign policies, and their foreign ministers were to meet at least as frequently. All decisions would require unanimity—though members could also abstain or refuse to attend, in which case they were not to be bound by the unanimous decisions of the rest. A political commission of high officials from the ministries of foreign affairs of the member states, with its seat in Paris, was to prepare and assure continuity between meetings. The European Parliament was not to gain in powers, though it could be consulted and could also advise on its own initiative. Perhaps the chief new feature lay in Article 16 of their draft for a Political Union:

> Three years after coming into force, the present Treaty shall be subject to a general revision, the object of which shall be to examine steps for strengthening the union, taking into account the progress achieved.

> This revision should have as its principal objectives the establishment of a unified foreign policy, and the gradual constitution of an organization centralizing within the union the European Communities mentioned in the preamble of the present Treaty.

The union was firmly closed against any states that were not members both of the Council of Europe and of the three existing Communities, and the admission of any new member state thus qualified also required the unanimity of those already members of the union.

The plan as submitted in November—and even more so as resubmitted early in 1962, after being edited, it was said, personally by President de Gaulle—ran into determined opposition. Federalists found it suspect: The inclusion of economic affairs in the purview of the heads of government might threaten the supranational character of the existing Communities, and, in other fields, institutions of the Gaullist kind, embodying the veto and lacking any independent Community organ, might impede more supranational institutions from being set up in due course. The other five governments also found the French plan unacceptable; they at first opposed it, and then submitted a series of amendments on which all five found themselves substantially agreed.

The opposition once more appears to have been led by the Dutch, though their objectives almost looked self-contradictory. On the one hand, they are the most federalist and the least confederalist of the Six: From their point of view, an intergovernmental body of the type that President de Gaulle suggests would be a step sideways at best, when the Bonn declaration seemed to promise far more. On the other hand, the Dutch are anxious to have Britain inside the Community, and that not merely for economic but also for political reasons: For, failing a higher degree of federal integration among the Six, British entry into the Community would provide an alternative safeguard against possible Franco-German hegemony. They thus feared that the French proposals were designed as a move to stymie Britain's entry into the Communities by altering the rules just when Britain was negotiating to enter.

The Germans and the Belgians, and to a lesser degree the Italians, too, joined the Dutch in their hostility to President de Gaulle's scheme, though they were on the whole more worried that it might sidetrack Community integration than that it would keep Britain out. For after all, in the Commons debate of August 3, 1961, Mr. Macmillan had gone out of his way to take sides in the internal disputes of the club he was asking to join and had specifically expressed his support for De Gaulle's notions of *l'Europe des patries* (a phrase President de Gaulle, incidentally, denies ever having used) as against the plans for Community integration favored elsewhere. But since Holland, Belgium, and Germany also favored Britain's entry, and it was taken for granted that once Britain entered, nothing more federal than the French proposals could be adopted, the argument in the Fouchet committee really became somewhat academic.

The talks dragged on in what became known as the Cattani committee when President de Gaulle appointed M. Fouchet as High Commissioner in Algeria, until they eventually broke down on April 17, 1962. A week earlier, Mr. Edward Heath, speaking to the ministers of the Six in the Western European Union, had stated categorically, "We shall be anxious to join the political union at the same time as we join the European Communities," and asked the Six to consider whether the British, "as impending members of the European Economic Community," should not also join the talks on the future political union of Europe. This suggestion was no more acceptable to the French than the French proposals were to the rest. "Never has an absent delegation won so resounding a victory," Mr. Spaak is credited with having said. And so the "third Community summit"—which had been scheduled to take place in Rome in June, 1962, for the signature of a political treaty—was put off.

The idea of such a "summit" was revived—at first sight surprisingly enough—by Dr. Adenauer, when he paid his state visit to Paris at the beginning of July. His days as Chancellor of the Federal Republic, are likely to be drawing to a close, he fears, and so any political treaty that would tie Germany further would now be worth his consideration. Clearly, he also wants a new demonstration of European solidarity vis-à-vis the East, and he may even wish to make sure that when Britain enters, there will be no misunderstanding as to the eventual extension of the Community concept to foreign affairs. The French have not shown themselves enthusiastic for an early summit, but if it is to be successful, it will be President de Gaulle's ideas rather than any more far-reaching ones that must be adopted. In a sense, therefore, the French are sitting pretty.

But whether the discussions drag on or whether a Gaullist document is finally signed, it would be unwise to believe that that could be the end of the matter in either case. Federalist forces will not so easily give up the struggle for supranational integration. France, for the moment, is the stumbling block. But behind President de Gaulle, there flourishes a vocal French public opinion which in no way shares his views. In May, 1962, the five MRP ministers of M. Georges Pompidou's new government resigned in protest against the President's European policy, and a few weeks later almost all but the UNR deputies walked out of the Assembly in a similar demonstration.

Moreover, whatever the immediate political tactics, the existing institutions are plainly inadequate for the tasks they are increasingly called upon to perform. They represent a quite deliberately planned anomaly, and the snowball of integration will be forced to take another turn before long. Federation or confederation, merged executives or political secretariats—some development of this kind becomes inescapable once countries have been caught in the wheels of integration. The foreign ministers already meet quarterly, and heads of government meet each other bilaterally with increasing frequency. Governmental cooperation in the cultural sphere will help rather than hinder European unity. And a political secretariat, even if intergovernmental, need not in the long run detract from the importance of Community institutions. Indeed, it may itself lead the governments into a limbo between intergovernmental procedures and supranationality of the governmental type in the harmonization of their policies beyond the economic field.

All these notions may seem a chamber of sinister horrors to those whose thinking is molded by insular traditions—but on the Continent, the framework of political planning, not only for Dr. Adenauer and Professor Hallstein, but even for President de Gaulle, is more and more transcending the nation-state. One may be tempted to dismiss these institutional possibilities on the Continent as the pipe dreams of ineffectual eccentrics. But heads have been buried in the sand before, and the skeptics have been proved wrong. The outlook for the future development of Community institutions may be uncertain: But at least the possibility must be recognized that the strategy of the Europeans might turn out to have been correct. An Economic Community may dissolve the bulk of interstate conflicts within it. In world affairs West Europeans are already in the same boat. A thoroughgoing community of economic interests will lead more and more to a political community of interests: And then a Political Community may not be far off.

IV

Europe and Africa

The Background

No aspect of the Rome Treaty is politically more delicate, none is more pregnant with long-range problems for power relationships in the world as a whole, than the association of overseas countries with the Community. And since this is the first time that we look beyond Western Europe, it is worth pausing for a moment to think of the world context in which the "little European" Community was formed.

According to the forecasts of the United Nations, in the year 2000 the United States and Canada will account for only 5 per cent of the world's population, the Soviet Union for 6 per cent, and Western, Southern, and Eastern Europe (excluding Russia) will account for only 9 per cent—together making up only 20 per cent of the world's population. For the rest, non-Russian Asia will by itself contain 62 per cent of the world's population, leaving 8 per cent for Africa, 9 per cent for South America, and 1 per cent for Oceania. European attitudes toward the underdeveloped countries are in any case of vital moral significance; these and similar considerations of hard power politics serve only to emphasize their practical importance.

In the past, Europe's relations with Africa and the rest of the underdeveloped world have been characterized by two sometimes simultaneous and sometimes alternating, sometimes contrasting and sometimes blending, sets of motives. On the one hand, there were motives of commercial exploitation and national aggrandizement which are sufficiently well known; on the other, the altruistic, missionary motives which inspired priests, doctors, and administrators to bring what they believed to be religious or medical, social or cultural, economic or political benefits to these countries. This second set of motives revealed fundamental differences of attitude between Britain, Belgium, and France that were to leave their mark even after decolonization.

British administrators, coming from a class- and color-conscious society at home, never saw the colonial peoples in their charge as potential fellow citizens to be integrated with the mother country. On the contrary, guided by the liberal concepts of "no taxation without representation" and of "government responsible to the people," their ideal was broadly that of education for self-government. Their charge, they considered, was a temporary one: to guide the establishment of a new state distinct from Britain, preferably with dominion status, under British external leadership.

The French, proud above all of their cultural tradition, saw it as their noblest colonial task to turn Africans into Frenchmen. There may be scorn for the uncultured majority which has not "evolved," but it is not on account of their skins. Color prejudice is far less acute in France than in Britain. French workers have never been protectionist along racial lines and hardly find Algerians more alien to themselves than the Poles and Italians alongside whom they have been working for generations. Deputies from France overseas were formally integrated into French political life. Thus M. Senghor, now President of Senegal, took a large share in the drafting of the Constitution of the Fourth Republic—if for no other reason than that he was among those in the Assembly who wrote the most polished French prose. In both the Fourth and the Fifth Republics, the Upper House was presided over by a native of French Guiana representing a metropolitan *département*. French policy at its best was aiming at full integration.

The Belgians, for their part, saw their main contribution to Africa in raising the living standards of the indigenous populations. They gave elementary education, because economic advance required foremen; but they restricted higher education so that orderly economic progress should not be disturbed by frustrated intellectual agitators hankering after political independence and personal power.

When nationalism came to fruition all over Africa in the years leading up to 1960, the consequences inevitably reflected the differences in the approach to colonization. When Britain withdrew, though the politicians sometimes had to be released from jail, she handed over to a nucleus of quite efficient African administrators. When De Gaulle gave independence to the African countries south of the Sahara, there were sophisticated French politicians with black skins ready to carry on a vigorous indigenous political life and by no means reluctant to maintain their links with France. When the Belgians moved out of the Congo, chaos ensued.

Earlier European Plans

We saw in the first chapter that Africa played a certain role in federalist thinking from the beginning. Indeed, at the first meeting of the Council of Europe in 1949, the Assembly conceived of an economic area which was to comprise not merely all the West European metropolitan states, but also the developing countries overseas that had constitutional links with them, including the independent countries of the Commonwealth.

Three lines of thought converged in this proposal. Firstly, the development of such an area as a single whole and the pooling of its complementary resources were to strengthen the economies of all these countries outside the dollar area; secondly, only such multilateral cooperation could bring the speediest benefits to the peoples concerned; and thirdly, the development was to be secured by a partnership, decisions being taken not by Europe for Africa, but by representatives of European and African countries together. Recommendation 18 of the Council of Europe, made in 1949, called for an economic conference representing all the countries of Europe and their overseas associates.

When the Ministers declined to follow this up, the Assembly itself convoked a group of experts to draw up more concrete plans. Thanks to the mechanism of the French Union, the Assembly from the beginning contained representatives of African countries, who now took their share in adopting what came to be known as the Strasbourg Plan.

The Strasbourg Plan was another example of the different strains of thought that mingled in the European movement at the time. Launched in 1951–52 under the impact of the raw-materials crisis and of the dollar deficit following the outbreak of war in Korea, it certainly aimed at convertibility in the long run. But for the short run, it outlined a system of preferential trade between Europe and all the overseas countries that had constitutional links with her: It sought to bring into the relationship those European countries which had no colonial responsibilities, and to multilateralize to some extent the relations of the Commonwealth and colonial countries—to link them with the whole of Europe and not only with their own metropolis.

The Strasbourg Plan called for increased purchases of overseas products by all the European countries, the abolition of quantitative restrictions, lower tariffs (if necessary, of a preferential kind), long-term contracts, and international raw-material agreements that would give greater security of income to overseas producers. It called for concerted efforts by all European states to supply the overseas countries with the specialist personnel they require for their development. Lastly, it proposed the setting up of a European Investment Bank: European countries without colonial responsibilities were thus to share in the financial sacrifices required to lay the foundations of economic development, and the unilateral financial dependence of any colony on its metropolis was to be replaced by a Eurafrican partnership.

The Association

Although the Assembly voted this recommendation almost unanimously, the colonial powers rejected it at the time. But four years later, the same ideas were adopted—though only by the governments of the Six. The Spaak Report had made no mention of the overseas countries with whom the Six had constitutional links. It was only at the Venice meeting of the foreign ministers in May, 1956, that France, by making an association of overseas countries a condition for going ahead with the Common Market project at all, got the question put on the agenda.

The French had weighty reasons for their stand: firstly, a technical one. How could France simultaneously be part of a European customs union and of a French economic area that lay largely outside it? How, in such a situation, could one prevent other European countries from re-exporting their manufactures across France to the overseas countries at the preferential rate of duty, and how could one prevent overseas produce from traveling duty-free through France to the rest of the Community?

Secondly, the French Government argued on economic grounds. A unique burden from which its other European partners were relatively free rested on the French economy. It had to provide the capital needed for long-term development in the French African possessions for administration, schooling, health services, transport, and basic energy facilities; and aid to these countries has, if anything, been stepped up since they were given their independence. The figures for France shown in Table IV are inclusive of the net cost of administration (that is, the cost after deduction of locally raised taxes), but even supposing this cost to have been $1 billion, the burden on the French economy and the benefit to the overseas countries (except for a part of administrative efforts in Algeria) remain. In addition, French industry often had to buy its raw materials at a price higher than the world level. How, given these burdens, could French industry compete on an equal footing with the rest of Europe unless her partners bore their share too?

Moreover, some of them at least, especially Germany, were already beginning to put commercial capital into the more immediately profitable enterprises in Africa, which could only be built up on the bases laid at French public expense; it was doubly unjust for them not to contribute to the nonrecoverable initial investment.

The same point could also be put in political rather than economic terms. France felt that in Algeria she was fighting both a military and an economic battle on behalf of the whole of Europe and the Western world. Algeria was a problem which the rest of Europe perhaps should not touch. But French investments in Africa south of the Sahara were also political investments for the whole of the free world. This burden, at least, she should not be expected to carry alone.

But there were other arguments of a much deeper political nature. Fundamental to the whole Eurafrican concept was the French historical and philosophical predisposition, which held as a matter of doctrine that France extended overseas, and that France with her possessions formed a cultural and political whole. France's civilizing mission overseas—so the matter was seen in Paris—could not be abandoned simply because of European integration: What the French language, French literature, and French philosophy had put together, no European arrangements should sunder.

Those, too, were the days when Algeria was still regarded as a permanent part of metropolitan France. The association of French Africa south of the Sahara with the Common Market made the position of Algeria within it quite natural and obscured any immediate issues about German, Dutch, or Italian attitudes on the future of the Algerian *départements*.

Lastly, and most obviously, there was of course the responsibility incumbent upon France to make the best terms for her overseas possessions. She herself was expecting major long-run

Table IV

PUBLIC AND PRIVATE AID TO UNDERDEVELOPED COUNTRIES, 1956–59
(billions of dollars)

	Private investment	Government grants	Government loans	Total	Percentage of national income
France	1.5	2.5	0.6	4.6	2.7
U.K.	1.8	0.6	0.3	2.6	1.3
U.S.	4.7	5.3	3.3	13.3	0.9
W. Germany	0.3	0.3	0.4	1.0	0.6
Rest of world	1.6	0.8	1.2	3.6	—
International Bank	—	—	—	0.9	—
Total	9.8	9.5	5.8	26.0	—

SOURCE: National Institute Economic Review, May, 1961, p. 33. For later figures, compare Table IX below.

economic benefits from entering the Common Market. How could she, at that moment, exclude from those benefits the colonial peoples in her charge?

A straightforward inclusion of the overseas countries in the Common Market would plainly have been impracticable. It could have prevented the development of infant industries, upset their fiscal systems, which are heavily dependent on tariffs, and done little to bring their social capital up to the European level. As a result, it was association, not inclusion, that was called for.

The Germans were not particularly happy about this French condition. Politically, they were anxious not to compromise themselves in the eyes of the developing countries of the Afro-Asian world: Untainted by colonialism since the Allies had so obligingly stripped them of overseas possessions in 1919, the Germans were scoring notable commercial successes in these countries, above all with supplies of heavy equipment. Had not Bismarck in fact been right in suggesting that all they needed was opportunities for commercial investment without political responsibility? Again, on the economic side they did not relish the idea of having to give away money for public investments in French Africa. One of the more obscene cartoons showed the Six settling down to their common meal with a swarm of little monkeys emerging from Marianne's skirts to partake of the feast. But finally, Dr. Adenauer, anxious to remove every obstacle to European unity, agreed. Part IV of the Treaty contains the main clauses on the Association, while an Annex and an Implementing Convention spell it out in greater detail.

Part IV of the Treaty sets up the Association. Its purpose is twofold: to further "the interests and prosperity of the inhabitants of these countries and territories in such a manner as to lead them to the economic, social, and cultural development to which they aspire," and "to establish close economic relations between them and the Community as a whole." *

Unlimited in time, the Treaty recognizes the obligation of member states to contribute to the investments required by the overseas Associates. Limited in the first instance until the end of 1962, the Convention sets up the European Development

* Article 131.

Fund of $581.25 million as a multilateral form of giving them nonrecoverable assistance funds. Table V shows the contributions made by each of the Six to the Development Fund, and the sums earmarked for those Associates of the four countries which had such overseas responsibilities. (The first and third columns of the table are here given to demonstrate that the lion's share of the Fund was secured by France for her Associates, while Belgium was either unable or not anxious to obtain very much for hers.)

Table V

THE DEVELOPMENT FUND 1958–1962

	Member's national income, 1959 *(billions of dollars)*	Contributions by members *(millions of dollars)*	Population of Associates *(millions)*	Allocations to Associates *(millions of dollars)*	Funds committed by December 31, 1962
Belgium	11.5	70	20	30	25.3
France	52.5	200	35	511.25	464.4
Germany	59.5	200	—	—	—
Italy	28.4	40	2	5	4.9
Luxembourg	.4	1.25	—	—	—
Netherlands	10.2	70	1	35	17.8
Total	162.5	581.25	58	581.25	512.4

The Treaty lays down that imports from the Associates will benefit from the same tariff reductions and the same elimination of quantitative restrictions as imports from European partners; but the overseas Associates, instead of having to eliminate their tariffs on European goods in return, merely have to extend to the goods of other members of the Community the same treatment they give to the European country with which they have special relations. Thus, while at the end of the transitional period no restrictions will remain on the Associates' exports to the whole Community, the Associates, provided they give equal

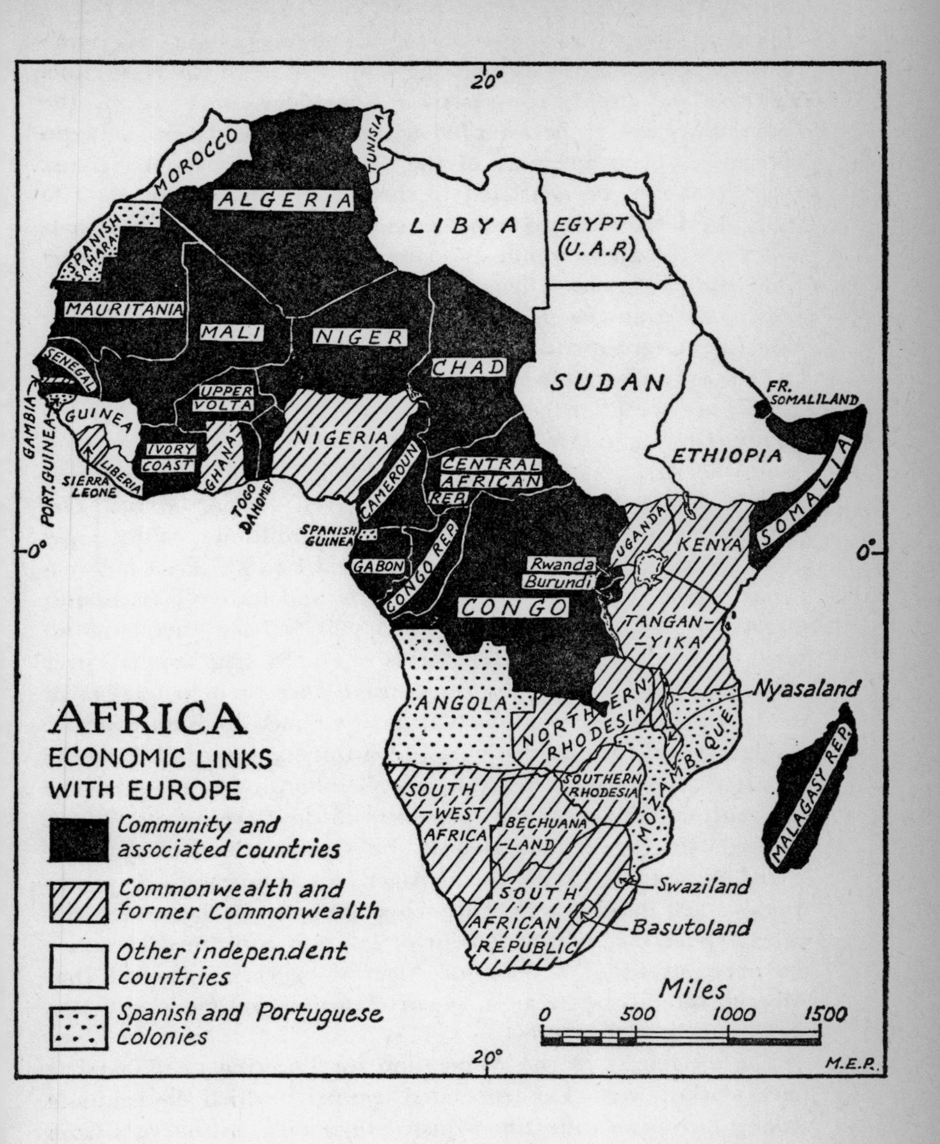

20°
MOROCCO
TUNISIA
ALGERIA
SPANISH SAHARA
LIBYA
EGYPT (U.A.R)
MAURITANIA
MALI
NIGER
CHAD
SUDAN
SENEGAL
GAMBIA
PORT. GUINEA
GUINEA
UPPER VOLTA
NIGERIA
FR. SOMALILAND
ETHIOPIA
SIERRA LEONE
LIBERIA
IVORY COAST
GHANA
TOGO
DAHOMEY
CAMEROUN
CENTRAL AFRICAN REP.
SOMALIA
SPANISH GUINEA
GABON
CONGO REP.
UGANDA
KENYA
Rwanda
Burundi
CONGO
TANGAN-YIKA
0°
ANGOLA
NORTHERN RHODESIA
Nyasaland
MOZAMBIQUE
MALAGASY REP.
SOUTH WEST AFRICA
SOUTHERN RHODESIA
BECHUANA-LAND
SOUTH AFRICAN REPUBLIC
Swaziland
Basutoland
AFRICA
ECONOMIC LINKS WITH EUROPE
Community and associated countries
Commonwealth and former Commonwealth
Other independent countries
Spanish and Portuguese Colonies
Miles
0
500
1000
1500
M.E.P.

treatment to all members of the Community, may levy any customs duties needed for their development or for their revenue. Tenders and supply contracts for investments financed by the Community are to be awarded without discrimination between enterprises from any part of the Community or its Associates, and are not to be restricted to the metropolitan country. The right of establishment is to be extended progressively to nationals and firms of all Community states. The movement of workers from the Community to the associated countries, and from the associated countries to the Community is, however, left for subsequent agreement.

The countries to which the Association applies under the Treaty are the French, Belgian, and Italian colonial and trusteeship territories in Africa, Madagascar and its dependencies, and —outside Africa—Netherlands New Guinea and a host of tiny French settlements in Oceania and even the Antarctic. The populations of these areas add up to 53 million people. Some of the Associates (the Congo and Ruanda Urundi, French Equatorial Africa, Togoland, the Cameroons, and Italian Somaliland) already applied nondiscriminatory tariffs, so that there was no need for them to adjust their tariffs at all. By stages spread over the transitional period, the rest must reduce their general tariff to the rate applied to imports from their metropolitan country.

Algeria and the other overseas departments were then formally a part of France and hence of the Community, but, under the Convention, they could also benefit from the Development Fund. Though the other countries of the Community initially preferred the Fund to keep out of Algerian commitments, expenditures of $20 million were authorized before Algerian independence. Where the free movement of labor is concerned, France's partners, afraid of a flood of Algerian workers, insisted that Algeria should be treated as an Associate rather than as a member.

The mechanics of the Association for lowering tariff barriers have worked well. The associated countries which discriminate among European countries adjusted their tariff on imports from other Community countries by a second 10 per cent of the differences on July 1, 1960. Madagascar has introduced a new tariff which gives free entry to all Community products. But commercially, nothing spectacular has happened. Understandably enough, there has so far been no very significant rise in the Associates' imports from other countries of the Community. But, more regrettably, there has also been no dramatic increase in the Community's imports from the Associates. (See Table III, page 32.) This is hardly surprising, since the products of the French Associates have traditionally been bought by France herself at highly inflated prices, so that even a 40 per cent reduction in the duties on tropical produce has not made these products competitive on the markets of the other member states.

As for the Development Fund, it was set up to finance investments of general interest—such as harbors, roads, electricity generators, irrigation, and flood-control dams—and certain social investments, particularly in hospitals, research establishments, and training schools. The European Development Fund was slow in starting its operations, and it took a year to lay down the regulations governing its work. The first decisions were taken in February, 1959, and by April, 1962, applications on behalf of associated states had reached a total of 1.017 billion—projects of a social nature accounting for 27 per cent, 216 economic projects accounting for 73 per cent of the sums applied for. The heavy emphasis placed by the associated countries on economic rather than social projects seems to be a healthy sign. By January, 1963, the Fund had authorized 162 social projects totaling $155 million and 142 economic projects totaling $265 million—$198 million of them in the field of transport and communications.

Altogether, it was estimated that the resources of the Fund could add up to 50 per cent to the French Government's annual grants for this kind of investment in the French-speaking countries south of the Sahara. Small as its operations may seem by comparison with African needs, the Fund, quite apart from its political significance, thus has an important economic contribution to make. Mention should also be made of the program of scholarships for nationals of the associated states: For 1961–62, 350 scholarships, each for a year, were awarded in economic, agricultural, and technical fields, and for 1962–63 there are plans to award 1,000 such scholarships.

The Association in Transition

Legally, the Convention setting up the Development Fund came to an end on December 31, 1962. It was deliberately concluded for a limited period in order to leave the way open for a revision in the light of developments. However, a general return to bilateralism in development finance is inconceivable today. Even if one or two member states have a preference that way, other member states have decided views against any such return to bilateralism, and both African opinion and world opinion generally will militate against it even more effectively. A new arrangement thus had to be negotiated by the end of 1962.

But whatever the legal position of the Convention, even the articles which form an integral part of the Treaty and are thus legally valid for an indefinite period are now out of date. They were based on a largely static conception of the political relations between the African countries and the metropolitan member states. In the past three years, that relationship has evolved beyond all expectations. Since the Treaty was signed, most of the Associates have become politically independent of any member state. The list is impressive: the Cameroons, the Central African Republic, the Republic of Chad, the Congo, Dahomey, the Gabon Republic, Guinea, the Ivory Coast, Madagascar, Mali, Mauritania, the Republic of the Niger, Senegal, Somalia, Togoland, and the Upper Volta. With the exception of Guinea, every single one of these new states has asked to remain associated with the Community. Guinea has been invited to do so too, but though not formally denouncing the Association, she has not applied its provisions, and her relationship with the Community must be considered to have lapsed.

The independence of all these countries obviously poses major problems for the Community. For a start, the Commission has invited the governments of these new states to appoint representatives in Brussels, so that they may feel independent of their ex-metropolis in their dealings with the Community. They thus, for example, have direct access to the Development Fund. (Under the original system, the Fund could not consider projects which were not forwarded to it by a metropolitan member state.)

But the overseas associates also have obligations to perform under the Convention and the Treaty itself. Thus, the Commission issued a directive in 1960 on nondiscrimination in the award of contracts for works financed by the Fund. Yet the overseas countries are not represented on the Commission, and one cannot expect countries to submit to political organs of the Community in whose decisions they do not have a vote.

Moreover, independence has brought with it new relationships among the African states themselves. In January, 1961, Egypt, Morocco, Libya, the provisional Algerian government-in-exile of the FLN, and the "union" of Ghana, Guinea, and Mali met in Casablanca primarily under the banner of anticolonialism. With the exception of Libya (which has since joined the "Monrovian powers"), these "Casablanca powers" have attempted, in spite of difficulties among themselves, to pursue something like concerted policies toward the rest of the world. On the other hand, in May, 1961, twenty out of the twenty-seven independent African states met in Monrovia, at the invitation of the Cameroons, Liberia, Nigeria, and Togo, and founded an Afro-Malagasy Organization for Economic Cooperation. Their heads of state met in Lagos in January, 1962, where they were joined by Tanganyika and the Congo (Léopoldville), though Libya and Tunisia dropped out. There, it was decided to create a permanent assembly of heads of state and a council of ministers, together with a permanent secretariat, to coordinate regional activities in the economic and social fields. Such Pan-African moves toward regional and continental unity may have a lesson to teach the Europeans; at any rate, they show how undesirable it is to project the barrier between the Six and the Seven onto the map of Africa. If political links between African countries associated with the Community and those not associated with the Community—such as the Monrovia grouping or the Ghana-Guinea-Mali arrangement—are strengthened, Europe's differentiation in treatment of the three categories—Commonwealth countries, Associates, and other independent countries—becomes all the more problematic.

Quite apart from the problems posed by Pan-African sentiment, the extension of the frontier between the Six and the Seven to the soil of Africa serves to accentuate the unhappy economic effects of the Balkanization of Africa. To take one simple example: If Nigeria dams the river Niger to make it navigable upstream well into the Republic of the Niger, this will make uneconomic the proposal—put before the Development Fund—to build a railway from the Republic of the Niger south to link with that running to the coast of Dahomey. The desperately poor Republic of the Niger can only profit from close relations with Nigeria. Even if no political arrangements are possible, at the very least technical and economic arrangements will have to be made between associated and nonassociated countries.

Politically, too, we need not suppose that the newly independent countries will necessarily find the present formula the most satisfactory from their own political point of view. While they were dependent overseas possessions, their association with the Community represented an escape from national apron strings: But this limited widening of their economic horizon may no longer satisfy them once they are independent states themselves, members of the United Nations, and wooed by the rest of the world in a manner that remained impossible until their day of independence. Now they may well wish to escape from a Community five of whose six members were themselves at one time or another colonial powers.

To consider all these problems, the first meeting of 103 Afro-Malagasy parliamentarians with the European Parliamentary Assembly was held in Strasbourg at the end of June, 1961. Fifteen African states, Madagascar, and the Six were represented. The resolutions which the conference unanimously passed pointed the way toward a far-reaching reform of the Association: For it was agreed that the Association must be retained for an unlimited period. The Strasbourg resolutions insisted on an absolute equality of rights between the Afro-Malagasy and European partners in the Association. They called for a repetition of the Strasbourg Parliamentary Conference, to be held alternately in Europe and Africa at least once a year, with committees assuring continuity between its sessions. They called for an Association Council with equal weight given to Afro-Malagasy and European representatives, and for Afro-Malagasy co-determination in the running of the Development Fund (which was to be renamed the Common Development Fund, and to which all would contribute something). An independent Court of Arbitration was to deal with any disputes arising out of the Association. The possibility of association with ECSC and Euratom was also envisaged; some of the low-cost reactors on which the Euratom program is now concentrating might have a distinct interest for African states.

On the economic side, the unanimous resolutions called for an increase in the resources of the Common Development Fund. The Common Fund was also to make loans as well as grants to finance measures of price maintenance. Its operations were to be speeded up, and more European technical counselors were to help the Africans draw up projects for it to finance. A jointly financed Afro-Malagasy Institute for Research and Development was to be set up, and the European member states of the Community were to pay more for technical education in Africa.

The resolutions also called for increased purchases of African products by the Common Market, to be encouraged particularly by a lowering of consumption taxes. It was clear that the Afro-Malagasy group was very conscious of the advantages to it derived from discrimination against the rest of the world. The resolutions called for the retention of tariff preferences and asked the European states neither to enlarge existing tariff quotas nor to introduce new tariff quotas for imports from outside the Association. Indeed, any changes in the external tariff on products of interest to tropical exporters were to be taken in common with the associated states.

Since the Strasbourg conference, three more new states have been born in Africa that are relevant in this context. Burundi and Rwanda, declared independent in July, 1962, have chosen to retain their Associate status, thus bringing the number of independent Associates up to eighteen. Algeria, declared independent in April, 1962, presents a much more complicated case. It could be argued that since the bulk of the Rome Treaty applies to her under Article 227, she is entitled to remain a member of the Community. On the other hand, she could gain her own representation in the Community's institutions only if the Treaty were amended, and this is unlikely to happen: Under Article 237, the Community is open only to European states. Nor is Algeria likely to wish for full membership. Under the Evian Agreement by which Algeria became independent, France promised that Algeria should remain economically associated with her (and therefore with the Community)—not perhaps a promise that France can make any longer by herself, but at least an interesting symptom of the wishes of the FLN in the matter. Indeed in December, 1962, the Algerian Government asked that it should be allowed to continue to benefit from the Rome Treaty's Convention on the Association of Overseas Countries, and the Community has agreed to maintain its existing commitments to Algeria; the future relationship between Algeria and the Community is to be worked out in due course. The transfer of Netherlands New Guinea to Indonesia, on the other hand, is bringing in its train the winding up of New Guinea's Association with the Community. There thus remain, over and above the eighteen independent Associated Overseas Countries, four French overseas departments: Guiana, Martinique, Guadeloupe, and Reunion, and a miscellany of surviving colonial territories: Surinam and the Netherlands Antilles, French Polynesia, New Caledonia, Wallis and Futuna, the Comoro Islands, French Somaliland, St. Pierre and Miquelon, and the French southern and Antarctic territories.

In the meantime the Six, after arduous negotiations among themselves finally, at the beginning of July, 1962, agreed on the terms they were prepared to offer to their overseas Associates under a new five-year Convention to replace the one that expired on December 31, 1962; but it then took until December 20, 1962, for the negotiations between the Six and the Associates to be completed and for the new Convention to be initiated by all the participating states: The formal signature is planned to take place in Africa, at Yaoundé, some time in 1963.

There were many questions to be faced before that agreement could be reached—notably the total of funds to be offered, the contributions to be made by each of the Six, the use to which those funds were to be put, and—at German and Dutch insistence—the whole problem of tariff levels on tropical products.

In the negotiations between the Six, France began by demanding $1.2 billion for the Associates over the next five years. Belgium and Germany in particular thought that such largesse was excessive, and in the end the Six agreed between themselves on a figure of $780 million. The Associates then demanded $810 million, and in the end a compromise was reached: $800 million were to be made available, $730 million to the independent overseas Associates, and another $70 million to the French overseas departments and the dependent territories.

While hitherto the Development Fund was able only to make non-returnable grants for economic and social investment, and of the $730 million going to the independent Associates $620 million would still take that form, two other methods of financing were instituted in the new Convention. $46 million were to be made available by the Development Fund as soft loans, differing from loans commercially available by longer periods of amortization, lower interest rates, and similar concessions. In addition the European Investment Bank (see p. 50 above) which has hitherto confined its activities to Europe will be able to make loans on normal terms of $64 million, while the Development Fund is empowered to use part of its non-returnable funds to reduce the interest charge in fact payable by Associates to 3 per cent. In addition the Fund can use its assets temporarily for short-term loans not exceeding $50 million to help stabilize the prices of primary products. The financial burden implied by this $730 million of national contributions was also redistributed: It might possibly have been appropriate in 1957 for Italy only to contribute just over half the Dutch share, but by 1962, her progress had been so rapid that this was plainly unfair. Under the present agreement among the Six, therefore, Italy's contribution has gone up from $40 million to $100 million, the Dutch and Belgian contributions have dropped slightly to $66 million and $69 million respectively, while Germany and France have increased their shares to $246.5 million each, and Luxembourg provides the remaining $2 million.

More important than the sharing of the burden is the use to which the new funds will be put. Here, the French felt that it was time the Community shouldered not only a part of the economic and social investment, but also part of the scheme of price guarantees which France has continued to operate in favor of its ex-colonies, the Community's Associates. The fall in world prices of tropical products has lately increased the sums needed to keep export earnings up and save these African economies from serious setbacks. Something like $80 million would be required annually to bridge the gap between world prices and the prices (particularly for coffee and bananas) which France has continued to guarantee.

As against this, France's partners in the Community saw no reason to subsidize the French consumer of tropical products from the former French colonies, and felt that commodity stabilization should be a world task accomplished on a non-discriminatory basis. Instead of $400 million over five years, they finally agreed to $230 million to subsidize uncompetitive growers, to increase productivity, and to diversify production. To make the point quite clear, the price subsidies were set to start at $125 million in 1963, and were then to taper off over the five years of the new Convention, as an incentive for growers to become competitive quickly, while the reorganization grants, on the other hand, would increase during this period. With $230 million spent on price subsidies and reorganization and diversification grants, $500 million was left for economic and social investments—almost the same figure as in the first five years.

Where trade is concerned, the Germans and the Dutch pressed for a halving of the common external tariff on tropical products. In order not to reduce the preference given to Associates too drastically, they offered in return to abolish the duties levied on tropical produce from within the Association, on January 1, 1963. The French thought that a quarter was the biggest possible cut in the common external tariff, and a compromise was finally reached: On coffee and cocoa, the duty will be cut by 25 per cent, and there will be a suspension of another 15 per cent, which can be annulled only by unanimity in the Council; in effect, this will reduce the duties to 9.6 and 7.2 per cent, respectively. The duty on tea was also to be cut from 18 to 10.8 per cent (and indeed, in August, the Six agreed to abolish it altogether should Britain join the Community). Other tropical products would have their external rates of duty cut by between 15 and 25 per cent, while within the Association, coffee, cocoa, tea, coconuts, fresh pineapples, and various spices move duty-free from the moment the Convention comes into force.

The first Convention had not explicitly provided for any Community action in the field of technical training and co-operation: but the Commission soon felt that it had to go beyond the technical activities directly connected with investment projects. The new Convention now gives the Community much wider scope in this field, and we may expect the existing scholarship, internship, and training schemes to be greatly enlarged over the next few years.

Closely following the recommendations of the Strasbourg Parliamentary Conference of 1961, the new Convention also set up four new organs to supervise its implementation: a Council of Association consisting of one member of the government of each Associated state and of representatives of the Council and the Commission of the Community, to meet at least once a year; an Association Committee consisting of one member of each of the eighteen overseas and six European governments and a representative of the Commission to ensure continuity under the Council's instructions; a Parliamentary Conference of the Association, meeting once a year, to which the Association Council must present an annual report; and a Court of Arbitration consisting of a chairman and four judges, two nominated by the European, two by the Association states.

Highly significant, in addition, is a new clause that makes the Association potentially open to other overseas states not associated at the moment with any of the Six—a clause on which the Dutch and the Germans in particular insisted so that some Commonwealth countries might have a chance of becoming Associates even if Britain is not a member of the Community.

Toward a World Approach

The Association, and particularly the development of it which has now been agreed, goes a considerable way. It recognizes the need for Europe to encourage the consumption of tropical products, and for Europe as a whole—and not only the countries with recent colonial responsibilities—to give away money for infrastructure and social investment in the poorer countries in order to allow their economies to reach "take-off level." In addition, France has been generous (after her experience with Guinea) in continuing her aid to her former colonies, quite apart from the Community. And for a whole range of products, the Association means more discrimination in favor of the poorer countries than Commonwealth preference means to Commonwealth neighbors.

But turning to the long run, one may wonder how far the Association can be of permanent significance. The French-educated African leaders are now for the most part still anxious to preserve their links with Europe—are trying, for example, to recruit more French schoolteachers—and will no doubt defend the Association for its economic benefits, provided it allows them to "deliver the goods." But they are still finding their feet in the wider sphere of the world politics where other alternatives are open to them as well. And it is difficult to see from Europe how far their peoples are behind them and whether they will in the long run wish or be able to continue with the Association in the spirit in which Europeans, sometimes for shortsighted reasons, hope that they will. In fact, very real problems remain —of both an economic and a political kind.

For a start, Africa is divided into two separate preferential areas, very much along the old colonial demarcations. For many tropical products, and especially for cocoa, coffee, and tea, there are now two separate preferential areas in Europe: the United Kingdom granting tariff preferences on imports from Commonwealth countries, and the EEC on imports from their Associates. In addition, there are countries such as Liberia and Ethiopia (or indeed Tunisia and Morocco), which are left outside either major preferential area. This whole situation is a political no less than an economic anomaly.

If Britain ever joins the Common Market, the obvious solution is that the African and the Caribbean countries of the Commonwealth should become Associates of the Community and benefit from the same tariff preferences from the whole of the enlarged Community. Such a solution might be seductive from an "Afro-European" or "Eurafrican" point of view, and would meet the demands voiced by the Afro-Malagasy group at the Strasbourg conference. But it would encounter the very grave misgivings of Asia and South America, and, in consequence, of the United States and of Japan. Nor would such misgivings be unjustified: The preference, instead of favoring certain producers against the rest, would then in effect discriminate against a minority of producers—chiefly in South America. Such a solution is plainly against the interests of the free world as a whole.

The time has perhaps come to ask what the point and purpose of tariffs on tropical produce might be. Only in a few cases, such as that of vegetable oils, can the tariff be regarded as protecting domestic interests. At a time when the richer countries are attempting to find money to help the development of tropical areas, it seems self-defeating to impose levies which not only distort the consumer's choice, but above all restrict the funds that these countries are able to earn for themselves. The German consumption tax on coffee, for example, brought in $180 million in the single year 1959—almost what Germany has to contribute to the Development Fund in the whole of the first five years.

In this situation, President Kennedy has come out in favor of a world-wide solution: the abolition by all industrial countries of tariffs, consumption taxes, and quantitative restrictions on tropical produce. There are signs that the Commission would not be at all hostile to such tariff disarmament. But, implying (as it would) the abandonment of discrimination in favor of former French territories, it would have to reckon with stiff opposition from both France and the present Associates. Such opposition could only be appeased if at the same time other measures of aid for tropical producers were instituted.

For tariffs and tariff discrimination are only a minor factor in determining the export income of tropical producers. Far more important is the world level of commodity prices. During 1958, the main tropical products, whose export was valued at $25 billion, proved subject to average price fluctuations of 23 per cent. In the same year, the United States, the United Kingdom, and France together gave assistance amounting to $3 billion to the Asian and African countries that are the main producers of such tropical raw materials. A drop of 12 per cent in the average price is thus sufficient to wipe out the entire inflow of money into these countries from development aid. The money may be used differently, whether it comes by way of export earnings or by way of aid; perhaps the latter contributes more to investment. But either way, the price stability of tropical products must be a subject of vital concern to all interested in the political stability of Africa.

The free world market is in fact the market of the free world. By buying up half of Guinea's banana crop for several years ahead, at a favorable price, the Soviet Union gained political sympathies in a way which vast gifts of capital might not have done. A rise in the world market price could, of course, complicate this situation. But the Soviet Union, with a centralized purchasing policy, can perfectly well give better terms to any who are willing to form political links with her. The Communist bloc, having reached its present stage in improving living standards, may soon become the fastest-growing market for tropical products in the world. No one in the West should attempt or even appear to attempt to put obstacles in the way of African countries concluding with the Soviet bloc such trade and aid agreements as they wish. But the West itself should also bear in mind the need to be an attractive partner.

This is a problem which the Six cannot resolve by themselves—or even in collaboration with Britain. Any solution depends on the cooperation of the United States, and here may well lie one of the most important tasks of the new Organization for Economic Cooperation and Development. The present Administration in Washington has thus suggested that if both the Six and the Commonwealth dismantle the protection in favor of their respective tropical clients, the United States could contribute to a general compensation fund designed to help the new African states stand on their own feet, regardless of the loss of special protection. If agreement is reached on the minimum each consuming country would pledge itself to buy, and the maximum each producing country would sell, the producers could draw on such a compensation fund in a lean year and pledge themselves to replenish it as prices improve. The idea is not new, and the practical difficulties remain stupendous. But if it can be done, we should not be sorry if the preferential aspects of the Association are dissolved in a world-wide arrangement.

The attitude in Washington, on the investment side of the Association, seems to be similar. From a world point of view, it is not rational that as rich an area as Europe should concentrate its economic aid on 53 million people in various spots of Africa which happen until recently to have had constitutional links with them and which by the year 2000 will constitute only 1 or 2 per cent of the world's population. The replacement of bilateral colonial relationships with the metropolis by multilateral (or oligolateral) relationships with the Community marks a step forward: But it remains a halfway house. The African leaders who champion it at home may find it increasingly difficult to defend a still narrow and recently tainted relationship. It will not be easy to convince their populations of the advantages of this historical accident as against freer choice in a wider institutional framework. And for those left out of the Association and of the Commonwealth, economic progress may well be unduly slow.

France in particular, the other five, and Britain too, if she joins them, should be given credit for the aid they now give to African development. But the time may come when we shall all be asked to match the aid given to our historical associates with proportional aid to the rest of the world. The technical and personnel problems may seem insuperable. The economic burden may be heavy. The proportion of funds apparently wasted may be dispiriting. But, in the long run, here as on the tariff side, far wider development plans regardless of past colonial connections might well be healthier for the political evolution of the world.

V

Britain vs. France and Her Partners

The Free Trade Area Proposals

In September, 1954, when the EDC had been thrown out by the French National Assembly, the Earl of Avon (then Sir Anthony Eden) assumed the initiative in Europe and, in a lightning tour of Continental capitals, put a few pieces together again. The Western European Union that was the outcome of his efforts benefited from British membership and British guarantees. But the moment of British leadership was brief. Western European Union assumed no greater importance than the Council of Europe, and, in 1957, Britain withdrew her Fourth Division from the Continent—less than three years after she had promised to keep it there until the year 1998. Indeed, from 1955 until 1960, British diplomacy was back in the old groove. Unable to understand that Germans and Frenchmen could really want to merge aspects of their national sovereignty, British leaders continued to be unaware of the strength of "European" feelings and aspirations on the Continent, and very few thought through the implications for the United Kingdom's position, should these aspirations succeed.

First British Reactions. The Messina Conference passed almost unnoticed in Britain. It seemed unrealistic to believe that, just after the failure of the EDC, the Six could pull off a gigantic new scheme such as a general Common Market. At the meeting of the Spaak Committee, Britain was represented by an official of the Board of Trade, but by 1955, it seemed pointless that a country that had no intention of being committed by the outcome should participate in the serious drafting, and so the British observer was withdrawn.

In 1956, when they accepted the Spaak Report as a basis for negotiation, the Six invited Britain to join in working out the Treaties. Once more, Britain refused. But by now, a few senior officials and one or two ministers began to wonder what would happen if the Six managed to pull it off. A series of plans were prepared as a staff exercise. While Mr. Thorneycroft and Mr. Macmillan, in favoring "Plan G," came pretty close to advocating British participation, Mr. Butler, concerned about the fate of British agriculture, was hostile. But the Cabinet and the Prime Minister were far more preoccupied that summer by events in Egypt, and the most that the government was prepared to do was to take up the suggestion, made in the Spaak Report itself, that a Free Trade Area could be superimposed on the Common Market. (A free-trade area, like a customs union, involves the mutual abolition of trade barriers; but, unlike a customs union, it does not involve common external trade barriers.) In late 1955, at the meetings of the Spaak Committee, the British representative had been unable to pledge Britain to participation in a free-trade area; in November, 1956—just after, but in no way because of, the Suez expedition—a European Free Trade Area surrounding the customs union of the Six became official British policy.

Here, then, was the first Community of the Six that was threatening to result in big, tangible disadvantages for Britain. The Coal and Steel Community might have touched vital British interests, but only in one sector, and has in fact hardly done so even there. The Defense Community was distinctly in line with British interests, and the Political Community was a draft treaty that remained far from realization. Now a new customs union was arising on the Continent where one-eighth of British exports were sold. Since most of British exports went to the low-tariff countries of the Community, the Six were, on average, to raise their tariffs on British goods, while tariffs on all goods from their partners were to be abolished.

The blackmail was in part incidental; but sooner or later it was bound to come, and, but for the EDC, it would have been felt years before. Moreover, the blackmail was reluctant: M. Jean Monnet, who had been the instigator of Churchill's offer for a union between France and Britain in 1940, had attempted in the early postwar years to interest Sir Stafford Cripps in a Franco-British Economic Community, and today it is poignant to recall that Jean Monnet, Etienne Hirsch, and Pierre Uri spent a week with Sir Robert Hall and Lord Plowden at Jean Monnet's home to mull over the project, which the Cabinet then resolutely opposed. It was only after this that Monnet went ahead with his plans for the Coal and Steel Community, declaring, in London: "There is one thing you British will never understand: an idea. And there is one thing you are supremely good at grasping: a hard fact. We will have to make Europe without you—but then you will have to come in and join us."

The Free Trade Area proposals were Britain's first move towards the Six; but on the Continent, having seen the British Government stymie the Council of Europe, the Europeans feared that this was yet another attempt at sabotage. The Six were anxious not to complicate the process of ratification by having a "soft option" all ready for those in their own parliaments who might feel that the Common Market went too far. At their request, Britain agreed to wait with negotiations until after the treaty was ratified.

Whatever the motives behind Britain's next move, this once more called forth a cry of "subversion" from the Continent. In December, 1956, shortly after the Suez expedition, Mr. Selwyn Lloyd put forward his "Grand Design" for a single European Assembly, in which the Consultative Assembly of the Council of Europe, the Assembly of Western European Union, the NATO Parliamentarians' Conference, and preferably also the Common Assembly of the Coal and Steel Community (and therefore, in due course, the Parliamentary Assembly of the Six) would be merged. Certainly the proliferation of assemblies was causing inconvenience and diluting their impact on the public. But the federalists saw in this "drowning of Europe in the Atlantic" a deliberate attempt to hamstring the political institutions of the Six. Thus the "Grand Design"—an unfortunate title if it really was concerned only with tidying up institutional overlaps—was laughed out of court, and the negotiations on the much more serious and substantial Free Trade Area proposals began under a political cloud.

Concrete British Proposals. The Free Trade Area proposals—which were designed to allow all member states of the OEEC to join—had this much in common with the Economic Community: They envisaged the abolition of internal customs duties and quantitative restrictions on trade in industrial goods. But the British Government refused to envisage a common external tariff; its scheme expressly excluded agriculture from free trade and refused to countenance a common agricultural policy; it included no specific provisions for freedom of movement of persons, services, and capital; it did not extend to the overseas associated countries and territories; and it contained none of the other provisions listed in Article 3 of the Community Treaty such as the Social Fund, the Investment Fund, and the measures of harmonization.

Britain's reluctance to see agriculture included in any agreement was dictated not least by considerations of domestic politics. But it was also felt that free entry from the Continent would detract from the Commonwealth countries' privilege of being the only duty-free exporters of many agricultural commodities to the United Kingdom.

Where a common external tariff was concerned, the mutual preferences granted on trade between the United Kingdom and Commonwealth countries seemed incompatible with British participation in a customs union with the Continent. Either Britain would have to cease giving preferences to Commonwealth imports, and therefore probably lose the preferences granted to her in Commonwealth markets; or, alternatively, the preferential system would have to be extended to the whole of the customs union—a solution which, quite apart from its doubtful compatibility with GATT, was not necessarily acceptable either to the Commonwealth or, for that matter, to British exporters.

The special domestic policies demanded by the United Kingdom's special position as banker to the sterling area, the fact that wages, hours, and holidays were largely decided by collective bargaining and not by legislation—these and similar arguments were used against the harmonization of domestic policies with those of the Six. Finally, neither industry, afraid of central planning, nor labor, afraid of permanent Christian and conservative majorities on the Continent, nor the government itself was ready at the time to commit itself to the execution of as yet undefined measures to be decided by government representatives without a formal power of veto and, worse still, from the government's point of view, proposed by supranational bodies representing not the component nation-states, but the Community as a whole. So the Free Trade Area, while a step forward from 1955, was the most that Britain felt she could propose.

France's Partners

Every one of the motives that impelled Western Europe to seek unity after the war applied with particular force, though sometimes with particular complications, to West Germany. The Germans had lost their fatherland in a sense that no other country had: It was morally discredited, geographically divided, and physically shattered. The escape forward into a united Europe was the sole secular ideal that remained to German youth. What for the rest of Europe was the problem of controlling Germany, was for the Germans the problem of working their way back to equal membership in the European family of nations.

To Dr. Adenauer and his group of Christian Democratic leaders, Franco-German reconciliation was not only a moral task arising out of the bitter past, but one of extreme political urgency. They feared a resurgence of nationalism, which could lead to deals with the Soviet Union: They feared nationalism in Germany, where reunification remained for years a hotly debated issue, and they feared it in France. On the other hand, none had grimmer experience of fighting Russia, or of Russian occupation, and European unity also seemed vital to them for defense against the East.

Nor must it be forgotten that the recovery of the German economy was closely tied to Marshall Aid, and therefore to the efforts made by the Americans and by the West Europeans themselves under the European recovery program. Until well after the outbreak of the Korean War, two years after the currency reform, Germany's credits from the European Payments Union were essential if she was to maintain her rate of imports and therefore her rate of growth. Very quickly and dramatically, in 1951, Germany once more began her career as an exporting nation, and so, both in the first stage and in the second, European economic integration seemed directly parallel with German economic interests. The philosophy on which German recovery was based after 1948 was one of free trade domestically, and it was natural that this market economy at home should be complemented by free-trade ideas in international economics. Economic ideology thus coincided with economic interest, steering the West German economy toward European integration.

Over the issue of the Free Trade Area, a substantial section of German opinion had been on Britain's side. The Minister for Economic Affairs, Professor Erhard, basically subscribes to free trade and distrusts the elements of supranational *dirigisme* he sees in the Rome Treaties. In 1957, he had referred to the Community as "economic nonsense" and "European incest." German industry was confident of its competitive position and was anxious to have access to the British and Scandinavian markets on equal terms with British industry. But Dr. Adenauer was far less happy with the British proposals. Anxious to tie the Federal Republic into a tight Western political framework before his death, he suspected any scheme that threatened to dilute the political content of the Common Market.

The Dutch welcomed the idea of a Free Trade Area: Their economic position was close to that of Germany, their prices were competitive in the industrial sector, and their tariffs low by comparison with those to be established by the Community as a whole. An enlargement of the projected area of free trade would thus simultaneously boost their exports and help keep down their consumer prices and manufacturing costs. If Britain had not insisted on the exclusion of agriculture from her scheme for a Free Trade Area, she could have had a much more wholehearted ally in the Dutch. Where politics were concerned, the Dutch strongly believed in Community institutions: For a small country, supranationality of the governmental type was not enough. But if they could not obtain supranationality of the Community type, they preferred to have Britain in to balance any possible Franco-German domination.

As in the Common Market, so in the Free Trade Area negotiations, the Dutch delegation often spoke not only for Holland but also for German business. For with Adenauer and the German Foreign Office asserting the primacy of foreign over economic policy, Erhard and the German business world were never allowed to put effective pressure on France to accept Britain into a free-trade relationship with the Six.

The Belgians and the Italians perhaps took up less pronounced positions on this issue. M. Spaak was concerned with preserving the supranational character of the Community; Belgian business was less sure of its competitive position than Dutch. Like the Italians, the Belgians were therefore reluctant to hurry France into acceptance of the British scheme.

But by now, the convinced Europeans on the Common Market Commission also had a hand in the game. They feared that the institutionally looser Free Trade Area would detract from the importance of the Community and that wider and more anemic plans would prevail. The whole negative spirit in which the Free Trade Area was discussed in Britain, purely as a measure of self-defense, only cemented this new alliance between protectionists and Europeans. Britain's breach of her promise to Western European union further swelled the already deep-rooted suspicion that such engagements to Europe as she might be prepared to undertake could justifiably be treated with skeptical reserve. In this, the Europeans made common cause with France. It was not on technical problems that the negotiations foundered; it was the underlying political factors which, at the end of 1958, led France to precipitate the breakdown of the talks. A press conference by M. Jacques Soustelle, De Gaulle's Minister of Information simply torpedoed the talks from outside when he declared that the whole principle of free trade area as envisioned in the negotiation was unacceptable to France.

French Economic Resurgence

In 1957, French postage stamps showed Europe as an open building site: In 1958, they depicted Europe as a completed chain of six links closed firmly in upon itself. Consciously or subconsciously, their designers not only anticipated economic developments: They also mirrored a revolution in French foreign policy.

When France wrecked the EDC, two arguments were among the most telling: that any integration of the Six would be dangerously unbalanced without British participation, and that it would lead to an Economic Community for which the French economy was unprepared. By 1958, on each of these arguments, feelings in France were, if anything, all the other way—and that, piquantly enough, just when the bitterest opponents of the EDC had at last come to power. On the political side, this reversal of French attitudes began well before the demise of the Fourth Republic. Indeed, after the great emotional upsurge over the EDC, it looked almost as if the French public had exhausted its more violent anti-German feelings. The later close alliance, when a German head of state could for the first time in history be received in Paris, had not yet been achieved. But sentiments about the Germans had become more neutral—more like those about the Belgians or the Dutch. And so, until 1958, French objections to European integration became less political and above all economic.

The Economic Seeds of the Fourth Republic. France had been if not the sick man, then certainly the hypochondriac of Europe. Massive industrial investments under the Monnet Plan, far-reaching contributions to the development of Africa, wars first in Indochina and then in Algeria, and the pursuit of an independent nuclear deterrent, combined with a generous social policy at home, entailed heavy expenditures. But successive weak governments were unable to raise the revenue which, together with United States aid, should have prevented inflation. The benefits of several devaluations of the franc were wasted by failure to hold the domestic price level: French exporters found themselves priced out of many markets, and the balance of payments was causing constant concern.

When the foreign ministers of the Six met at Messina, in 1955, the French had been prepared to agree to cultural projects, to joint atomic programs, to transport integration—but the Benelux countries and Germany succeeded in obtaining agreement on the wider scheme of an Economic Community. To make it more palatable to France, her partners gave her the benefit of the doubt throughout the detailed negotiations on the Treaty. France had the external bargaining power that comes to an unstable government dependent on a volatile assembly. We have seen in earlier chapters how she was bought with concession after concession. The French had not really thought that the plan for an Economic Community would become a reality. (They were not the only ones to take that view.) Maybe they would have been content with less. But, bluff or not, their tactics succeeded. And since, substantially, all their demands were met, neither the government nor the business community felt able to oppose the Rome Treaty in the end.

Paradoxically enough, it was Britain that helped to bring about the conversion of French business interests to the Six, for their reversal of attitude was in part a tactical move. Only by turning champions of the Six, some felt, could they torpedo the Free-Trade Area. Traditional French protectionism certainly could not swallow the British scheme. That France should open her frontiers not only to the other five, who had granted her such far-reaching concessions, but to some half-dozen or dozen other countries as well—and all that without special concessions and without harmonization of at least some elements of production costs—seemed too much to those who had accepted even the Common Market only reluctantly, and who expected to make full use of all the escape clauses provided to fit their special needs. Put in more abstract terms, they considered it unfair that all the trading advantages should be obtained by those who proved unwilling to shoulder all the other obligations contained in the Rome Treaty (and without which, the French had insisted vis-à-vis their own partners in the Six, free trade was unacceptable to them): the contribution to investment in Africa and in southern Italy and other backward regions, the social fund for the conversion of enterprises and the retraining of workers, and the harmonization of agricultural and other policies. Absence of the first two at least, they argued, showed a selfish or callous spirit. Moreover, they argued that it was technically impossible to operate the British scheme. Britain, they felt, had taken up a curiously dogmatic standpoint for such an empirical nation, and it became an intellectual sport in Paris to knock down every device that the British put up.

The Economic Harvest of the Fifth Republic. There followed the fateful May 13, 1958, the installation of the Fifth Republic, and, at the very end of the year, President de Gaulle's new economic program of *vérité et sévèrité:* a frankness which recognized the depreciation of the franc by a devaluation of seventeen per cent, and a discipline which prevented the advantages of this devaluation from being frittered away in a new bout of inflation. The new President was determined to keep his Treaty obligations, and no escape clauses ever had to be invoked. For, once the currency adjustment had been made, the basic health of the French economy stood revealed; and having taken the plunge, French business, much to its own surprise, soon found its wings in the new air of competition and expansion across national boundaries.

The Fifth Republic here reaped the benefit of the policies of the Fourth—policies which had in no small measure contributed to popular dissatisfaction with the old regime. The Monnet Plan had put investment first—and investment in the basic energy sector and heavy equipment before the development of the consumer industries. As a result, industrial production had risen by nearly one-half between 1953 and 1958, a rise only slightly below that of the Federal Republic.

This remarkable performance was achieved in spite of a rise of only seven per cent in industrial employment, while the Federal Republic, through the absorption of refugees and migrant labor, and thanks to the crop of Third Reich babies, was able in the same period to expand its industrial employment by twenty-six per cent. The Fourth Republic was in fact not only making physical investments, but carrying a heavy burden of human investment as well. For the past ten years, the number of young people coming on to the labor market each year has been less than three-quarters of the number of new mouths to be fed. And through a system of family allowances lavish compared with the British system, that burden has been borne by the community as a whole. Only now, as a reward, will the opposite trend set in with a consequent sudden expansion of productive capacity. (In Germany, the low birthrate of the postwar period will shortly produce just the opposite effect.) It is hardly surprising if Frenchmen now feel that their economy has turned its tightest corner and that they have good structural reasons for economic self-confidence.

There has been a real revolution in the mentality of French business. This is partly due to natural factors: A new generation of more dynamic young Frenchmen, born in the 1920's, whose formative years were marked by the upheavals of the 1940's, are

Table VI

YOUNGER ELEMENTS IN THE FRENCH AND GERMAN POPULATIONS
(millions, January 1, 1960)

Age	France	Germany	Difference
20—25	3.0	4.5	— 1.5
15—20	2.7	4.1	— 1.4
10—15	3.9	3.4	+ 0.5
5—10	4.0	3.8	+ 0.2
0—5	4.0	4.2	— 0.2

SOURCE: *Annuaire Statistique de la France,* 1961, p. 15; and *Statistisches Jahrbuch für die Bundesrepublik Deutschland,* 1961, p. 46.

taking over from the more easy-going protectionist "old guard." French business is fast losing its inflation complex: It no longer takes it for granted that anything produced can be sold at good profit margins at home. It is beginning to take a real interest in modern business methods, in rationalization, expansion, and exports. Often nationalized industries are setting the pace. Where formerly France was suspicious of foreign investment, today American firms are welcomed. Organizations such as the *Jeunes Patrons* and the *Comité Franc-Dollar* foster the new spirit, which has come to imbue even the *Conseil National du Patronat Français*. The Common Market has acted as a tremendous psychological shock; devaluation and the underlying soundness of the economy have permitted that shock not to depress but to elate.

Indeed, the first results achieved by French business under

the new dispensation have been impressive. Exporters decided to make Germany a test market. Here was their chief competitor: If they could beard him in his own den, the whole new structure would work. At the Hanover Fair in 1960, France was the leading foreign exhibitor, and in some sectors German industrialists quickly began to complain of French inroads into their market.

The effects may be traced in the development of the French balance of trade. While exports had been stagnant between 1957 and 1958, they rose rapidly from the beginning of 1959; by 1961 French exports to EEC partners were running at more than twice the 1958 level, and other exports were up by twenty per cent. Imports from the rest of the Community were up three-quarters, while imports from the rest of the world were still below those of 1957. The heavy trade deficit of 1957, when exports paid for little more than four-fifths of imports, had been turned into a respectable surplus by 1959, and this has been well maintained since.

Table VII
French Balance of Trade
(monthly averages, millions of dollars)

	1957	1958	1959	1960	1961	1962
EEC						
Exports	106	95	127	170	202	226
Imports	109	102	114	154	175	210
Trade Balance	− 3	− 7	+13	+16	+27	+16
Rest of World						
Exports	315	332	341	402	400	388
Imports	401	365	310	369	381	416
Trade Balance	−86	−33	+31	+33	+19	−28
Total Trade						
Exports	421	427	468	572	602	613
Imports	510	467	424	523	556	627
Trade Balance	−89	−40	+44	+50	+46	−14

Source: *EEC General Statistical Bulletin,* No. 12 (1961), pp. 130–34; and *ibid.,* No. 2 (1962), pp. 91-97.

European Business Integration. Both in conjunction with the new export mentality, and perhaps even more in order to exercise at the new level of the Community institutions those pressure-group activities to which business has accustomed itself on the national level, French businessmen are now meeting their opposite numbers from other countries in a big way. They have been leading spirits in the formation of a host of new international industrial and business associations, of which there are literally hundreds. They vary from the all-embracing *Union des Industries de la Communauté Européenne* and the Permanent Conference of EEC Chambers of Commerce to the EEC Mustard Industry Committee and the European Union of Publicity Organizations in Brussels, the Common Market Committee of the International Hairdressers' Federation in Paris, the European Ribbon and Elastics Association in Arnhem, the European Union of Milk Traders in Bonn, and the Working Party for EEC Problems of the Sanitary Chinaware Manufacturers in Milan. Hardly a week passes without a whole string of sessions at which common problems and common attitudes toward the Commission and the national governments are discussed.

The last four years have also seen a vast crystallization of Franco-German industrial and commercial agreements and measures of business integration directly provoked by the Common Market. Peugeot and Mercedes-Benz, As de Trefle and Agfa Leverkusen, Fouga and Messerschmidt, Desmarais and BV-Aral, Rhone-Poulenc and Bayer Leverkusen, Centrale de Dynamite and Hoechst, Breguet and Dornier, Lip and Holzer, Lavallette and Bosch, Manurhin and Auto-Union, Nord-Aviation and Focke-Wulf, to mention only some of the more famous names in the aeroplane and motor, chemical and mechanical industries of the two countries, have all concluded various kinds of agreement: for the exchange of patents, for manufacture under license, for the marketing of each others' products, for the joint manufacture of new products. Much the same kind of activity is going on between French and Belgian firms, Dutch and Italian firms, and almost all the combinations possible between six partners. Having once begun to make their plans on the basis of the Common Market, it is not surprising that even French businessmen were soon demanding the acceleration of its development.

But while French self-confidence was equal to the first stage of the Common Market, it was far from rising high enough as yet to face free trade. French agriculture—not the least powerful lobby in the country—feared that any arrangement with Britain would have to include an arrangement with the Commonwealth, which would be bound to harm the French farmer. As for industry, the *Conseil National du Patronat Français* supported the 1960 proposal for acceleration, but opposed the reduction in the external tariff of the Community and demanded a speeding up not only in the mutual tariff reductions, but also in the harmonization of national policies. Just as French industry's conversion to the Common Market had in it a very real element of avoiding the greater of two evils (the Free Trade Area), so in 1959–60 there was a trace of ulterior motives about the demands of French industry for the acceleration of the Common Market's time-table: a quicker pace of continental integration would render less likely any free trade arrangement with the British and the rest of Europe. French industry did not fear British competition in France herself so much as in Germany and in other partner countries. And no doubt—a more dubious motive—there were also those who felt that, in spite of the trust-bust provisions of the Treaty, agreements restricting competition (as against agreements principally lowering costs) can be made more easily in a smaller framework. As one official of the *Patronat* put it: "We are getting to know the Germans and we like working with them. We think less and less about Britain: We realize now that we can get on very well without you."

De Gaulle's Bid for Leadership

Parallel with this conversion of French business to the Common Market, there had been a revolution in the thinking of the government. Certainly President de Gaulle has gone out of his way to praise the healthy effects of the Economic Community on the economy of France. But it was above all on the political side, and for political reasons, that he changed his position to the point of a *volte-face*.

With President de Gaulle's accession to power in 1958, British hopes for an accommodation with the Six had risen. Neither President de Gaulle nor, later, M. Debré could be classed as enthusiasts for a Little Europe, or as enemies of Britain and friends of Germany. (M. Debré had voted against every single European Community). Yet it was only under the new regime that a forthright statement of France's real intentions at last could be heard. M. Soustelle's famous press conference of November 14, 1958 removed the whole basis on which the negotiations had been carried out. There is a French comedy film in which a deaf man relevantly replies to all remarks addressed to him: *"Ah, si on avait un gouvernement!"* This heartfelt wish of France's neighbors had at last been met; but for Britain, the answer, delayed for so long, proved a bitter disappointment.

The new emphasis on France's national greatness, far from leading President de Gaulle into making gestures of friendship towards Britain, led him rather into consolidating his relations with Bonn. In the race for nuclear status, Britain, not Germany, was the rival. In North Africa—the very problem to which the new regime owed its existence—it was Britain, not Germany, who had delivered arms to Tunisia, whose attitude in the United Nations had lacked the enthusiastic solidarity expected from a fellow colonial power, and whose whole African policy was an embarrassment to the French. As British forces on the continent were reduced while German rearmament progressed, President de Gaulle could feel that it was the German Army, not the British, that stood between the Soviet Union and Rambouillet. Dr. Adenauer, on the other hand, needed French support against Mr. Macmillan over the Berlin question, and was prepared to pay a heavy price to secure it, both in political support and in cash. France needed short-term funds to settle her foreign exchange debts and she needed long-term funds for overseas investment; both these could cross the Rhine, but not the Channel. In fact, for the new French Government, the Economic Community was a Eurafrican as much as a European scheme. The implementation of the Common Market, far from having to reconcile France and Germany, thus became in part a by-product of the new Paris-Bonn axis.

But President de Gaulle was concerned as much as anything else with France's weight in the councils of the West. Formally, this preoccupation with "Anglo-Saxon hegemony" took the form of his demand for a tripartite directorate in NATO, in which France, too, would rank with America as a leading great power. In material terms France is, of course, too small to fill such a role by herself. So, too, is Britain. But according to President de Gaulle's premises, what had given Britain a special relationship and influence with the United States was not simply a shared language and traditions, nor even just her possession of nuclear arms, but above all her role as leader of the Commonwealth. Fundamental to President de Gaulle's thinking was his determination to use the European Community to buttress French weakness: As leader and spokesman of the Six, France also would have a key place in the inner circle of the free world.

This new mood of French self-confidence was not confined to the economy. Diplomats who for years had been representing weak governments or even mere caretaker administrations suddenly found themselves listened to again with respect. Some of the French vetoes seemed almost to represent a working-off of accumulated feelings of inferiority: Indeed, one Frenchman described the failure of the Free-Trade Area negotiations as "our revenge for your having liberated us in 1944." Given the Quai d'Orsay's experience and its exceptionally able personnel, given French prestige and the peculiar historical position in which Germany is placed, given the weight of her African Commonwealth behind her, and her role as the hinge between Europe and Africa, France felt assured of the leadership of the Six.

It followed that for political no less than for economic reasons, France had no interest in British participation in the European Community. As the fear of Germany had evaporated, so had the craving for Britain to act as a balancing factor to Germany within Europe. On the contrary, British participation would snatch her unique position from France and only reinforce Britain's own influence—with effects which, in some French eyes, might be disastrous. Some Frenchmen felt that, for a battle won by the Prussians, Britain has had a sufficient spell of world leadership since Waterloo.

It is understandable that France should at this juncture have attempted to reserve this dynamic new structure of the European Community for her very own. Frenchmen were tremendously conscious of the speed with which Britain seemed to them to have lost her position and prestige in the years 1956–60. And some French officials were gloomy about Britain's economic prospects if she should separate herself from her Commonwealth. As one of them, alluding to Greece, somewhat bluntly put it: "We are having to take on a desert peninsula in the south; we do not want to take on a desert island in the north as well."

However, one should see nothing rootedly anti-British in all this. France might in fact well want to see a strong Britain with a consolidated Commonwealth that could stand beside France against the less experienced, less sophisticated, but fast upsurging younger nations of America, Africa, and Asia. Visionaries in Paris see a French or European sphere of influence that stretches around the Mediterranean over the area of the old Roman Empire, and a British or Commonwealth thalassocracy in partnership with it. (Some even believe that both the Mediterranean and the Commonwealth blocs could be strengthened, without violation of GATT, by a gentlemen's agreement between bankers of the two blocs, with each side extending longer export credit facilities than conventionally granted for exports—provided these exports go to within their own area.) Though Britain is the hereditary enemy of France, the Commonwealth could become the natural ally of the Common Market. Between them, two such structures might guide America and uphold European values and traditions vis-à-vis the rest of the world. An economic directorate of three might be at least as useful as a strategic one.

The European Free Trade Association

By early 1959, the bridges were blown, the Community had begun to function, and Britain stood well outside the long-range plans of the Six. Daily, there was news that more Continental firms were planning to integrate their investment and production programs. United States capital, in particular, was being diverted from Britain to the Common Market. Many British firms were hastening to establish plants or set up subsidiaries on the Continent. The British Government found itself in a paradoxical predicament. In 1957, it had set out to reassure industry that it had nothing to fear from free trade with Europe: By 1959, industry was convinced it had a great deal to gain. The government had taken great pains to advertise its medicine; industry fancied it as a cordial—and now the government could not deliver it. The demand which the government, as a sorcerer's apprentice, had itself raised now forced it to look for some alternative solution.

The Formation of EFTA. In this situation, five main courses of action were canvassed. Some advocated a retreat into the Commonwealth; some proposed that Britain should join the Community outright; some wanted to see the whole Commonwealth brought into a Free-Trade Area; some felt that Britain should wait and see; and some urged that Britain should set up an alternative grouping and invite the remaining OEEC countries to join.

This last scheme seemed particularly seductive to a government in a not quite unjustified state of pique. Through it, all kinds of different objectives could be pursued simultaneously. Had the French claimed that free-trade areas were impracticable? Here one could be demonstrated at work. Was the Community preparing to discriminate against Britain? Here Britain could shut the Community out of a grouping of her own. Did Britain still wish to join? This way, pressure could be brought on the Six: Shut out of Scandinavia, the Six might be willing to let Britain into Europe. If the phasing of customs reductions between Britain and Scandinavia parallelled that of the Six, the mutual abolition of customs barriers between the two areas would be a simple matter. This way, at least, the other OEEC countries would be held together to negotiate as a bloc, and would not be forced to negotiate singly against the Six. And in these other countries, British industry could find some compensation for the hopes that had been dashed, and the sales that might be lost as a result of the breakdown in negotiations.

The industrial and employers' federations of the countries concerned had already published such a scheme in April, 1958: What was then a bargaining threat now became a second-best solution. In July, 1959, a White Paper set out a draft plan, and in December, the final Convention was signed. Austria, Denmark,

Norway, Portugal, Sweden, Switzerland, and the United Kingdom joined this European Free Trade Association (EFTA). Finland became associated with it in 1961.

The Convention provided for the mutual reduction of duties by twenty per cent on July 1, 1960 (the Rome Treaty provided for the second installment of an average of ten per cent on that date), and then for reductions parallel with those demanded by the Rome Treaty, until sixty per cent of tariffs had been cut. The abolition of tariffs would thereafter be completed in four annual installments by 1970. Agricultural and marine products were excluded from these cuts, but, as a last-minute concession from the United Kingdom to Norway, frozen fish was included among industrial products. Britain was also to abolish the tariff on bacon and a few other commodities of particular interest to Denmark. Every import quota was to be increased by twenty per cent each year, except where special difficulties arose. For the rest, the rules of competition, those to prevent deflection of trade, and the institutional machinery to carry through the Convention were all simple in the extreme.

The Flaws in EFTA. But whatever the intrinsic merits of this scheme, it was highly doubtful from the start whether it was really adapted to fulfill its particular objectives. The process of demonstrating that re-exports within a free trade area can be controlled by certificates of origin was perhaps not really necessary. The Six themselves, after all, are using analogous papers to control re-exports among themselves until their external tariffs have been integrated; and additional experiments could add little to the experience already gained from the Commonwealth system. As for the wider problem of how far mutual tariffs can be lowered without detailed provisions for the harmonizing of cost structures and legislation, the experience of a unit as scattered as EFTA and as clearly dominated by one country (which alone contains well over one-half of the total population of the area) was scarcely to be regarded as conclusive.

Again, the argument that it would be easier for Britain to enter into a free-trade relationship with the Six if she had previously established a free-trade area with Scandinavia was dubious. The ultimate common external tariff of the Six agreed to in the Rome Treaty is not so very different in its average incidence from the present British tariff; and if the Commonwealth problem could be solved, a customs union between Britain and the Six was by no means to be excluded. But free trade with Scandinavia, where tariffs are low, could well make a customs union with the Six much more difficult to achieve. Negotiations might be easier, it was thought, if the Six were to accept the Seven as a single negotiating partner; but in June, 1961, this belief, too, was recognized as mistaken. Moreover, the substantive problems to be settled among the Six and some of the other partners in EFTA were in some respects rather more intractable than those between Britain and the Six: Swiss, Austrian, and Swedish neutrality are an obvious example.

For the export prospects of British industry, EFTA was plainly a poor second-best. The proposed Free-Trade Area, including the Common Market of 170 million, would have opened up access to a new market of over 200 million people—four times as large as the population of the United Kingdom. EFTA, on the other hand, added only about 38 million people to the domestic market. Moreover, Scandinavian tariff rates were on the whole low: The abolition of these tariffs was unlikely to make a dramatic difference to British exports, which have in fact grown no faster to the Seven than to the Six. (Each of the other partners gained rather more tariff preference than Britain; their domestic markets are multiplied by the inclusion of Britain, and British duties are on the whole substantial.) Transport costs also tell against the EFTA unit: At its heart lie the German industrial areas.

Then, there was the hope that EFTA would change French attitudes to the establishment of a free-trade area. Yet French exports to the EFTA countries were of little importance; only fourteen per cent of French trade was with EFTA, as against twenty-six per cent for Germany. Commercial pressure on Germany, in so far as it might have been achieved, was in any case unlikely to change the mind of President de Gaulle. On the contrary, there can be little doubt that this rival scheme aroused resentment in a nation not in a mood to be coerced and to be coerced least of all by discrimination from the very country which objected so loudly, and for so long to the discriminatory character of the Common Market. When EFTA wanted to set up its headquarters in Paris, the President's reply was: *"Mais Paris n'est pas un hotel!"* And by July, 1960, Europe was divided into two trading blocs discriminating against each other.

Britain in Isolation

It was lightly assumed for the first postwar decade that the fundamental problem in European politics was the reconciliation of Germany and France. But perhaps more fundamental is the relation between Britain and Europe—Britain, Germany, and France. The breakdown of the Free-Trade Area negotiations was followed by a period in which not only Anglo-French but also Anglo-German relations reached a nadir.

November, 1958, saw the beginning of the new threat to Berlin. While President de Gaulle was prepared to stand fast by his Community partner, Mr. Macmillan traveled to Moscow, and the worst was suspected. On the other side, in Britain, it was feared that Dr. Adenauer's rigidity would sabotage any attempt to reduce international tension. In the first half of 1960, when swastikas were daubed on the Cologne synagogue by two ruffians from a splinter party, and NATO moved to establish German supply bases in Spain tempers were not sweetened on either side. France and Germany were thrown very much into each others' arms while Britain, not the Continent, was left isolated.

Moreover, Europe by this time consisted not only of France and Germany, but also of the "Europeans" in charge of the institutions of the three Communities—led in particular by Professor Hallstein, President of the Common Market Commission. By a master stroke of diplomacy, Professor Hallstein and the Quay d'Orsay were able to adopt a totally new strategy in 1959. The balance of payments of the United States was just beginning to give serious concern. The Americans were therefore all the more reluctant to countenance any new larger areas that would discriminate against them. The move to convertibility, in December, 1958, played right into their hands, for with the dissolution of the European Payments Union, the larger Europe of the fifteen or eighteen could be argued to have lost its economic relevance. The whole problem could thus be placed into an Atlantic framework: And there the United States could be relied upon to support the Community for political reasons, and to oppose British schemes for economic reasons. Moreover, the Commission particularly stressed the problem, important to the U.S.A. at this time, of a coordinated effort of aid to underdeveloped countries overseas. At the Atlantic Economic Conference in January, 1960, it was decided to replace OEEC by an Atlantic grouping: the Organization for Economic Cooperation and Development. The Commission and the French had thus downgraded the whole framework of the Free-Trade Area proposals, and taken yet another step toward treating Britain like any other country in the world outside the Six.

At the same time, they drew the logical conclusion from the surging prosperity of all their countries and from the pressure put on them by Britain: the "Hallstein plan" to accelerate the implementation of the Treaty. This was a compromise between two lines of thought. The French and the Belgians wished to consolidate the Community in order to make it more difficult for any wider European grouping to absorb and "drown" it: Their preoccupations were met by speeding up the internal tariff reductions and making the first alignments toward the common tariff. On the other hand, the Germans and the Dutch were already reluctant to raise their external tariff up to the common tariff and their objection was met by the national reduction of the common tariff by twenty per cent.

Where Britain's foundation of EFTA had served to consolidate the Six in 1959, a remark made by Mr. Macmillan in Washington in February, 1960, in private, but published through a deliberate indiscretion, helped unite Continental opinion on acceleration: Referring to Britain's historical fear of a single power dominating the Continent, he talked of counter-measures reminiscent of the alliance with Russia in 1813. The U.S.A. clearly came out in favor of the Six, and indeed published a communiqué in favor of acceleration. Acceleration was decided upon in May, 1960. At the same time, Britain, seeing the Six draw away from her, convinced at last that the Six were here to stay and a force to be reckoned with, changed both her strategy and her tactics.

Mr. Selwyn Lloyd had admitted in January, 1960, that it was

a mistake that Britain had not participated in the Schuman Plan negotiations. In May, rumors were heard that Britain would be willing to join a European Customs Union. In June, Mr. Profumo announced British willingness to consider membership in the Coal and Steel Community and Euratom. In July, Mr. Selwyn Lloyd admitted that free-trade solutions had no chance of success and that a settlement must be both general and political; he defined three difficulties: Commonwealth free entry, British agriculture, and safeguards for the partners in EFTA; and he asked the Six for their ideas of a solution. That also was the month in which the Prime Minister reshuffled his cabinet, putting Messrs. Heath, Sandys, and Soames, all noted for their positive attitude to European unity, into key posts. Then came Dr. Adenauer's invitation to Mr. Macmillan to come to Bonn. The failure of the Summit had both highlighted the seriousness of the rifts in the Western camp and made Mr. Macmillan less dangerous from Dr. Adenauer's point of view. It was after their meeting in August, 1960, that a new spirit entered British pronouncements on Europe, and at the Scarborough Conservative Party Conference, in October, Mr. Heath, the new Lord Privy Seal, for the first time put on record the British Government's positive admiration for the economic achievements and the political enterprise of the Six.

One step at a time, but with surprising swiftness, as both the Berlin and the sterling problems seemed to grow worse, the British Government then moved toward Europe and abandoned one alternative policy after another. If all along the government's lead had been required to force the country to face the issue, it was the tough line from the Continent which finally narrowed down the issue. The first alternative to go was EFTA as a rival bloc, and today even the quarters from which this idea originated admit that this aspect of EFTA's formation was not the most brilliant move in the annals of British postwar diplomacy.

Implicit in the ambivalence of EFTA was the alternative notion of "bridge-building"—or, as it was put less happily, "the Six joining the Seven." This alternative proved just as impracticable as the rival bloc, and soon EFTA was even abandoned as a unit of collective negotiation. Once the peculiar problems of

Britain have been fully explored with the Six, it is hoped that satisfactory arrangements for the rest of the Seven should not be too difficult to invent thereafter.

Thus, in February, 1961, Mr. Heath put forward once more the idea of a modified customs union between Britain and the Common Market: On goods not coming from EFTA, the Commonwealth, or the Common Market countries and their overseas Associates, Britain would be willing to harmonize her external tariff with the Six. It needed only a moment's reflection to show that, in practice, very little is left after these wide exceptions: and if this was dressed up on the British side as, in principle, another step toward Europe, no one can have thought it to be a solution acceptable to the Six. Like the Profumo suggestion of 1960—that Britain should join Euratom and the Coal and Steel Community, but not the Common Market—this proposal was interpreted by French and European officials as yet another attempt at sabotage by perfidious Albion. The Foreign Office cannot have been altogether unaware that this would be the reaction: And so one can only conclude that Mr. Heath's method of "leaping a precipice in little hops" was aimed primarily at the British public and not at Continental governments.

The Community had for two years rejected both these alternative means of obtaining commercial advantages without political commitment—"bridge-building," and a customs union between Britain and the Six. In the spring of 1961 it was also made clear that the obverse notion—political consultation without economic commitment—would not be allowed to develop farther than the very minor degree implied by the existence of Western European Union. A concerted foreign policy, the Six maintained, can be based only on a community of interest, and this implies an economic community. British political participation, without economic participation, would only arrest the political development of the Six.

So, as all of the other avenues were explored and found to lead nowhere, it was not a rival bloc, or bridge-building, or a customs union, or purely political consultation, but full-fledged British entry into all three Communities that became the burning issue in the Western world for the next two years.

VI

Britain at the Crossroads*

The Spaak Report was published more than six years ago, the Rome Treaty signed more than five years ago, yet until early in 1961, all the problems that the existence of the Community raises for Britain occupied a very slight place in public debate. In the 1959 election, only 8 per cent of the Conservative and almost none of the Labour candidates mentioned European trade problems in their election addresses. The fact that half the Liberal candidates did so, and that the Liberal Party wanted Britain to join the Common Market, was perhaps a harbinger for the future, but it did not seem to commend the cause to a wide public. And the popular newspapers, which are today falling over each other to explain the urgency of the issue, may be combed in vain for any references to the Community during all the years when Britain was in an incomparably better position to join on her own terms than she is today.

Remaining Uncertainties

It needed the government's lead to force the country to face the issue: But if the debate has now begun in earnest and has

* This chapter and the following chapter, representing an abridgment of the arguments put forward in favor of Britain's entry to the Common Market until the end of 1962, are retained in this American edition after the failure of Britain's application for a purpose: Not only do they describe Britain's basic predicament, but *mutatis mutandis* their insistence on interdependence does not toll for Britain alone.

finally focused on the alternative of full British entry or no, there nevertheless remain uncertainties that do not make it any easier to conduct.

The first problem is perhaps whether there is any problem at all: Is membership of the Common Market actually open to Britain? Formally, under Article 237 of the Treaty: "Any European State may apply to become a member of the Community." But any one government, or any one ratifying legislature of the Six, may veto the application. The Community is "open" to applications for membership, but "open" to new members only by the unanimous consent of the old:

> It shall address its application to the Council which, after obtaining the opinion of the Commission, shall give a unanimous decision thereon.
>
> The conditions of admission and the adjustments to this Treaty necessitated by it shall be the subject of an agreement between the member states and the applicant state. Such agreement shall be submitted for ratification by all the contracting states in accordance with their respective constitutional requirements.

No one in Britain can be quite certain that the French Government will not attempt to delay and complicate the negotiations to an extent that will make it very difficult indeed for Britain to join: The more special conditions Britain feels she must demand, for the sake, in particular, of the Commonwealth, the easier will it be for anyone on the Continent who wishes to keep her out to "go slow."

A second uncertainty obviously remains: What, finally, will be the precise conditions on which Britain can gain admission? However many protestations there are to the contrary, the whole history of the negotiations leading up to the Rome Treaty shows that it constitutes no abstract scheme of eternal justice, but a highly political, delicately balanced compromise—a bargain between the interests of the original participants. Britain is late in applying and cannot expect many questions to be reopened. But the Treaty will clearly need substantial adjustment if what suited the constellation of the Six in 1956–57 is to be applied to seven or more countries in 1962. Thus the precise content of the document that Britain would be asking to sign is incompletely known.

But even after Britain is inside the Community, she, like the other members, will not know what common policies, demanded but in no way defined by the Treaty, will be evolved in the interplay between Community institutions and national governments. On the price levels set as targets for the Community will depend in large measure its "inward"- or "outward"-looking character in the agricultural domain. The common transport policy is yet to be worked out. A Community business-cycle policy is in its infancy. And a host of details of implementation remain to be settled in almost all fields. The member states have agreed to agree; but what the contents of their agreements will be, none of them can know in advance. All are certain that the Community spirit will spill over the framework of the Treaties themselves and will, in due course, lead to forms of cooperation or integration in wider domains.

Nowhere, of course, is the uncertainty greater, and on no subject is it more important than on the political side. The ultimate political and constitutional implications of the Community remain a mystery—even to the Six. Those who invite Britain into the Common Market alternate between calling it a commercial arrangement, which need pose no major constitutional problems for Britain, and a first step toward a United States of Europe, which none who does not already today accept federal objectives should enter.

The right answer is somewhere in between. To call the Communities a purely economic arrangement is a facile and short-sighted method of persuasion. A country that has been accused for so long of prevarication may be justified in feeling that there are times when good fences make good neighbors, and that she should not—in her own interest any more than in that of European unity—sign what some would construe as a blank check she might later fail to honor. The honest "European" must admit, and indeed insist, that to sign the Rome Treaty with the intent of only carrying out its letter would sooner or later lead to tensions and frictions. To sign the Treaty is to accept certain processes of decision-making. On further development toward Community supranationality Britain, too, would have a formal veto, but the spirit of "an ever closer union" expressed in the preamble would be the guiding one. To join the

Community in sincerity is thus an act of faith, of which the full consequences cannot be foreseen now with any accuracy. Indeed, it would be inappropriate, and in conflict with the whole spirit of the Community, to attempt to delimit its nature by a legal contract. As in a marriage, the legal instruments to be signed by the partners are no more than a minimal basis for the relationship that will evolve with time—an interrelationship simultaneously both cause and further consequence of internal changes (which naturally result as a function of the relationship itself) in each of the partners.

Criteria of Decision

The government may now have decided on a course of action, but Parliament must in the end give its approval, and the issue is of such dimensions that one can only hope for a further development of the whole debate, with a full statement of the case by both sides, in the coming months. The resolve required to carry through the implications of this step is so fundamental, that the British must themselves work through the issue not only in rational, but even in emotive terms. France was able to put the past behind her only after the bitter debate over the EDC had acted as an emotional catalyst. Similarly, it may be that in Britain, too, the issue must be fought through relentlessly to its logical conclusion by a much wider circle than that of the professional politicians and economists. The challenge of the Common Market is not an economic, and not even simply a political one: The challenge is, in the end, a psychological and a social one. Self-analysis cannot be an entirely pleasurable process. But it may be better not to join the Community at all than to slide into it gaily, unaware. Perhaps it is only after a sharp political battle—and one which may point to the real parting of the spirits irrespective of party allegiance—that this great, grave, and to some minds immensely exhilarating decision can reveal the full wealth of its dangers and opportunities alike.

In the first five chapters we have described the historical, economic, and institutional factors involved in the creation of the European Communities. Broadly speaking, those chapters set out to present a body of "agreed fact," in which both the advocates of British adherence to the Rome Treaties and its opponents can equally recognize the ingredients of their arguments. An unweighted catalogue of the *pros* and *cons* of the question may be found elsewhere.[1] But in the controversy of this nature and magnitude, the game of alternating between the roles of counsel for the defense and counsel for the prosecution, however respectable it may be academically, must be replaced in these last two chapters if not by a judicial summing up, then at least by the role of *amicus curiae.*

In that case, a guide must once more declare his own position. I can see a number of irrefutable arguments against Britain's going in. I can also see some irrefutable arguments against Britain's staying out. But to stay out is as much a policy decision, and no less fraught with long-run consequences, than to go in, and policy decisions must in the end always be taken by striking a balance between very uncertain considerations. The one thing Britain cannot choose, even should she want to, is the *status quo.* Taking the arguments on balance, weighing their importance and their probability, the scales seem to me to come down clearly in favor of Britain's joining—*if, but only if,* she does so not just for economic, but for political reasons, and is determined not to freeze European unity at its present level, but to let it develop, and to make her own unique contribution to its success.

But it is essential at the outset to establish one's criteria of decision. What are the overriding ends that political acts are to serve?

First one must insist once again that it is not so much economic as political issues that are at stake. Whether Britain likes it or not, the logic of integration will force us to take all economic decisions in this country with constant reference to the decisions taken in common with partners on the Continent; indeed, a good many of the decisions will be taken in Brussels itself. The content of the decisions may be economic, but where, and by whom, and under what sort of procedure they are taken is a political question—as political (or, rather, vastly more so) as whether steel investments shall be decided upon in a private boardroom or by a nationalized body: And what these decisions

1. *The World Today,* June 1961, pp. 233–54.

are will deeply affect many of the issues that have formed the stuff of British politics in recent decades.

Then there may be some professional politicians for whom the next election provides the effective intellectual horizon—but if there are, they must be left to think through their own tactical problem. A long-term decision such as British adherence to the Common Market cannot responsibly be taken for reasons of short-term expediency. To join the Community would be an irreversible decision, and a more vital step than ever before toward international, rather than national, decision-making: Any short-term advantages are relevant to it only if premonitory of bigger things. In this discussion, at least, we must try to envisage Britain and Europe ten, twenty or thirty years hence and ask: Would Britain be sorrier, then, if she now joins or if she stays out?

Again, what is the frame of reference of our decision? It is here, perhaps, that many will find it hardest to make the semantic, and indeed psychological, adjustment. We are so used to talking of "the British interest" or "the interests of the Commonwealth" that we forget the historically episodic nature of this type of association. What are the "interests of the Commonwealth" over and above the interests of Canada, Ghana, India, the United Kingdom, and its other component states—unless it be the world interests which the Commonwealth may happen to serve? What are the interests of Britain over and above the interests of her people? We would in major questions regard it as preposterous today to argue in terms of the Berkshire interest: Given modern techniques of production, communication, government and warfare, the citizens of Berkshire find their ends best served in a framework that is "supracounty" in extent and organization. Over a whole range of subjects, what is good for Britain is good for its component counties: And where there may be conflict on any particular issue, the benefits of union over other issues still far outweigh the particular problem.

This does not mean that we should argue in terms of the "European" rather than the British interest. On the contrary, the interests of Europe are at least as artificial an abstraction as those of Britain. In the last four decades of the twentieth century, no mature country will be able to think of foreign policy in terms of its own interest, or of that of a narrow grouping of states. Continental nationalisms—European, Pan-African, Arab, or other—are a welcome sign that the nation-state is no longer taken as a God-given absolute, but they are as inadequate as any other partial frame of reference. The absolute entities in terms of which such problems must be seen are two: the individual human being, and the totality of human beings today and in the future.

Looking at the problem in these terms, we must reconcile ourselves to the fact that whether we like it or not, we are living today in the seventh decade of the twentieth century. The explosive progress of science and technology has placed in our hands undreamed of powers: to abolish poverty the world over, to fight disease, to make available resources for universal education and culture, and to wipe ourselves off the face of the universe at one blow. This is the context in which our major political decisions must be taken today.

The really big issues facing us now would seem to be three: defense and disarmament and our whole relationship with Communist China and the Soviet Union; trade and aid and our whole relationship with the underdeveloped two-thirds of the world; and economic growth and stability within the West, by which, in part, our capacity and our manner of dealing with the other two will be affected. The scale of each of these problems is vastly greater than the separate national institutions that for the past century or more have been taking responsibility for peace and order, for foreign affairs and defense, economics and social welfare. The nation-state has become too small to face any one of the three problems that now challenge our intelligence.

Certainly the nation-state as an institution has splendid work to its credit: It was excellently suited to progress in the nineteenth century. But when we failed to transcend it in the first half of the twentieth, two world wars resulted, the West was tarred with Auschwitz and Hiroshima, the Sino-Soviet bloc was established, and nationalism came to condition responses throughout the underdeveloped world. By now, the attempts of industrialized nations to maintain their independence have failed, and national interdependence can no longer be concealed.

It is not the institutions we are forced to set up, but the sheer scale of our problems, that has made us interdependent.

Fortunately, mankind's ultimate interests are the same, so that we can hope to develop world institutions to cope with world problems. But we shall never have them presented to us on a plate all at once, full-fledged without effort: We can only work toward them piecemeal, with regional advances and functional experiments in different fields. In the short run, we have one major political asset: North America, the Antipodes, and Western Europe (including Britain) are already in the same boat. And with our interests and aspirations so closely related, we have been able to begin to face these problems together.

We have tried to act simply through intergovernmental co-operation. But this has proved neither conspicuously successful nor particularly democratic. Firstly, the starting point has too often consisted in national policies—designed originally to solve national problems, in part by deflecting difficulties onto the rest of the world; and all too often the upshot has been the highest common factor of agreement in a welter of national governments. Yet what is needed are institutions that can face the problems as a whole and solve them as such—institutions that can begin to attack states of affairs regarded as misfortunes only until there were institutions able to diagnose them as problems and to meet them as such full-square. Secondly, intergovernmental cooperation has largely escaped democratic control. Each government has gone back to its parliament after the event and explained that the other governments would go no further, that they were hemmed in by the hard data of intergovernmental bargaining, and no alternative was open to them. It is no wonder that much of our national politics has become meaningless when the vital decisions are increasingly being taken right outside its framework. That is why responsibility for international action must be placed squarely upon responsible joint institutions: Once these are under joint democratic supervision, our control over environment becomes vastly greater, and our political life becomes meaningful again in terms of alternative solutions to problems that are real.

Now if we believe Britain has a role to play in the twenty-first century, in a world in which—whether we like it or not—powers have influence because their populations are measured in hundreds of millions, then Britain cannot cling to the symbols of a sovereignty that has been hollowed out by the sheer progress of events. In economics, in foreign affairs, and in defense, Britain is interdependent with North America, the Antipodes, and Western Europe, and can be effective only in collaboration with them. Britain must thus ask whether she should join in controlling the events that have pushed us together, or whether she should stand aside, leaving Washington and Continental Europe to settle matters between them. The European Community in its present form may not be the best of all possible Communities for Britain to join in the best of all possible worlds. But it is the only unit open to her that might meet her requirements. In the end, nations, like individuals, cannot choose the form in which a challenge presents itself; if they could, perhaps it would cease to be a challenge.

Such are the broad basic grounds on which the political issues of Britain's entry into the Community, or its decision to stand aside, must be judged. Their elaboration *in vacuo* would be dull if not trite. For the remainder of this chapter, therefore, it is not so much the arguments for, as the arguments against, on which we shall focus our discussion.

Foreign Policy and the Communist Bloc

By far the most forceful argument against British signature of the Treaty of Rome is that this would reduce the factors making for international and interracial understanding more than it would increase them. If this is true, then economic advantages to Britain, if such there are, plainly must be secondary. But whether it is true, it is impossible to prove. On the other hand, if British adherence would strengthen the forces against international and interracial tension, then any economic disadvantages to Britain should not stand in her way.

There are three variants to this line of argument: the argument from "third force" concepts of various kinds, whether of the type that prompted Mr. Macmillan's trip to Moscow in quest of a summit meeting, or of the type that calls for unilateral nuclear disarmament and British withdrawal from NATO; the argument alleging that the Community is essentially an "inward-looking" rich man's club, forgetful of the less-favored nations of the world; and the argument from the concept of the multi-racial Commonwealth as a stabilizing factor in a world torn by racial antagonisms. All three arguments, if proven, would seem to be unshakeable in the sense that they should override others.

Such evidence, however, depends on the minor premise that Britain could not fulfil her role with the same effectiveness, or at all, if she were a member state of the Economic Community. And it is here that the crucial appreciations must be made. Would Britain—wanting a summit meeting and anxious to avert a Berlin showdown—be in a more influential position outside the Community, or within? Would British diplomatic initiative have greater chances of success if Britain were forced to compromise to some degree to carry her European partners with her, or if she "went it alone"?

Even today, Britain cannot "go it alone" very far—a reason why some, on the extreme right as on the extreme left, want her to withdraw from or loosen the existing alliances. All this is a matter of degree, and one personal guess is perhaps as good as another. But, giving it no more weight than that, one may as well maintain that if Britain's relative importance in the world generally declines—whether because of constant sterling crises, or a stagnating economy, or a withdrawal from the continent of Europe, or simply because of the crystallization on the Continent of a strong single power (an event which, in the nineteenth century, the whole of British foreign policy was designed to prevent), or because of the emergence of new powers with large populations (not only China and India, but Brazil, Argentina, and perhaps Indonesia), or because the United States sees herself defended against Russia and aided in world economic development far more by the Continental Europeans than by the British—then the weight of British influence in Washington, Moscow, and, for that matter, in New Delhi and Peking, is also likely to decrease. If one believes that even today Britain has a unique contribution to make in foreign policy, then one may well wonder whether, by giving up what in twenty or thirty years' time may look a rather spurious independence of action, Britain would not, on the contrary, gain in effective influence if she were to enter the Community. Then, it can be argued, she should join, for here would be a sounding board that could, if vigorously utilized, give the voice of Britain more than national strength in a world dominated by the new great powers of continental size.

This line of argument of course runs ominously parallel to that of the France of President de Gaulle and, for that matter, to the line of reasoning employed in the past against European unity by those who feared German hegemony. Each partner seems confident that he can make the others toe his line. Someone must be wrong, at least some of the time. When agreement is found, however—and it need not be total or unanimous agreement, but at least "a sense of the meeting" in the Community—then this combination of European states indeed will carry substantial weight, over and above the political weight that each already carries on its own. And the very fact that each is a component of this Community, on whom in part its joint decision depends, lends extra strength to each in his own dealings with the rest of the world.

But there is also a negative side to this argument. French statesmen have always argued in favor of tying Germany into Western Europe so firmly that she can never make any deals with the East for the sake of the German territories beyond the Elbe. They regard a divided Germany, with full freedom of action, as a danger to peace. Dr. Adenauer himself strongly holds this view, and has for his part also argued the case for a united Europe in terms of his fear of a Franco-Russian *rapprochement* at the expense of Germany and of Western Europe as a whole. Analogous accusations against Britain's going behind the backs of her Allies were loudly voiced on the Continent in 1959. And now, in turn, it is argued in Britain that both de Gaulle and some successor to Adenauer might be tempted to deal with the Soviet Union independently of Britain. There are thus today canny observers who, distrusting the Continent, feel that, if only as a precaution, Britain must be able to influence the foreign policy of a united Europe from within. A political development of the European Community might at the very least give each country a veto on any foreign policy that would take one of them too perilously far out of step with the others. It is a matter of judgment whether this would in the long run be a factor making for good sense and stability in the world.

This sort of argument about national "leadership" is apposite within the present context, and the argument about national vetoes—at least on possible joint foreign policies—is relevant also to the misnamed Political Union as discussed for the moment in the Fouchet-Cattani Committee (and for at any rate the first three years after its adoption). But in the long run, if we are looking forward to a Political Community, the argument from "maintaining the strength and power of Britain in the world" (all too often still used by the Government) really becomes anachronistic. National vetoes, or vetoes for combinations of states under qualified majority rules, will no doubt remain for a generation to come: But positive leadership within a Community is not really a matter that can be discussed in national terms. Does leadership of the United Kingdom lie with Scotland? Or leadership of the United States in Massachusetts? These questions may not be strictly analogous for many years yet, but they do point to the salient implications of the Community concept as such: that "leadership" will increasingly be exercised not by national institutions as against other national institutions, but by creative individuals, groups, and parties regardless of nationality—as and when they formulate ideas that gain acceptance by the requisite majorities in the Community. For the moment, this kind of "leadership" is confined to the three existing Communities, and national concepts are still the main ones relevant to foreign policy. But it is only fair to enter this caveat against the "leadership" concept in the present debate, for we cannot yet tell how long it will remain valid or when we ourselves will decide that it can or must be superseded.

But regardless of "leadership" and precise forms of integration, it can also quite generally be argued—and has been, particularly from the British Left—that any political consolidation of Western Europe only increases tension between the Soviet countries and their neighbors. There are those who hope for a gradual softening up of the Communist bloc at its Western edges and see this happening as a result of, or parallel to, a softening up of the edges of the Western world toward the East. A Communist or near-Communist Italy or a Germany, governed—an almost unimaginable prospect—by some less rigorously anti-Communist party than the Social Democrats, is thought of as preparing the path for a withering away of Soviet rule in Czechoslovakia, Eastern Germany, and Poland.

This argument is quite different from that which wishes to see radical social reform and clearly apparent improvements in living standards for the workers in the countries adjoining the Soviet satellites: For that argument naturally favors the existence of a prosperous Community, in which wages are rising fast, prices are almost stable, and social benefits are being leveled up toward the best standard in each separate social category. No—this is the argument that demands a neutralist foreign policy from the satellites' neighbors.

The withering away of Communist regimes is obviously an aim to be ardently, but wisely, pursued. But however laudable the aim, the process of argument seems to contain two very curious jumps. A Nenni Government in Italy, and some imaginary government in Western Germany—by splinter groups now barely in existence—may or may not make a healthy change for these countries: But it is difficult to see why they should contribute to the downfall of Soviet regimes in the Peoples' Democracies, and it is even more difficult to see why Britain, standing aloof from the Community, should make this contingency more likely.

We are not in a position to argue whether there should or should not be a strong European Community adjoining these Communist states. There is, and—unless Britain were to enter and sabotage it—no amount of wishing it out of existence will alter the prospect that the Community is likely to grow stronger and more compact. All we can ask ourselves is whether Britain should be presented by that Community with *faits accomplis* in its own foreign policies, or whether Britain is to have a share in its decisions and their execution.

Much the same must be said to those who see in the creation, existence, and prosperity of the Community a provocation of the Soviet Union. It is perfectly true that the Soviet Union has opposed West European unity from the beginning, while

Soviet actions have had no little share in helping its progress. The question once was whether the Soviet Union would be made more nervous by a strong West Germany, free from any tight international commitments, than by one which feels bound to consult with the Benelux, Italian, and French Governments; but even that is not the question today. All we can ask now is whether in the future a Community without Britain would seem a greater or a lesser danger to the Soviet Union and to world peace than one in whose councils the United Kingdom has an important voice.

Others see the Community as essentially a constituent part of the Atlantic Alliance—incapable of independent action—and would like to take Britain outside this "cold war" building of blocs, to form, together with the Commonwealth, a third force between West and East. The white Commonwealth countries seem to have no wish to join such a formation, and whether the SEATO and CENTO countries of the Commonwealth would follow such a line may also be questioned. We may be left with India, Ghana, and a few other partners to play this role. It might not be very effective, but those who feel that we should attempt it, almost on grounds of conscience alone, are fully entitled to their view.

But they must then reckon with the possibility that to take a place in the Community and seek to affect its policies, might be a more effective—though less "pure"—means of pursuing the same objective.

AN "INWARD-LOOKING" COMMUNITY?

The second major line of thought opposing British entry derives from the fear that the Six may be turning in on themselves and forgetting about the needs of the rest of the world. We saw in Chapter II the extent to which the Six have in fact increased their imports from the rest of the world since the institution of the Economic Community: In 1962 imports from outside the EEL were 35 per cent higher than in 1958 (as against a rise of 18 per cent in corresponding British imports). Of course these are over-all figures, and what matters more, from a world point of view, are the imports made not from Britain,

EFTA, or the United States, but from the developing countries outside the OECD area—chiefly Asia, Africa, and Latin America, though we shall here consider Australia and New Zealand as well.

The rather simple argument in static terms—that the Six do not import as large a percentage of their national product from outside Europe as Britain—is of course silly: No one with a knowledge of economic geography (let alone a palate) would expect Germany to import as much wine from South Africa, France as much cheese from New Zealand, or Italy as much dried and tinned fruit from Australia as does Britain. More sophisticated economists have therefore argued in dynamic terms: that the Six were striving for autarchy and independence from the outside world, while it was in providing the developing countries of the world with rising export revenues that Britain was pre-eminent in the world.

Unfortunately for this argument, the postwar figures, set out in Table VIII, tell just the opposite story. It would be unfair to

Table VIII

IMPORTS FROM OUTSIDE THE OECD AREA
(MONTHLY AVERAGES, MILLIONS OF DOLLARS)

	The Six	Britain	U.S.A.	Six-Britain	Six-USA
1950	383	358	465	+25	−82
1951	561	522	551	+39	+10
1952	533	451	538	+82	− 5
1953	531	452	510	+79	+21
1954	586	450	489	+136	+97
1955	632	490	531	+242	+101
1956	716	487	570	+229	+146
1957	777	510	589	+267	+188
1958	734	474	574	+260	+160
1959	738	507	630	+231	+108
1960	838	530	634	+308	+204
1961	857	510	608	+347	+249
1962	931	526	683	+415	+248

stress that Britain actually provided the countries outside Western Europe and North America with less export revenue in

1961 than ten years earlier, for 1951 was the year of the Korean boom in raw material prices. But a comparison of imports by Britain and by the Six in each successive year eliminates the distortions due to price changes and shows quite clearly that it has been the Six, far more than Britain, who have provided these overseas countries with rising export revenues. In 1950, the Six paid out only $300 million (or 7 per cent) more than the United Kingdom for imports from outside the OECD area: In 1961, the Six were already $4,200 million (or 70 per cent) ahead of Britain and by early 1962, the Six had surpassed Britain by more than 80 per cent—hardly evidence of the creation of an "inward-looking bloc."

The inclusion of the United States in our Table leaves no doubt as to the relative importance of these three markets to the rest of the world: The Six have been forging ahead of the United States in their imports from developing countries ever since 1954. And those who argue that the Six are likely to reduce their trade with Eastern Europe for political reasons should note that the Community's imports from that part of the non-OECD world rose by over 60 per cent between 1958 and 1961—from $57 million to $90 million a month.

Where aid is concerned, the comparison between Britain and the Six is almost equally instructive, particularly when we remember that West Germany has had no overseas constitutional links since 1919, and that Italy has links with only one tiny African territory. Table IX breaks down the total flow of financial resources in grants, loans, investment, and similar non-trade payments made to underdeveloped countries in 1960, according to the countries of origin and the types of assistance. Its figures are so important and so neglected in the current discussion that they are worth restating in words. The flow of funds to underdeveloped countries from France alone is one and a half times that from Britain, and outright grants given by the French Government are more than four times as large as those given by the British Government. (The figures for official grants is all the more important as British Government loans tend to be made at the rates at which the Government can borrow, plus a small management charge: And as private investments tend to flow more to such countries as Kuwait or Rhodesia than to the really poor countries of Asia or "black" Africa.) If we include all forms of assistance, we saw in Table IV (p. 102) that France in 1956–59 was devoting more than twice as much of her national income to overseas development as Britain. Incomplete figures now becoming available suggest that Germany has stepped up her total contributions considerably and is likely to overtake Britain both in grants and in loans and investment in 1963 if indeed she has not already done so. All in all, in fact, the Six today provide well over one-third of the world's financial assistance to underdeveloped countries, while Britain supplies less than one-ninth.

Taking the two flows of money—trade and aid—together, we

Table IX

TOTAL CONTRIBUTIONS TO UNDERDEVELOPED COUNTRIES AND MULTILATERAL AGENCIES (MILLIONS OF DOLLARS)

	1959	1960
United States	3,276	3,781
The Six	2,513	2,626
United Kingdom	896	857
Other OECD countries	317	469
Japan	195	256
Sino-Soviet Bloc	161	178
Total	7,358	8,167

OF WHICH IN 1960

	Official grants, etc.	Official net loans	Private lending and investment	Multi-lateral agencies	Total
France	708	75	435	69	1,287
Germany	70	172	270	105	616
Italy	16	23	169	89	297
Netherlands	26	−2	199	21	246
Belgium and Luxembourg	86	−4	64	33	180
The Six	906	264	1,137	317	2,626
U.K.	165	133	470	89	857

Source: OECD The Flow of Financial Resources to Countries in Course of Economic Development in 1960, pp. 10–12.

can make a rough calculation: In 1957, Britain provided export revenues of $6.1 billion and nontrading payments of $0.9 billion, making $7.0 billion in all. Three years later, this figure was still $7.0 billion. The Six, on the other hand, in the year before the Rome Treaty came into operation, were providing export revenues of $9.3 billion and aid of $2.1 billion, making $11.4 billion in all. By 1960, that combined figure had risen to $12.7 billion. No one would dare claim that either totals were sufficient to cover the needs of the developing countries: But to accuse the Six of not increasing the supply of money to the developing parts of the world fast enough is at least the pot calling the kettle black, if not indeed reminiscent of the parable of the mote and the beam.

All these comparisons, invidious up to a point, are set out here to explode certain arguments used in the current discussion and to point to the sort of policy changes that will be required of us in the future. But of course they are in themselves of limited relevance to the immediate issue at stake. For if we are asking whether Britain should enter the Common Market or not, then the proper form of the question is not "who has helped developing countries most in the past," but "will the developing countries in future receive more export revenue and more aid from Western Europe as a whole if Britain is inside, or outside, the Community?" In other words, will Britain's entry into the Community leave the Six, Britain, other European countries—and, indeed, even the United States—more protectionist, or less protectionist, than if she stays out?

No one in Britain has yet argued that British entry into the Community would make the Community less outward-looking than before. The only fear has been that Britain might become more protectionist, even if the Community becomes more liberal. Let us remember that the effects on the Community will be much more important than similar proportional effects on Britain: If the Community raised its outflow of funds in trade and aid by 10 per cent, while Britain reduced hers by 15 per cent, the developing countries would still be better off. But let us turn from the arid arithmetic of economic theory to ask to what extent, if at all, Britain's contributions to the underdeveloped world in trade and in aid could be increased or decreased by her entry into the Community and by her standing aloof, and what consequences should be drawn for future policy from such considerations.

It has been argued that for Britain to join the Economic Community would constitute the biggest step backward to protectionism since the abolition of the Corn Laws in 1846. This is certainly untrue where manufactures are concerned. Britain will, within seven years, have to abolish all tariffs and quantitative restrictions on a trade which, even now, amounts to a quarter of her industrial imports, and which is bound to increase fast. Admitting such competition from some of the most highly industrialized and efficient manufacturing countries in the world can hardly be called a protectionist measure. It will have a stimulating and selective effect on British industry and indeed, by forcing her to become more competitive, also reduce her need for protection from the rest of the world.

On trade from outside the Community, Britain would, within seven years, align her tariffs to the common external tariff. But this tariff is on average already lower than the existing British one, so that if Britain joins she will automatically also substantially lower her tariff on a whole range of manufactures from the rest of the world.

More important are the effects on the Community as a whole: And there are solid grounds for believing that once Britain is inside, she will become more liberal still in her commercial policy as time goes on. Of course the Community, in its early days, was suspected of being designed as a protectionist bloc. But in the meantime we have seen it take the lead in unilaterally reducing its external tariff by 20 per cent in anticipation of the "Dillon Round" of negotiations in GATT, and several of its member states, notably Germany and Holland, are anxious to reduce the common external tariff still further. If Britain joins them, she, in turn, can reinforce this already considerable pressure for lower tariffs on manufactures entering the Community. Indeed, one may wonder what purpose such a tariff serves once the industries of Germany, Britain, and France are all freely competing against each other. Industries that can stand this kind of competition should be able to deal also with that of the United States, and even of Japan. And we shall see in our last chapter what chain reactions toward freer world trade the British application to join has already triggered off.

So much for manufactures. As for industrial raw materials, the bulk of these—wool, cotton, jute, rubber, copper, iron, tin, to mention but a few of the most important—are imported into the Community duty-free. In the case of two industrial raw materials for which there is to be a common external tariff—woodpulp and aluminum—any country that wishes may import woodpulp for its own use free of duty, and Germany and Holland can import their own requirements of aluminum at a tariff of only 5 per cent. On raw materials and tropical foodstuffs from the Community's African Associates, all tariffs and quantitative restrictions are to be abolished by the end of the year—though a more determined attack on consumption taxes is needed in the near future.

That leaves the problem of temperate foodstuffs—in which, indeed, the Community will probably expose itself badly to the charge of protectionism. We have seen on pp. 136–37 that, in the case of cereals, the system of levies will give the Community's farmers first chance of supplying the Community market at any given price: Thereafter, the rest of the world can supply what is left of the market, imports being subjected to a levy to bring up their price to the target price set by the Community. We do not yet know what the target prices will be: But plainly the higher the target price, the more will be produced inside the Community, and the less will be imported from outside. The German high-cost peasants want a high price, which will allow them to continue production: The French, on the other hand, want a lower price, which will restrict production in Germany, yet allow them to produce profitably and sell their surplus on the German market. Here, French farming interests are thus far less "inward-looking" than the German.

British farmers will naturally want the highest possible price, too: However much they expand their production, Britain will still not be self-sufficient, so they will be able to sell all they produce; a lower price, on the other hand, could lead British farmers to curtail production and then other suppliers—in Europe or in the Commonwealth—would gain a greater share of the British market. The interests of British farming are thus diametrically opposed to the interests of Commonwealth farmers: British farmers, like those on the Continent, have a vested interest in an "inward-looking" Community where agriculture is concerned.

Economically, there is little justification for maintaining a higher-cost temperate-zone agriculture in Europe, when the wide-open spaces of Canada and Australia can produce food more cheaply. But before we condemn the Community outright, we should perhaps remember that, underlying the political pressures, there remain certain social reasons for maintaining some farming communities in Europe, and it has not yet been proved on egalitarian grounds that the Italian peasant with his one goat, or the Morvan peasant's wife bending over the village stream must be sacrificed immediately for the Australian farmer with his combine harvester, his American car, and his dishwasher. Temperate foodstuffs are a very different problem from that of the underdeveloped countries of Asia and Africa. But here we must turn from the problem of overseas countries in general to the special problems arising out of the preferential nature of Commonwealth trade.

The Commonwealth

The third argument against British entry was that the Commonwealth, as a multiracial unit, would be a more effective factor for world peace if Britain stood outside the Community than if she joined it. On the one hand, there are here economic arguments that have political repercussions. On the other hand, a constitutional matter is in question: Can Britain surrender any part of her sovereignty and still remain within a Commonwealth which is a free association of sovereign states? And there is also the general political question: What will the whole Afro-Asian world think of a United Kingdom that has joined in a Community with the European Continent?

On the economic side two general points must be made before we turn to the specific problems. It may be objected, of course, that British exports to the Community, which are threatened by discrimination if Britain remains outside it, are not very important compared to British exports to the Commonwealth, which might be threatened by Britain's joining the Six. But the matter cannot be seen in purely static terms. What matters is not where what trade went in the past, or is going now, but what future course of action will result in what future prices and quantities of exports sold. We do not know much about such hypothetical questions. What we can say is that the old pattern of trade set by the classical trade treaty with Portugal two and a half centuries ago, of wine for textiles, is becoming less important compared with the intensive exchange of industrial goods between industrial countries. British trade with the Commonwealth is comparatively stagnant. British trade with Europe is expanding faster than with any other region. In 1956, the discussion, based on 1955 figures, was in terms of 48 per cent of British exports going to the Commonwealth, 27 per cent to Western Europe. By the first half of 1962, Britain's exports to Western Europe had risen above her exports to the Commonwealth: Of total exports worth on average some $903 million a month, only $286 million went to the Commonwealth, while $316 million went to Western Europe—$168 million of them to the Six, $123 million to EFTA.

The share of the Commonwealth in British exports has thus been declining—and Britain's share in Commonwealth markets has been declining faster still. If we concentrate on the exports of the United Kingdom, the United States, the Common Market, and Japan, Britain's shares in these exports to New Zealand fell, between 1954 and 1960, from 85 per cent to 72 per cent, to Australia from 72 per cent to 51 per cent, to South Africa from 53 per cent to 42 per cent, and to India and Pakistan from 48 per cent to 37 per cent.

Reductions in discrimination in Britain's favor are only one factor in this relative decline, which occurred even where the discrimination had always been negligible or nil. At least as important is the fact that firms from other countries have gone vigorously into Commonwealth markets, and that Commonwealth importers and consumers, steadily becoming more aware of the choice of goods available from other suppliers, are comparing British with other exports. In such competition, Britain is not always able to hold her own.

Just how many Commonwealth countries have thus far turned

away from Britain to other suppliers has perhaps not been fully appreciated in Britain, because British exports, having risen less than those of some other big exporting nations, have still gone to the Commonwealth in only slightly diminished proportions. The absolute expansion of Commonwealth purchases has thus masked the progressive thinning out of the Commonwealth as a close trading unit. Similarly, the stagnation of British imports, together with the rise in Commonwealth exports, has resulted in increased dependence of certain (but not all) Commonwealth countries on the rest of the world for their earnings —in particular on the Commmunity, the biggest and fastest-growing importer in the world. Nigeria, Ghana, and the Federation doubled their exports to the Six between 1955 and 1959, while their exports to Britain dropped by 15 per cent. Ghana and Malaysia sell one and a half times as much to the Six as to Britain, and Pakistan sells about as much to the one as to the other. Table X gives a breakdown of overall exports

Table X

Exports from Commonwealth Countries by Destination, 1960

	Percentage to		Total Exports
	U.K.	The Six	£m.
Canada	17	8	1,982
Australia	24	18	704
Malaya and Singapore	12	18	532
India	28	8	476
New Zealand	53	17	302
Hong Kong	15	5	246
Rhodesia and Nyasaland	44	20	206
Nigeria	48	30	165
Pakistan	17	17	140
Ceylon	28	10	134
Ghana	24	37	105
Tanganyika	29	25	55

Source: H.M.S.O. Britain and the European Communities, p. 36.

from the main Commonwealth countries.

At the moment, Britain grants preferences to the Commonwealth on about half her imports from it: This preference amounts to around 8 per cent of the value of these imports, making an average preference on all imports (including those which receive none) of 4 per cent. This preference is of vital importance to some Commonwealth countries, notably to a country such as New Zealand. British signature of the Treaty of Rome as it stands would mean not only the ending of this preference, but also, in some cases, a rise in import duties on Commonwealth produce (or the imposition of a variable import levy) just at the very time when tariffs against Common Market producers would be dismantled. The Commonwealth may not depend for its political existence on commercial preference: But it would be politically difficult and undesirable to impose anti-Commonwealth preference in favor of the Community without giving Commonwealth producers reasonable assurances that they would not be left stranded without markets for their produce. The effects of a simple adherence to the Rome Treaty without such assurance would make themselves felt not only in British domestic politics but also in the sense of loyalty of Commonwealth countries toward each other, and in the economics (and thus perhaps even the domestic politics) of developing countries in Asia.

There is a lesson here not only for Britain, but also for the European Community. One cannot insist too strongly that at least with respect to the underdeveloped countries of the Commonwealth, Britain within the Community should be able to do more for their exports and provide or obtain more capital for their development, than if she stayed outside the Community. Indeed, quite apart from British influence on Community policy, this would become possible automatically, if British economic growth is stimulated by her entry into the Community: For both aid and trade are largely limited not only by political will, but by economic resources; imports are clearly far less affected by tariffs than by economic growth; and willingness to admit the simpler manufactures will be greatly strengthened by a rapid development of those more complicated manufacturing processes that depend on heavy investment and large markets for growth.

Of course just how far the world political benefits of the Commonwealth are dependent on commercial advantages is a subject on which opinion is divided. Where the "white" Commonwealth countries are concerned, it is unlikely that the import of Canadian Moffat cookers, or of New Zealand lamb, has any vital bearing on the interracial stability of the world. For tropical products, the interests of the Commonwealth producers lie in gaining free access to the Common Market and any other expanding markets, rather than in retaining preferences in the United Kingdom. Asian manufactures remain perhaps the only —though very important—example of a Commonwealth preference that has direct bearing on the stabilizing role of the Commonwealth in the world. But this is a question about favorable terms for which Britain must make a stand at the conference table (and which she has a good chance of winning), not a matter of whether she should seek membership or not. If Britain secures generous treatment for these Asian manufactures, then these Commonwealth countries will be substantially helped by the new relationship.

The argument from capital exports to the Commonwealth has already been implicit in our discussion. It is not irrelevant to recall that the mother country is able to contribute only just over one-tenth of the capital committed for 1961 and 1962 to the third Indian Five-Year Plan, and well under one-tenth of that for the second Five-Year Plan of Pakistan. Western Germany alone is providing almost one and a half times as much as Britain to India, and exactly one and a half times as much to Pakistan: of $2,225 million committed to India and $549 million to Pakistan, only $250 million and $42 million come from Britain, while $364 million and $63 million come from West Germany. One may well ask whether the Commonwealth would not be weakened rather than strengthened if Britain were to stand aside from Continental Europe, which, after the United States, is not only the second largest provider of development assistance for the world, but also of such importance for the Commonwealth. Here, as on the commercial side, the juxtaposition of Europe's Association links and Britain's Commonwealth links should in the short run help, rather than hinder, the cause of cooperation between poor and rich countries. In the long run, as we have argued in Chapter IV, we should work for a more open framework to replace the preferential aspects of both.

We come thus to another variant of the Commonwealth argument: the view that Britain's membership in the Economic Community is incompatible with the spirit of the Commonwealth. The crudest variant is the one that simply maintains that if trade negotiations between Britain and her Community partners on the one side, and the Commonwealth countries on the other, are carried out by the Economic Commission in Brussels, then this procedure itself impairs the whole Commonwealth relationship. If Englishmen and Australians no longer meet to talk wool, they will not meet to talk cricket either. But this argument distorts the probable behavior of the Commission, and of the British member of the Council of Ministers. During the transitional period, it is in any case the member states and not the Commission who, under Article 111, must take the necessary steps to adjust their tariff agreements with third countries to the common tariff. And even thereafter, under Article 113, it is the Council that authorizes the Commission to negotiate commercial agreements, issues the necessary directives, and appoints a special committee to assist the Commission in the negotiations. The Commission would naturally find it in the interests of the Community itself to choose the negotiators most likely to be acceptable to the other side in the negotiations. It is hardly conceivable that an Englishman should not be playing a major part in such talks—even if by any chance a Ghanaian team should find itself talking to Italian or German negotiators with less self-consciousness and suspicion than to their British colleagues.

Much more sophisticated and cogent is the view that membership in the Economic Community would constitutionally conflict with membership in the Commonwealth—a view sometimes taken to the opposite positive conclusion: that the Commonwealth would form a much better basis for an Economic and Political Community for Britain to join than the Six. If it were possible to form a Commonwealth Economic and Political Community then there can be little doubt that this would, from many points of view, be a better unit for Britain to enter than the European Community: Its far-flung membership, its multiracial character, its differences of income and stages of economic growth, could—if the Commonwealth, the United States, and Europe worked closely together—provide great scope for world peace and development. But of course this notion is totally unrealistic.

Commonwealth free trade has never been accepted, even in principle, by any Commonwealth country except the United Kingdom: Indeed, at the very moment when the Canadian Government was pleading for the maintenance of preference on its exports to Britain, it placed a 10 to 15 per cent surcharge on the tariff it levies on British exports to Canada. Few except those financially interested might weep for the disappearance of large sections of the British textile industry, but Commonwealth fair trade would also mean the abolition of subsidies to British farming. Debating points of this kind aside, it would be most unfortunate, from a world point of view, if India and Pakistan, Ghana and Malaysia were to throw their infant industries to the mercies of British competition. Commonwealth free trade would tend to restore the position of overseas Commonwealth countries as hewers of wood and drawers of water, hamstring their industrialization, and force them to rely on the production of just such primary produce as is subject to the greatest price instability on world markets. Under such conditions, private capital, whether from the United Kingdom, from the Six, or from America, would hardly find it worthwhile to flow into these developing countries.

Nor is there any political reason to believe that Nkrumah and Makarios, Nehru and Wilensky, Ayub and Menzies, could form a political unit of the kind that is required by the world situation, and which is at this moment crystallizing on the Continent as partner to the United States. Indeed, few of those who are most opposed to British entry into a European political unit would relish the prospect of becoming members of a Commonwealth Community of which only 50 out of 700 million inhabitants would be living in the United Kingdom, in which the biggest single power would be India, and the overwhelming majority would be Asian and African peoples. On neither side is there a political will for any such tightening of Commonwealth bonds.

The Commonwealth is a historical association of countries with centrifugal tendencies, rather than a centripetal attempt to overcome historical divisions. It has a role in the world—and an important one at that—as a forum of discussion between colored and white, poor and rich countries, with certain cultural links, meeting in somewhat more intimate conditions than the United Nations, and with a certain sense of belonging to (or reacting against) the mother country, whatever their domestic political regimes (many of which are far less like our own than those of the Continent). But the Commonwealth is not, and has no wish to become, a unit of action that could take the place of the European Community.

The choice is thus not a simple one between Europe and the Commonwealth—but may, on the contrary even be one between Europe combined with a more dynamic Commonwealth on the one hand, and exclusion from Europe combined with a more archaic or obsolescent form of Commonwealth association on the other. If Britain gains influence through her membership of the Community, she will gain in interest and attractiveness for the members of the Commonwealth. If, on the other hand, she is either swallowed up in Europe, or left as a quaint island off the shores of a vigorous Community, then the Commonwealth may indeed lose in centralized cohesion (the speed with which newly independent Commonwealth countries established diplomatic missions in continental capitals may be symptomatic here). But even then, it has not been proven that a Commonwealth in which Britain is less independent (or even one in which she occupies—except for Buckingham Palace—a less central place) would necessarily be less of a force for interracial partnership in the world. All would depend on the type of political freedom of action surrendered, and the type of political influence gained in return. Similes are dangerous, but can illuminate as well as mislead: And perhaps the now frequently used image of the Commonwealth as a bunch of keys is worth remembering. Each member can open doors in a part of the world among its neighbors and friends. The Commonwealth as a whole might well wish to consider whether or not it needs such a key to Western Europe, not just as the most dynamic market and second or third provider of capital for the Commonwealth's developing countries, but also as one of the biggest political factors in the emerging new pattern of the world.

Thirdly, there is a very general political and psychological point. The European Community contains Belgium, which, until very recently, was a colonial power; France, whose Algerian problem is only just solved, and whose atomic explosions in the Sahara have made her none the more popular; and Germany, whose new-found wealth is not exactly hidden under a bushel. Is this not essentially a rich men's club in a world divided largely along racial lines between the rich and the poor? It is that which might make the membership of the Community incompatible with the spirit of the Commonwealth. How can Britain —an African might ask—make common cause with Belgium? How can Britain, a Pakistani might wonder, associate herself with recent policy in Algeria? Is not this the moment when pigmentation is thicker than language—and when the colored peoples of the Commonwealth, for their part, should draw the same conclusion and band together against a neo-colonialist Europe?

Guilt by association—particularly when attributed as an argument to others—is always a slippery concept. Those who wish to argue that way can already point to various far more pointless British gestures of solidarity, with far older allies than the Six, and to plenty of other associations between Britain, Belgium, and France—in the Commission for Technical Cooperation in Africa south of the Sahara, OEEC or OECD, WEU, NATO and the rest. Those, on the other hand, who do wish to be able to distinguish between one white government's policy and another's, or between one white government five years ago and the same country's government today, will not be helped by Britain standing aside from the Community or confused by Britain's joining it. Responsible African leaders are far more likely to ask themselves whether Britain will be less or more able to help them economically, and whether the Continental sources of aid for development will be less or more likely to help them if Britain joins; and whether British colonial and development policy will become less or more enlightened, and whether the Community's development policy will become less or more enlightened if Britain is in the Community.

It is just as well to remember that now that Algeria has become independent, Britain is left with substantial territorial responsibilities in Africa in the company only of Portugal and Spain. It looks very much as if the problems of Kenya and the Central African Federation will be with us for some time to come. "Guilt by association" could thus also work the other way. A "holier-than-thou" attitude in British policy on colonial questions may thus be a little out-of-date.

Some people might even ask why it is that fifteen newly independent African states asked to remain associated with the European Community in 1960, and why, in June, 1961, their parliamentarians were sitting with an equal number of European parliamentarians in the Assembly Hall at Strasbourg to discuss how the Association could best be renewed indefinitely. The Six—so far from making "neo-colonialist" attempts to retain the African countries as primary producers for Europe's growing industrial machine—are providing capital and training facilities to help industrialize and diversify the economies of their African Associates. So far from attempting to "divide and conquer" Africa, the Community is fostering the equal economic treatment of all its Associates and forcing them to act together politically in a united front, and let one African country represent others vis-à-vis Europe in institutions based on Afro-European parity. The Africans are interested in a single African common market: British entry into the Community would go a long way to making Europe treat the bulk of Africa as one economic unit, and to letting the Continent share the burden of stepping up development assistance to the Commonwealth countries of Africa. By standing aside, Britain could thus even lay herself open to the charge that she is not prepared to join the grandiose and costly venture of Afro-European partnership developed by the Community.

How much weight this last point will carry with some of the African and Asian countries not associated with the Community is questionable. Already there are suspicions in other African states that these former French possessions are not determined enough in shaking off all vestiges of the imperialist yoke. The danger that Britain will be misunderstood in Africa and Asia if she joins the Community is thus very real. It is one which must be borne constantly in mind, and one which should be a spur to additional effort. But in the last resort, Britain must do what she conceives to be her duty, even toward the Afro-Asian countries, without overanxiety as to who will misunderstand her. To make her attitude crystal clear, and to prove her sincerity, must be a matter of subsequent concern, and one to be dealt with not by omissions in Europe, but by action in Asia and Africa.

Both the economic and the political arguments from the Commonwealth stand thus seem to point in the same direction. The old notion that Europe and the Commonwealth are alternatives is inadequate. The maintenance of the Commonwealth today seems to demand a strong Britain in a strong Community. Britain's influence in a few years' time will perhaps be at its best precisely when she is acting as the hinge between the two.

Anglo-American Brotherhood

From the balance of foreign-policy arguments derived from the Commonwealth as a stabilizing factor in world affairs, let us now turn to Britain's relations with the United States. Here, once more, we must think back to Britain's position in the world at large and in the free world in particular, for whose leadership the United States has for the moment assumed primary responsibility.

In some of the current discussions, a third course is implied as an alternative to a tighter Commonwealth or entry into the Community: that of steering Britain toward the status of a fifty-first State. All the arguments about Britain's influence in the world as part of a larger unit would apply with roughly equal force to Britain's entry into the United States of America.

But such an idea also faces all the problems of supranationality and of sovereignty raised by the European issue, only in a vastly more acute form: no one in Europe has yet proposed sending federal troops into the member states. The sense of kinship with the Americans might or might not carry one through. But then there is much less reason to believe that Britain would be welcome in the United States than on the Continent. The Atlantic Alliance today is not an Anglo-American, but a European-American partnership. A United States of America and of the British Isles is far less likely than a United States of America and Europe. British adherence to the Rome Treaty can thus hardly stand in the way of an Atlantic confederal arrangement; on the contrary, it might, if one wished, provide that balance within the Atlantic Community that could even commend an Atlantic confederation more easily on both sides of the ocean. Once more, in the American as in the Commonwealth context, a Britain that is also a member of the Community would seem a more attractive partner than one that stands alone.

More usually, in less cut-and-dried form, fears are heard that Britain's privileged position in Washington would be threatened if she entered the Community. This might be a serious argument, though it would weigh less heavily than some of those connected with the Soviet and the underdeveloped parts of the world. But what becomes of it under closer scrutiny?

Britain has been naive, probably for years, in imagining that a unique relationship with the United States was anything other than one-way. Ever since the early fifties—under the leadership of Secretaries of State Acheson, Dulles, and Rusk—Washington has been at least equally interested in the unifying Continent. At any rate, the new Administration will recognize power and dynamism where it finds it. When Mr. Macmillan, in early 1961, asked President Kennedy if Britain's participation in the European Community would not threaten her special relationship with the United States, President Kennedy just did not understand what special relationship Mr. Macmillan meant. And there is no reason to believe that Mr. Dillon or Mr. George Ball (the Common Market's chief legal and political adviser in Washington until he entered the Administration) have changed their views now that they are working for Mr. Kennedy.

The first argument, then, is that by standing aloof from Europe, Britain may find herself cut off from the main axis of power in the Western alliance. Both for ideological reasons and for reasons of power politics, Washington will be tempted to work at least as closely with Bonn, Paris, and Brussels as with London—if London's stake on the Continent is confined to a few divisions on the Rhine (and we do not know how long Britain can afford to keep them there). If Britain's influence within the Commonwealth declines rather than increases if she remains outside Europe, then her influence in Washington is even more likely to dwindle if she stands apart.

There is no doubt that the Kennedy Administration, like the Eisenhower Administration before it, would like to see a politically united Western Europe, able to buttress her Western defenses without perpetual diplomatic and economic assistance. The United States is quite prepared to see a certain amount of commercial discrimination against herself in the pursuit of this greater aim. The Kennedy Administration feels that there are far more sensitive parts of the world requiring its attention and its resources, and that the time has come for Europe to lend a hand instead of asking for more. For defense, political, and economic reasons the quarrels between the Six and Seven must seem petty while Washington is concerned with a Berlin crisis, Laos, the strategy of space stations, disarmament, and the challenges of starvation in South East Asia and of poverty in South America, and of the upsurge of a China of 650 million people.

Of course no one likes to be told what to do—least of all by the first of its rebellious colonies. But if the United States is anxious for wider political consolidation in Europe, then it is difficult to see how British influence in Washington could survive after Britain's refusal, but perfectly possible to see how British influence might increase if she did take up a leading place in the European Community. The problem, in any case, is not how important British influence in Washington will be, but what sort of influences there will be and how heavily they will weigh. What does it matter whether they are called British or European, provided they are of the right kind?

There is every reason to believe that the free world would be helped by a strong, united Europe, able to stand by the side of the United States. There is no political rivalry between Western Europe and America. In the world situation of today, the burden of leadership and the burden of economic assistance is running close to the limits set by American politics itself. Economic difficulties within the United States make it none too easy for the Administration to intensify an active policy of world development. But if other nations are sinking their past differences, however great, in order to face the tasks of the future, then this could have a major effect: Americans might no longer feel alone in the world with a few sometimes recalcitrant retainers, but see themselves as one half of a partnership between Europe and America—in which America need not even, in some years, still be the leading half. The population of the Community, even without Britain, is already bigger than that of the United States, and neither its skill nor its prosperity need remain below those of North America. British adherence to the Community, whatever it might mean in international law and commercial life, could be of far more dramatic importance: It could, as it were, bridge a gap in the circuit and galvanize the free world into a new phase of action. British adherence to the European Community could thus do much to transform the whole power structure of the world.

The Politics of the Community

So far, we have discussed Britain's entry into the Economic Community in terms of foreign policy toward the Soviet bloc countries, in terms of the Commonwealth and the "uncommitted" Afro-Asian countries, and in terms of Anglo-American relations. Consequent on a change of scale in the world, the choice in each case seems to be one between more independent but less effective, and less independent but more effective action vis-à-vis the rest of the world. But even if there were no non-European world to be considered, Britain's relations with the Community across the Channel would pose their own political problems: the nagging doubts in this country as to the domestic political stability of more than one leading Community power; the doubts as to the balance of national and political influences within the Community; the fear in Britain of supranational entanglements; and more genteel cultural and psychological factors. Each of these arguments must be looked at in turn.

The facts can be put dramatically. Both Germany and Italy were under Fascist dictatorship less than twenty years ago; France has narrowly escaped several *coups d'etat* in the last few years. Belgium, after the earlier excitement over the royal question, in 1961 suffered from a general strike in which the difficulties between Walloons and Flemings came to the surface once more; Holland has had several cabinet crises lasting, in one case, for three months. If these countries cannot govern themselves, the argument runs, their political ineptitude may well drag Britain into awkward predicaments.

Now, quite apart from any diagnosis of the domestic politics of the Six, what sort of "awkward situations" are really envisaged in this argument? How much more will political instability on the Continent affect Britain if she is inside the Community than if she is only inside NATO, OECD, WEU, and the Council of Europe? How much more was Germany affected by the attempted coup of 1960 in Algeria than was Britain? How much more were the Dutch affected by the Belgian strikes than the Danes?

It may be objected that for the moment, domestic instability (provided it is not of a Communist variety) may be irrelevant, but that in an ever closer union, its effects would soon be felt. But would not a more closely knit larger unit also be more stable than any of its component parts? A Communist majority in Italy could prove very troublesome if Italy were wholly independent: Its effects on the position of Yugoslavia would be difficult to foretell. But a Communist majority in the geographical area of present Italy would be a small and ineffectual minority in the political institutions of a real United States of Europe. The problem is how best to arrange to live with the Continental countries in the narrow peninsula on the fringe of Eurasia on which, together, we represent the foothold of the Western world. If it has any effects on this score, British participation can only add to European stability. Britain's interest, traditionally, has been in stability in the Low Countries and in friendship with them. Under modern conditions, all of Western Europe has become Britain's Low Countries.

But though all this reasoning based on Continental instability has its importance (and tells in favor of British entry into the Community), its premises must be seen in perspective. Of course no one can guarantee the stability of any country's politics. Since the independence of Ireland and the general strike, British politics have enjoyed a period of calm. But at least one well-known British commentator has wondered whether the boot may not by now be on the other foot—whether economic stagnation in Britain compared with Continental prosperity may not soon result in a restive atmosphere here. (Other people's countries always look different from ones' own—indeed the readers of the illustrated papers in Germany may already be asking themselves whether, with intermittent strikes all over Britain, Mosleyite demonstrations in London, race riots in Notting Hill and Worcestershire, and attempts by unilateral "disarmers" to enter American bases, life in West Germany is not by comparison rather dull.) In fact, the only country where there has been serious instability at any time in the past ten or fifteen years (as compared with cabinet crises that are equivalent to ministerial reshuffles, and often less drastic than the government reorganization of July, 1962) is France, where the Algerian question has so long poisoned political life: Now that she has disposed of her Algerian problem, her surging economic progress, like that of Italy and of West Germany, has drastically reduced the possibility of any Fascist or Communist regimes. The turbulent experiences of recent decades have sobered down Continental politics: ideology is fading as a political factor, and economic progress is not only a tribute to the essential stability of the Continent over the past fifteen years, but also a warrant for continued stability in the future. Indeed, perhaps it would be salutary to reflect that except for the creative imagination brought to their problems by the Six, and except for the remarkable success they have made of their politics there would have been no Community today for Britain to join.

Then there are the fears over the political balance within the Community. Will the Community be dominated by France? Will it become, as the *Zollverein* once was for Prussia, the harbinger of a new German domination of the Continent? Or will France assume the diplomatic, and Germany the economic leadership? Or will the two big powers form a coalition to which the Benelux countries will have to submit while Italy is gathering strength behind the Alps? Any of these interpretations would provide a *prima facie* reason for Britain to take a hand. If Britain stands outside the Community, she can hardly affect it. It has frequently been argued that each time Britain withdrew from the Continent, she had to return to fight a war and to sort out the mess that resulted. Those who still think in national terms may argue that the French have far more need of Britain to balance Germany in the Community than France herself, in her present mood of buoyant self-confidence, is apt to realize or admit.

But in fact it is of course inconceivable that any one nation should come to dominate the Community. Anyone who asks why has only to turn back to Chapter III, in which we analyzed the voting arrangements for the Treaty: All the countries that signed the Rome Treaty were at least equally concerned to avoid such a possibility then as Britain would be now. In any case, conflicts within the Community will increasingly be between sectional interests rather than between nations—between farmers and consumers, cartels and importers, rather than between Frenchmen and Germans as such. And the whole concept of national domination is invalidated *a fortiori* within the Economic Community for all the reasons that we already adduced in discussing the notion of "national leadership" in a Political Community. It is precisely the fear of a hegemony of one or two big countries in Europe that points to the Community-type of institution—in which smaller countries are up-valued in terms of votes, and in which national predominance becomes irrelevant as problems cease to be national and come to require Community solutions.

As a result, too, the problem of what regimes are in power in various nation-states begins to look different. The character of a national government in one country retains its full importance only while traditional or Gaullist intergovernmental views of cooperation prevail over Community integration. Within EEC already no one national government can veto the decisions to be taken by a qualified majority: And the more authority is transferred to Community institutions, the less does the complexion of the Italian Government affect the conduct of the Dutch economy.

Rather more serious, perhaps, than the fears of a predominance of any one nation, are the fears of some one-party or vested interest, with consequent effects on the policies which, it is thought, Britain must therefore also pursue. To Labour people, the balance of electoral forces does not look too promising: At the last respective national elections in Britain and the Six, of 122 million voters, 11 million voted Communist, 35 million

Socialist, 35 million Christian Democrat, 25 million Conservative and other parties of the moderate right, 7 million Liberal, 3 million for parties of the more extreme right (above all in Italy), and the remainder is even more difficult to classify.

Today, the biggest party group among the Six are the Christian Democrats, and in an ultimate Political Community they might well hold the balance—though their coherence should not be overestimated. Their character has at times been grossly misunderstood. The days when German Christian Democratic leaders called themselves "Socialists out of Christian conviction" are over: But the influence of the Christian trade unions remains significant. One former Labour minister who has worked with Continental parliamentarians was heard to say that had he been a "Continental," he would have been a Christian Democrat; and a German CDU parliamentarian has declared that, given the relative absence of Marxist ideology in the Labour Party, he might well, had he been an Englishman, have joined the Labour Party. This does not mean to say that the two can be equated—very far from it; some Christian Democratic parties contain elements that could only be described as reactionary; but the gamut of views and interests represented within the Christian Democratic parties overlaps both, or rather all three major British parties.

Christian Democrats tend (though not always) to be opposed to nationalization; but they have set up or helped set up some of the best social and welfare services in the world, and the upward harmonization envisaged somewhat vaguely in the Treaty could mean major advances in a British welfare system which has mostly stood still over the last ten years. There may not be a single Socialist government among the Six today, but French, German, and Italian workers work shorter hours and have longer paid holidays than do the British. French women workers by law get equal pay with men, and the rapid rise in their national incomes will allow their social systems to be further developed—in the German case, for example, pensions will by law automatically rise roughly in line with productivity. There are plenty of issues on which the Christian Democrats will side with Conservatives rather than with Labour. But it is too easy to write off the European movement as either a papist or a planners' plot, to try to impose the outdated categories of the British two-party system on the totally different often even more outdated constellations of Continental parties and to draw the wrong conclusions.

With right-wing nationalist parties, by their very nationalist antitheses, liable in part to neutralize each other, three or four party groups would then be left to form probably changing majorities in different situations: Christian Democrats of widely differing social and economic persuasions, Socialists, and Conservatives, with some Liberals thrown in for good measure. How right wing, it may be asked, would such majorities be likely to be? In a sense the very question exposes the inadequacy of our political vocabulary, coined in the national context, for exploring the variety of attitudes to the international problems we now face. Traditional party labels do not help very much. "Right-wing" in the new context presumably means inflexible in defense and foreign policy toward the East, illiberal in economic assistance to the underdeveloped world, and disinflationary, *laisser-faire,* and reluctant to extend the welfare state in managing the economies of the West. The welfare state, the degree of nationalization of the economy, and the amount of assistance to underdeveloped countries would put the three big countries of the Community possibly rather to the 'left' of Britain. None of the party groups would score high marks for right-wing attitudes on all three criteria; indeed, the line between left and right would have to be drawn right across most of the national parties we know: On the British scene sheep and goats would part over the treatment of textiles, with the champions of Lancashire's, whatever their party label, as vested interests on the right, and the champions of Hong Kong on the left.

Moreover, it is not so much the national parties that are relevant here as those of their aspects that reflect themselves on the European level. We have seen already that the Socialist group in the Assembly has been at least as active and successful as the Christian Democrats in imposing its demands on the Communities—and that without reinforcement from a strong British Labour Party. The strong representation of the trade unions in the institutions of the Communities has also often moderated the character of the Liberals on questions of European scale:

as though in return, European Socialists have perhaps been more productivity- and less class-conscious in Strasbourg than at home. No one would claim that the Community is a Socialist scheme, but every Socialist party in Europe except the Italian Nenni group voted for it, and its policy—if not the Treaty—has been not a Socialist but a social one. As such, it is one that most of the younger Conservatives in Britain would also accept wholeheartedly. So far in fact, possibly because there has not yet been any need to shadowbox for the benefit of an electorate, the atmosphere of the Assembly, and even more so of the other institutions, has been far more one of constructive integration of different viewpoints than one of clashes in the name of party shibboleths. Direct election might affect this atmosphere—but methods and habits of work once established need not necessarily break down; the problems, being largely new, can be approached with less doctrinaire prejudice, and the whole spirit of a forward looking team successfully building a new structure militates against skirmishing for merely party-political victories.

To those used to the ping-pong matches of the British two-party system and the plebiscitary aspects of British general elections, all this may seem lacking in the proper spirit of partisan democracy. But more serious criticism of the indirectness of democratic control over the Community's institutions can be made with greater justification, and has indeed been borne out by our arguments in Chapter III (esp. pp. 89–96 above). The Assembly is not yet directly elected, the High Authority and the Commissions are not directly enough responsible to it, and the Council of Ministers (who are not corporately responsible to anyone but only severally responsible to national institutions) remains the chief decision-making body. Directness and indirectness are relative terms; much more depends on the spirit and the actual practice than on the legal chains of responsibility, and in the breaking of new ground and in the initiation of altruistic or highly enlightened policies toward the outside world—some would argue—there may even be advantages in a certain removal from the immediate pressures of vested interests in the political constituency. But when all that is said, no one would pretend that the Community's institutions have reached their final shape.

Concrete proposals going beyond the direct elections envisaged in the Treaty have been put forward elsewhere.[2] Indeed, some of the most ardent champions of British entry into the Community will, if Britain enters, turn around to criticize the present institutions with less inhibition, and will press for major reforms —just as some of the most acute critics of Britain's entry will champion further integration once she is inside, precisely to give the Community greater planning and executive powers and to democratize its institutions. President de Gaulle may believe for the moment that he would have Britain's support for his concepts of a Europe of States. But he may well be in for a surprise: Britain's economic needs and Britain's parliamentary traditions may lead her in just the opposite—that of the Community concept. Once he loses control of French foreign policy, there will be no obstacle to such a development of European institutions. To argue that Britain should wait until the institutions have reached their final state is to miss not merely the only opportunity of joining she is ever likely to have, but also the opportunity of helping mold the institutions into the shape she feels they should have.

The Width of the Channel

As on the economic, so on the political side, one is ultimately left not with issues of institutional mechanisms, but with people and their attitudes, with groups and their spirit. On any political question rationalizations are rife on both sides. There are plenty of reasons why the cause of Europe should have been taken up by the particular group of people now associated with it. Every one of them can probably, by self-inspection, find all sorts of nonrational, accidental, social and psychological factors in his attitude. Similarly, on the side of the opponents of British entry into the Common Market, those who would be happy to buy Italian shoes more cheaply may fear that Italian men would obtain offers of employment in Britain. However much such workers would be paid at union rates and however much they might contribute to national income, their very presence in the community would make them uncomfortable. The line of

2. Cf. U.K. Council of the European Movement Recommendation to the Munich Congress of the European Movement, London 1962.

thought that at its crudest takes the form of "Niggers begin at Calais" runs through reflections like "Foreigners don't like cricket" to misgivings in terms of the differences between English law on the one side and Continental (and Scots) law on the other, and the absence of a common spiritual and emotional experience formed by a common language, literature, and history.

On the other side, there are those who obtain positive psychological satisfaction from the thought that Britain must abandon effortless superiority, that she can no longer set up solar systems in which all her partners are only satellites, that she must adapt herself to reduced circumstances, and come to terms with nations of her own size as an equal. And there are those who have a taste for German wines, Italian holidays, and French films, and whose Europeanism is directed more at a wider choice in consumption than at the tasks which a united Western Europe can take in hand. More constructively, radicals of all three parties—or of none—hope that insular complacency, not simply in sections of industry and commerce, but in the whole range of intellectual and social life, might be broken by increasing contact and competition with the Continent. In the worlds of social organization and town planning, architecture and design, literature and the arts, interest in Continental achievements, once confined to a narrow upper class, is already widening. Entry into the Community, it is argued, would provide the right sort of stimulus for further exciting discoveries and mutual cross-fertilization of ideas. As communication across the Channel in creases, so standards will rise and become more eclectic, taking the best that each nation can offer: And once Europe makes a real impact, a much more openminded attitude to all sorts of other countries beyond Europe and to their achievements should further serve to goad and inspire British performance.

The very heat with which the issue is discussed is evidence of the deepseated temperamental factors that enter into it. As freedom of movement clashes with xenophobia, so the problem of supranationalism touches the deeper suspicions against the outside world. In defense, Britain has long abandoned independence; in economics, a country as heavily dependent on the rest of the world can only be master of its own fate to a very limited degree; but the formal merger of decision-making procedures, the absence of a formal veto on proposals made by a body on which the British Government is not itself formally represented, go against the grain of many who, on most other grounds, would like to see Britain join the Community. Very few people in Britain actually welcome the idea of taking decisions in common with the representatives of other countries. We have seen that economic integration today inevitably involves decisions taken together. That is the whole logic behind the Rome Treaties, and it is one which each can rethink for himself. Supranational decisions may not yet extend very far in the Community, but the issue of supranationality is not one that should be played down. Those who, rejecting arguments as to the world implications of the choice, would rather be unfettered masters in their own houses even at some expense of political influence and economic advance, are perfectly entitled to their view.

But on the once war-torn Continent, supranationality is regarded by many as a good in itself, quite apart from its functional necessity for economic integration. The strength of the opposite sentiment in Britain is obvious, and has become even more so since May, 1961. This subjective phenomenon presents the Europeans, and those who regard a political Community in Europe as important for world politics, with an objective dilemma. Would Britain within the Community, however loyally she accepts the letter of the Treaties, drag her feet once again when it comes to implementing the spirit of the preamble "to establish the foundations of an ever closer union among the peoples of Europe?" We have seen that Europeans fearing such sabotage have not been in a hurry to see Britain join until Europe was well on the path toward "ever closer union." Is it not perhaps still too early for Britain to join? The answer depends on the sort of European unit—its extent and its tightness—that we feel the world context requires. The answer may once more be impossibly difficult to give, but that is no excuse for not posing the question.

This, indeed, is the question that is pondered all over Europe today. The Commission's President has been quite blunt on the purpose of the Community: "We are not in business, we are in politics." And in politics even the right thing done for the wrong reason can spell disaster. If Britain sees in the chief purpose of the Community its biggest drawback, if she is willing, but only for commercial reasons, to sidle in with a whimper, then it may in the long run be better if she stays out. But if the country feels ready to accept a new challenge, if, instead of anxiously counting the safeguards, she welcomes its economic and political opportunities and is prepared to think in political terms through and beyond the Community, then there is every case for going into Europe—better late than never—with a cheer. For what matters about the Common Market, after all, is not so much what Britain can get out of it, as what she can put in. And the real argument for Britain's entry is not to be found in Britain's short-run self-interest alone, but above all in the role that an enlarged Community including Britain would play in the world, and in the wider initiatives, outlined in Chapter VII, to which her entry would provide the best launching pad.

VII

A Historic Reversal

It is said that a one-sentence memorandum from Prime Minister Macmillan was circulating around the ministries of Whitehall in late spring, 1961: "What has changed since we decided to stay out?" What indeed?

Only two years earlier, the government had enumerated all the reasons why it was out of the question for Britain, with her Commonwealth connection, her special relationship to the United States, her own conception of an independent role in the cold-war world, and her own peculiar legal, constitutional, political, religious, and social traditions, to join the politically unstable low-wage countries of Europe in a customs union that would damage British sovereignty. In October, 1959, the Macmillan government had gone to the country in jaunty self-confidence, with the slogan "We've never had it so good," and the statistics on comparative rates of growth in Europe, flourished occasionally by Labour hecklers at Conservative election meetings, were brushed aside: Nor did they constitute for the Labour Party anything but a brick to heave at the government, for not even 1 per cent of Labour candidates troubled to mention the problem of trade with Europe, let alone any institutional relationship with Europe, in their election addresses. The Free Trade Area negotiations had failed in November, 1958, the European Free Trade Association had been instituted in the summer of 1959, but only 8 per cent of Conservative candidates mentioned European trade in their manifestoes to the electors. The Liberal Party, it is true, took the problem more seriously: About one-half of their candidates referred to it, usually in a free-trade spirit, but the electorate, though it gave the Liberal Party 6 per cent of votes, almost certainly did so for other reasons. It may be doubted whether more than a tiny minority, even among the politically conscious, paid any heed to the rapid consolidation of the Economic Community, and few thought through the implications of an accelerated decline in Britain's relative position in the world.

We saw in the first few pages of this book how, at the end of World War II, Britain found herself further removed in outlook and psychology from the countries of Western Europe than perhaps ever before. The strategic significance of the Channel was interpreted as the peculiar resilience of Britain's national institutions, and the accident of Allied victory obscured the inevitability of Britain's relegation to the second division of international powers. Britain had helped to win the war: Once more it had looked as though the British were best. But the result of that victory was complacency on the one hand, and illusion on the other. It took Britain fifteen years to realize how profoundly her international position had shifted since 1939, let alone since 1914.

When the European movement began to crystallize on the Continent, there were only a very few in Britain who felt that their country was not qualitatively different from the rest of Europe. In the economic field, Britain had suffered incomparably less than the Continent. Awareness that the flow of unearned income from abroad was diminished percolated slowly into general consciousness. Few could believe that wholesale destruction was the best precursor of industrial modernization, and that, within a decade, Britain's Continental competitors would be rather better equipped than Britain over a whole range of production.

In the political sphere, the wartime alliance with America buttressed the notion of an Anglo-American condominium and a special peacetime relationship of which London (or, for that matter, Paris) was increasingly rather more conscious than Washington. Even the surrender of India, Pakistan, and Ceylon to independence was seen as a moral, not as a power-political phenomenon: While Churchill had not become His Majesty's first Minister to preside over the dissolution of the British Empire, Attlee clothed the inevitable with Socialist dignity and generosity.

Under his Labour Government, British European policy was, in fact, an extension of British economic policy: socialism in one country and national planning protected as much as possible from international influences. To have joined in a closely integrated Europe would have been to abandon economic sovereignty, the right to plan the British economy, and to extend the welfare state in what was then one of the richest European countries, independently of a unit that might prove to be predominantly nonsocialist.

Even in opposition, Sir Winston Churchill, alternately revered as the Saint John or reviled as the Judas Iscariot of European unity, had made it clear that the United States of Europe he proposed in his Zurich speech had no application to Britain, any more than to the United States, or to the Soviet Union. Though his pronouncements on the European Defense Community were somewhat differently couched, his government, after 1951, invoked the doctrine of the three circles: Britain's links with the Commonwealth and the special Anglo-American relationship were held to preclude excessive ties with Europe; each of the three connections was to be maintained simultaneously with Britain at the point of intersection of the three, and thus the traditions of British foreign policy—to hold the balance, but never to become too closely involved in Europe—reasserted themselves in a new guise.

The great European divide of 1950 came in the period at the end of the Labour Government, but it was Sir Winston Churchill, paradoxically enough, who from the Opposition's front bench gave the Government's refusal to join any supranational scheme. Faced with the question "Would you agree to a supranational authority which has the power to tell Great Britain not to cut any more coal or make any more steel, but to grow tomatoes instead?" Sir Winston was unequivocal: "I should say, without any hesitation, the answer is 'No.' But"—and this was where he disagreed with the Labour Government, which had refused to join in any negotiations over the Schuman Plan—

"why not be there to give the answer?" In the same debate, unremarked at the time, Mr. Edward Heath made his maiden speech: It was a plea for the Government to reconsider its decision, and to join in this economic and political venture, if only for the sake of the underdeveloped countries of Africa. But the decision was taken largely by default—its full import recognized by only a few.

In earlier chapters, we traced the progress made by the Six from 1950 onward: And the division between the Six and the rest that originated in 1950 was not bridged by Britain's support for the EDC, nor by Lord Avon (then Mr. Anthony Eden) in his lightning tour around Europe to set up the Western European Union in 1954. Indeed, when the Conservatives, in opposition, had flirted with the European movement, the most conspicuous absentee had always been the Shadow Foreign Secretary, Mr. Anthony Eden; it was he who was at the height of his power as Prime Minister when Britain refused the invitation to Messina, and it was in the last few weeks of his period of office that Britain finally withdrew her observer from the Brussels talks.

Looking back, one can perhaps see five steps by which postwar illusions crumbled within five years. The beginning of 1961 really came at the end of 1956: It was the failure of the Suez expedition that first tore the veil from Britain's postwar illusions in no uncertain way. Suez demonstrated that Britain, even allied to France, could no longer "go it alone" even against minor countries of the Middle East. In 1957, the White Paper on Defense (insisting on reductions in conventional forces) left Britain almost isolated among her NATO allies and 1958 saw, simultaneously, the nadir in her relations with both France and West Germany. The warm glow spread by the professional public-relations men in the election year of 1959 proved the sundown of national euphoria: The fiasco of the Paris Summit, six months later, marked the failure of Mr. Macmillan's attempt to play an independent role on the world diplomatic stage and ended more illusions on Britain's margin of maneuver in foreign policy. 1960 also saw the collapse of "Blue Streak" and the end of the policy of an independently delivered British nuclear deterrent. By the end of 1960, Britain's sluggish economic growth compared with that on the Continent could no longer be ignored, and, over the economy, the gathering clouds that burst in the balance-of-payments crisis of the spring of 1961 finally exploded economic complacency. In early 1961, it was only the central banks of the Continent that by their Basle agreement saved the pound sterling from devaluation. Suez, "Blue Streak," Paris, the "Growth League Tables," and Basle—these marked the five stations on Britain's road to Europe.

It would be pleasurable to record that the small band of devoted Europeans that does exist in Britain made a major contribution toward that change by its zealous preaching of the gospel. It may be that the switch in British policy would have been more difficult without the scores of British MP's who, by 1961, had served an apprenticeship in the Consultative Assembly of the Council of Europe in Strasbourg. But beyond that, it seems difficult to establish any effective extragovernmental influences. The organizers of the Common Market campaign found that British industry, while seriously concerned about the problem and in many cases anxious to enter the Common Market, was unwilling to exert much pressure on the Government. The Common Market campaign itself did not begin to deploy its propaganda until the government had clearly decided upon the direction of its policy. It sometimes seemed that the United Kingdom Council of the European Movement was more responsive to the governmental influences encouraging its educational activities than the government was responsive to the European movement.

The newspapers were on the whole late in taking up cudgels —indeed *The Times* appeared reluctant to follow the government's lead to the last and remains far from firmly committed. *The Economist*—and possibly *The Financial Times* and *The Guardian*—began to take the question of actually joining the Community seriously by the end of 1960: But the *Herald,* the *Mirror,* and the *Telegraph* were only converted at the eleventh hour—the *Mirror* announcing its "Damascus" with a flourish, on May 10, 1961. Lord Beaverbrook's *Express,* on the other hand, ran a virulent campaign with daily arguments against Britain joining from spring, 1961 onward, to be joined by the Socialist *New Statesman* and *Tribune* at the other end of the political spectrum.

Table XI

GENERAL INDICES OF INDUSTRIAL PRODUCTION

	Belgium	Luxembourg	France	Germany	Italy	Netherlands	The Six	United Kingdom	U.S.A.
1950	93	89	89	72	78	88	80	94	82
1951	106	99	99	85	89	91	92	98	89
1952	100	109	98	91	91	91	95	95	92
1953	100	100	100	100	100	100	100	100	100
1954	106	103	109	112	109	111	110	108	94
1955	116	116	117	129	119	119	122	114	106
1956	123	124	128	139	128	124	132	114	109
1957	124	126	139	147	138	127	140	116	110
1958	116	121	145	152	143	127	144	114	102
1959	122	127	150	161	158	139	153	120	116
1960	129	138	167	178	182	157	171	129	119
1961	135	142	175	189	200	160	182	130	120
1962	143	135	(192)	198	222	165	(193)	131	130

Source: OECD *General Statistics,* July, 1963, p. 2. (Preliminary estimates are in parentheses.)

The decision to apply for membership was in fact an outstanding example of the extreme centralization of British decision making. A handful of civil servants, the Prime Minister, and a few members of the Cabinet sufficed to reverse the policy Britain has pursued toward Europe for four hundred years. The "rot," or the "dawn" (depending on one's point of view), appears to have started, in so far as any date can be assigned to the spread of what the French pictorially call an "oilstain," in the early summer of 1960—at the time when the Prime Minister, after the tragicomedy of the abortive meetings "at the Summit," must have been considering what his particular contribution to Britain's political history would be, and when the senior officials of the Treasury (by convention anonymous) were growing seriously worried about Britain's economic stagnation. Dr. Adenauer's invitation of Mr. Macmillan to Bonn, in late summer, 1960, marked a new beginning on the diplomatic stage. Opinion in Whitehall suffered a landslide in the autumn and winter, and Mr. Macmillan's meeting with President Kennedy in January, 1961, seems to have clinched matters in the Prime Minister's mind. The Cabinet's formal decision was probably taken only shortly before the announcement of July 31, 1961: But by that time, the stage had been set so effectively that it would have taken a weak Prime Minister indeed not to be able to force his Cabinet's resolve along lines he thought right.

Thus, on July 31, 1961, Mr. Macmillan announced in the House of Commons that:

> Her Majesty's Government have come to the conclusion that it would be right for Britain to make a formal application under Article 237 of the Treaty for negotiations with a view to joining the Community if satisfactory arrangements can be made to meet the special needs of the United Kingdom, of the Commonwealth, and of the European Free Trade Association.

On August 3, the House of Commons approved this decision (by a vote of 313 to 5, with the bulk of the Labour Party abstaining) and accepted the government's undertaking:

> no agreement affecting these special interests or involving British sovereignty will be entered into until it has been approved by this House after full consultation with other Commonwealth countries, by whatever procedure they may generally agree.

On August 9, Britain formally applied for membership, and on August 10, Denmark did the same; Ireland had already applied on July 31, and in the summer of 1962 Norway followed suit. In October, 1961, the neutral states of EFTA, Austria, Sweden, and Switzerland jointly announced their wish to negotiate not for membership, but for association with the Community. Turkey had already applied for association earlier in the year. In fact, since Spain and Portugal, embarrassingly, also made applications in 1962, only Finland and Iceland of all the European countries listed on p. 9 have made no formal application to the Community.

On September 27, the Council of Ministers of the Community replied to the British and Danish applications, unanimously approving their requests for negotiations. But for the benefit of all applicants, the Ministers stated expressly that:

> application by a country for membership of the Community implied unreserved recognition of the aims and rules of the Treaty as well as accession to the two other existing Communities.

On October 10, Mr. Heath, now in effect Minister for European Relations, analogous to the Secretary of State for Commonwealth Relations, duly appeared in Paris at a meeting of representatives of the six member states. In a long declaration, couched very much in the idiom of the Community, he declared that the United Kingdom wished "to join in the bold and imaginative venture of the Six" and insisted that the United Kingdom was ready to play its full part in the institutions of the Community. He particularly referred to "the progress of the Six toward greater unity in fields other than those covered by the EEC Treaty"—meaning, of course, above all in the political field. Mr. Heath explicitly referred to the Bonn declaration of July, 1961, when the Six had decided to "enable a statutory character to be given to the union of their peoples" and stressed that:

> the British Government shared the aims and objectives of those who had drawn up the Bonn declaration and would be anxious, once they had joined the Community, to work with the Six in a positive spirit to reinforce the unity they had already achieved.

Satisfactory solutions would, however, have to be found to the three problems of Commonwealth trade, United Kingdom agriculture, and EFTA. But he felt that these could be dealt with by protocols, and should not call for amendment to any of the articles of the Treaty, though some articles would, of course, require adaptation consequent upon the admission of new members. In the case of the Commonwealth, he thought some countries might want "a suitable form of association with the Community," though others might need different solutions for their problems. The United Kingdom was ready to participate with the Six in a common agricultural policy, though an adequate transitional period might be required to safeguard the essential interests of British farming and horticulture. As for EFTA, his statement that "it had always been the British view that the present division of Western Europe into two economic groups should be brought to an end" may have sounded a little odd to some of his hearers; but he felt it necessary to remind them of the decision that the EFTA ministers had reached—very much against the advice of the British civil service—in June, when they agreed to maintain EFTA "until satisfactory arrangements had been worked out . . . to meet the various legitimate interests of all the members of the European Free Trade Association, and thus enable them all to participate from the same date in an integrated European market."

For the rest, Mr. Heath envisaged no major problems. Britain was ready to accept the structure of the common external tariff and saw no need for an item-by-item renegotiation. He did foresee, however, that tariff levels would have to be lowered to satisfy GATT and third countries: He favored a uniform cut, with special treatment for some items. He also agreed that the United Kingdom would at one fell swoop reduce the tariff against her Community partners by whatever percentage they had reduced theirs against each other—obviously at least 40 per cent—and would be willing to join Euratom and the Coal and Steel Community.

First Reactions in Europe

The immediate Continental reaction to Mr. Macmillan's announcement of July 31 was one of public enthusiasm in Holland,

Germany, Belgium, and Italy—very roughly in that order of warmth. Public opinion in France seemed a little more reserved; and both French government and business circles, and also many in the ranks of the Community's officials, felt qualms and misgivings. "An elephant cannot get into a bathtub": However sincerely she might wish to, Britain by definition cannot join the Six. And so there are fears that the Community will be a totally different thing once Britain is in.

French Political Preoccupations. "Of all the forms of integration," President de Gaulle is credited with having said, "I like best the Europe of the Six. But the others seem determined to bring in Britain." Certainly it looks as though the French President has been caught in a dilemma by refusing to believe for so long that the British might actually apply for membership in the Community. President de Gaulle's European policy has been one of purely confederal arrangements: Yet once the Irish and the Danes, the Norwegians and the British take part, what remains of the Europe that was to bolster France's position in the world? How will these intergovernmental consultations differ in intensity and effectiveness from the hundreds of others going on every year all over the world? De Gaulle's conception of Europe made Europe easier for the British Government to accept. Now British adherence may not only put an end to his hopes of hegemony in Europe, but may even dilute Europe to the point of emptying it of significance for world power politics.

This line of thought is followed through by those French civil servants who believe in playing the game for the same stakes as they played it in and after the Free Trade Area negotiations: They would like to bypass the British application if they could, to annul a victory over Britain which they never wanted, which some of them tried to prevent, and in which, up to the last, some of them had hopefully refused to believe. One can imagine what their tactics would be if they could determine French negotiating policy. Obviously, they could not torpedo the talks. The free world cannot afford ill will in Western Europe, and the Community itself would be severely threatened if France were to reject Britain obviously on any terms. But the negotiations could perhaps be diverted. French officials have already sought to play some Commonwealth countries against Britain as Britain has played Germany against France. (One of them even claims to have had a hand in organizing Mr. Sandys' reception in the Antipodes in July, 1961.) Again, Britain's economic incentives to join might also be reduced if world measures could be initiated to stabilize the pound sterling. Perhaps the Community could be induced to pay in cash for measures that, in effect, would keep Britain out. Once more, as in 1958, the tactics could be to drown in Atlantic or world economic discussions Britain's own particular concern to find a settlement with the Six. At the same time, the terms might be made so stiff, and the negotiations so protracted, that the British Government would be worn down in a war of nerves and abandon its attempt to force its way into the Community.

French Economic Interests. The terms, in that case, are likely to concern mainly the economic aspects of the question. For the qualms felt by many French civil servants and diplomats are also shared by French business circles. French employers had from the beginning insisted on a dual balance within the Treaty: The liberalization of trade in agricultural produce must keep step with that in industrial goods, and progress toward harmonized internal policies must keep step with progress toward Community free trade. In principle, the *Patronat* would thus like to see another acceleration of the Treaty, but only if agricultural and other common policy measures were accelerated alongside tariff disarmament. The swiftness of the British application really took the *Patronat* by surprise. They feared that decisions on common policies might be held over until Britain is in—and this fear was shared particularly by French agriculture. (The peasant riots of the early summer, painted by some British newspapers as a revolt against the Common Market, were, on the contrary, a protest against the delays in implementing it.) Both agriculture and industry fear that concessions might be made that would give special privileges to the Commonwealth and thus restrict the outlets for French agricultural production and give British industry access to cheaper food and raw materials than the French can obtain.

If the conditions are satisfactory, however, only particular branches of French industry—tractor producers threatened by British competition, and papermakers threatened by Scandinavian competition—might feel seriously opposed to an enlargement of the Community. British competition would be appreciable, but the British market would also become more accessible, while, on the whole, French industry is by now confident enough. Only if the pound were devalued (as was the franc on the eve of the first tariff reductions) would French industry really feel insecure.

The Spirit of the Community. Over and above French civil servants and businessmen, the other group that had strong reservations about Britain's application was to be found among the enthusiastic champions of the Community as a political enterprise. They fear that for Britain this is an economic scheme and that she will veto its political development. Nevertheless, some federalists, and notably such dynamic Europeans as M. Jean Monnet and his Action Committee, have welcomed the British candidature wholeheartedly, because they have always considered Britain essential to their enterprise and because they believe that, however grudging Britain's acceptance of the political implications of the Treaty may be today, she will play the game once she is in. All the positive reasons that make her join will make her realize that she, too, requires a Community with strong institutions, above all at times when she feels economically or financially weak. Once the context of Britain's problems becomes European, British thinking will become European too.

But there are others who regret Britain's application because they fear that, whether the negotiations fail or succeed, the Community's character will be transformed. If the negotiations fail, the Dutch and the Germans, while they will hardly renounce the Treaty, may well cease to implement it in the spirit of loyalty and goodwill without which it would be unworkable. During the time of the negotiations, the Six and Britain would have grown so many political and economic tissues into each other, that a break would mean open wounds on both sides. But what if Britain joins? Mr. Macmillan has spoken of guiding the Community from the inside. It is not surprising that French and Community officials feel that they have done sufficiently well without British guidance and against British opposition, and that guidance ill becomes those who have just landed themselves in an unenviable economic situation. Indeed, those who built the Community as a racing car to keep up with the Eastern bloc are unhappy that it may now be thumbed as an ambulance to pick up the "British invalid."

The French, and other Europeans, must anticipate the internal institutional problems created by British, Danish, Irish, and Norwegian adherence. Hitherto, the Germans have tended to give a little more than they took in Franco-German compromises: And these, in turn, have rarely encountered serious opposition from the rest of the Six. This process will be upset by the new membership, and majorities will become more unpredictable and less easy to handle. As a result, the common policies may take longer to formulate and go less far. The West does not have much time to overhaul its economic structure and intensify its productive efforts: It would be disastrous, they fear, if all the plans of the Community were held up for months or years, before and after British adherence, by attempts to fit too many countries into a looser mold.

Such, roughly, are the main misgivings on the Continent. No one wants the negotiations to break up: But in the last resort, it was Britain who asked for them to begin. It is not that the Six have failed and have asked Britain to rescue them; the Six have been conspicuously successful, and Britain, after disdaining membership for so long, is now asking to be let in. It is Britain, therefore, and not France, who will be asked to pay the price: And on the whole, it is France and the Community, rather than Britain, who can afford to wait for the price to be agreed. The plain fact is that in economic terms Britain is negotiating from tactical weakness.

That, perhaps, is the least reason—but it is still an additional reason—why Britain must think about the Community in political terms. In a sense, it is almost a pity that there may be economic advantages for her in joining it. True, without these—and without her economic embarrassment—the country might never have become interested in the first place. But now that public discussion has turned from the profits of cucumber-growers to the institutional politics of the question, it is time to relegate both the economics and the constitutional law to where they belong: They are important only in so far as they impinge on Britain's and Europe's role in the world at large.

Economically, at least in the short term, there may not be very much that Britain is able to offer. But if Britain talks politics, she can bargain from strength. *Il faut prendre les choses par le grand bout.* Only if Britain treats her entry into the Common Market as a momentous political step—for herself, for the Six, and for the rest of the world—will it offer her not simply a shelter from the harsh winds of economic change or an acclimatization chamber to it, but a key position from which to contribute to the political and economic future of the world as a whole.

The Brussels Negotiations

The negotiations began in earnest in the rue des Quatre Bras, in Brussels, on November 8. Formally, this was a negotiation between Britain (the applicant) on the one side, and the six present member states on the other, with the Commission (representing the Community as distinct from the separate interests of each of its member states) sitting in with the right to speak.

The talks were carried on at three levels. At the top level were the Ministers: M. Couve de Murville, the Foreign Minister of France, M. Spaak of Belgium, M. Luns of Holland, M. Bech of Luxembourg, though other ministers from these countries also sometimes came in. Italy was represented by Signor Colombo, the Minister of Trade, while Dr. Erhard, the Deputy-Chancellor and Minister of Economics, and Dr. Rolf Lahr of the German Foreign Office, were the chief German representatives. The British Minister was the Lord Privy Seal, though Mr. Duncan Sandys, as Secretary of State for Commonwealth Relations and the Colonies, and Mr. Christopher Soames, as Minister of Agriculture, also attended on occasion. These Ministerial meetings were held roughly once a month, for two days or so at a time, until summer, 1962, when the pace quickened.

Below the ministers came their deputies: to the Permanent Representatives of the Six in Brussels was added Sir Pierson Dixon, British Ambassador in Paris, while in his absence Sir Eric Roll, of the Ministry of Agriculture, carried on the negotiations at this level. The deputies met in the middle of almost every week, from November until the summer. On a third level came various expert working parties to deal with different problems—tropical produce and the Association, Asian manufactures, agriculture, and so forth.

Outside these formal multilateral negotiations there were of course constant bilateral contacts—at the summit (when Mr. Macmillan paid a weekend visit to President de Gaulle at the Chateau de Champs, at the beginning of June), at ministerial level (as when Mr. Heath repeatedly toured the capitals of the Six), and at deputy and official level between national delegations and between the delegations and the Commission and its staff.

From November, 1961, until May, 1962, this negotiating machinery was warming up. Problems had to be defined, statistics and other information had to be assembled—and only then could the real process of bargaining begin. The British delegation, apprehensive at first of stalling by the French (or possibly even by the Commission) found that their negotiating partners in fact exploited none of the opportunities for delay or sabotage that presented themselves, and the Commission's staff appeared to be working genuinely toward bringing Britain in, provided the Community's rules and spirit were respected. (When the smoke from Continental cigars and British pipes in the conference room led the British to demand open windows while the negotiators of the Six preferred centrally heated fog, the Commission, transcending cross-channel differences with an integrative gesture, had air-conditioning installed.)

Some people, perhaps, were growing impatient with the length of time needed for this preparatory phase: But the Commission had a good many other things to worry about. In spite of overwork, it was disinclined (even if it could have found the money and the right people) to increase its staff to deal with this bulge in its work—particularly since new member states, which would in any case claim posts in the Community's civil service when the bulge of work might be over, were about to make their appearance. The decisions on the agriculture of the Six, on cartels, on the passage to the second stage, and on yet another acceleration of the Treaty, were being taken during this period: Major negotiations for a new Convention were going on with the African Associates; tariff negotiations with the United States as part of the "Dillon round" went on until January 1962; and the opening of negotiations with Ireland, Denmark and Norway, no less than applications from Austria, Switzerland, Sweden (and later even from Spain and Portugal) had to be considered. Indeed, the manifold problems of the Community's external relations all seemed to converge on it at once.

Moreover, it must be remembered that the Rome Treaty had taken nearly two years to negotiate—from its inception at Messina to its signature on the Capitol—though the problems then were comparatively homogeneous and mainly intra-European, though the negotiators began more or less with a *tabula rasa* where rules and institutions were concerned, and though there was a single politician to act as driving force. The British negotiations, on the other hand, have hinged mainly on the problems of some 600 or 700 million people spread over five continents, and have concerned the merging, reconciliation, or adaptation of two complicated agricultural and trading systems. Thus even the technical phase of defining the problems was necessarily a lengthy one.

But Britain's Commonwealth links also posed a far more fundamental problem. The British application suddenly compelled the Six to face the whole problem of their external relations—particularly their foreign economic policy, which the progress of the Treaty of Rome had not yet posed with such acuteness, and on which they had had very little need to define their attitude before. What some thought of as a problem of fitting Britain into the Community structure turned into a problem of fitting the Community into the whole structure of the world economy. (The dialectic by which the problem was thus transformed was closely allied to the way in which the German problem had, fifteen years before, raised the problem of European unity—a dialectic which we traced earlier in this book.) Britain demanded special conditions that would have created a preferential relationship with overseas Commonwealth countries. Such a relationship might be acceptable to the Six and to the contracting parties of GATT where 60 million Africans were concerned, but a preference for 700 million Asians, Canadians, multi-racial societies in Africa, and inhabitants of the Antipodes was a totally different matter. The Six had, earlier and largely in response to the British Free-Trade Areas proposals, formulated the doctrine of non-discrimination between third countries. From this antithesis between intra-Commonwealth arrangements and extra-Community nondiscrimination, there was only one logical way out: to submerge Britain's preferential demands for trade guarantees into worldwide solutions to worldwide trade problems. It is hardly surprising if, for this purpose, the negotiations proved too restricted, the partners too few, and the time too short.

When the expert groups had finished their examination of specific problems, the Deputies, in May, presented the Ministers with their report, defining problems and setting out a range of possible solutions. From that moment on, the negotiations changed gear: The process of bargaining could begin. The Commission, acting—as it had to—for the exising Community rather than for an enlarged Community not yet in existence, at this stage necessarily receded in importance; and the negotiations in fact came to be conducted in two dimensions: between Britain and the Six, then among the Six themselves, and then again between the Six and Britain. No small part of the time involved, and no small share of the frictions that have arisen, were due to disagreements among the Six. Faced with British demands, they felt it vital to present a united front toward the applicant state; and it is no wonder that the negotiations did not go too smoothly, since, once the Six had reached a compromise among themselves, a reopening of discussion would cause immense complications each time.

Time, on the other hand, is not on Britain's side. Mr. Heath, pressed by domestic deadlines, chiefly the Prime Ministers' Conference set for September 10, asked for an outline of the whole "package deal" to be ready by the end of July—August being a summer month in which all the harrassed officials, let alone their masters, felt they needed their long-deserved rest, while the Commonwealth Governments were to be given that month to study the outline.

The British negotiators were of course in a difficult position. They were asking, at one and the same time, for Britain to join the club, for special exceptions to the rules to be made in her favor (or more particularly in favor of her overseas family), and for certain of the rules of the club in effect to be changed also for its founder-members. It is a pity that the British Government did not feel able to go into the negotiations without too many prior pledges and seek to solve more of the special problems after entry, rather than before. It could also be asked whether under the circumstances it was wise to impose deadlines on the negotiations. But in fact there was never meant to be a time limit in the sense that, if it were exceeded, Britain would withdraw her application. The end of July proved one of those deadlines that have been used in the Community's negotiations before —deadlines that were broken, but had their effect nonetheless in speeding negotiations: The ordeal by night-session (based on the same principle as the old confinement of a jury), by changing the rhythm of negotiation, largely changes its character.

The negotiations came to a head at the end of July and in the first few days of August, culminating in an all-night session that lasted until 7:30 A.M. on the morning of Sunday, August 5. There was speculation at the time that the French had deliberately launched a torpedo that night, and others surmised that the suspension of talks was on the contrary a long-planned trap for the French engineered by Mr. Heath, who wished to hamstring debate in the Commonwealth Prime Ministers' Conference and in the party conferences, by leaving the final terms of accession uncertain. Neither view seems borne out by the evidence. It had, in fact, become abundantly clear a week or two before that much would have to be left over, that there was no chance of tying up a neat package before the holidays, and when disagreements between the Six as to the interpretation of one of their own earlier decisions on the financing of the Agricultural Fund cut across the discussion of temperate foodstuffs, physical exhaustion before the intellectual and diplomatic complications of the whole matter made a suspension of the talks until the autumn seem almost inevitable.

The Partial Package Deal of Conditions

Between May and August, a good deal was in fact achieved, and the greater part of the "outline package" has become clear. On so many different issues of such immense complexity, it would have been impossible to take all decisions simultaneously in one final session, yet compromises on one issue were naturally to be offset by compromises on another. Decisions were therefore taken one by one on different issues. Until the over-all decision as to whether Britain should join or not is taken, all these decisions on particular methods of solving the problems arising from Britain's entry must of course be regarded as provisional. But it would be foolhardy to think of them as much more provisional than that: To reopen any part of the agreements already reached might well lead others to reopen other issues and thus place the whole package deal in jeopardy.

Africa and the Caribbean. The British Government felt particular pride in having persuaded the Six to offer Association not only to the bulk of British colonial possessions, but also to most of the newly independent countries of Africa and the Caribbean. In spite of misgivings on the part of the present Associates of the Community (who are worried about the dilution of their trade and aid privileges) the Six are thus willing to give Associate status to Nigeria, Ghana, Sierra Leone, Tanganyika, Jamaica, and Trinidad, with a joint population of 60 million, as well as a long list of British colonies. The question of associating the Federation of Rhodesia and Nyasaland was held over for future decision.

Asia. It was agreed that comprehensive trade agreements should be concluded between the enlarged Community and India, Pakistan, and Ceylon at the latest by the end of 1966: Their object would be to "develop trade and so maintain and increase the foreign exchange earnings of these countries and in general to facilitate the implementation of their development plans." These trade agreements would cover tariffs, quotas, export policies, the promotion of private investment, and the provision of technical aid.

In the meantime—in other words for a period hardly likely to be longer than the three years from 1964 to 1967—the Six are already making advance concessions to India, Pakistan, and Ceylon. The 18 per cent common tariff on tea would be abolished, though nothing has been said on consumption taxes on tea. Just how important tea is in this context—particularly to Ceylon—can be seen from the fact that it accounts for 62 per cent of Ceylon's exports, and for 19 per cent of India's. The Six would also abolish the external tariff on a few minor manufactures, notably sports goods. (They hardly have much to lose by allowing cricket bats into Europe duty-free.) Jute is already imported into the Community free of duty, but special arrangements would be made for jute goods. The Community has agreed to suspend the duty on cashew nuts, and Britain has asked for nil duties on some other products, such as hand-knotted carpets, coir matting, and East India kips (which are partly tanned hides).

More important among manufactures are textiles, which at the moment enter Britain duty-free, but on which there is an agreed export quota. The Community's common external tariff of 18 per cent is to be imposed by Britain when the common external tariff comes to be fully applied throughout the Community—presumably at the latest by 1970; in the meantime, Britain is allowed a slower rate of adaptation of her tariff than that laid down in the Treaty: a fifth (roughly 3.5 per cent) on accession, another fifth eighteen months later, another 30 per cent a year after. But "the enlarged Community would take steps without delay to restore the situation" if, as a result of the progressive application of the common external tariff by the United Kingdom, exports to the Community were to decline. The United Kingdom would restrict its imports of cotton textiles to about the present level, while the Six would increase theirs in accordance with the Geneva agreement on the subject.

Manufactures from Canada, Australia, and New Zealand. Compared with the Treaty, which demands a 60 per cent adaptation of national tariffs to the common tariff by the beginning of 1966, Britain will apply 30 per cent of that tariff on accession, and 30 per cent from the beginning of 1967, the full tariff being applied from 1970 onward. Consultations are provided for in 1966, and in 1969, prior to the second and third phases in applying the common tariff, in case there should be violent dislocation of trade.

Raw materials and canned and processed foodstuffs. Britain has asked for nil tariffs for a whole list of raw materials (most of them metals) including, notably, aluminum, lead, zinc, woodpulp and newsprint. The Community has just reduced its aluminum tariff from 10 to 9 per cent: In essence, this is a battle between Aluminum Ltd., of Canada on the one side, and Pechiney on the other—though there is of course a general case for the free importation of raw materials. Britain has also asked for a nil tariff on canned and processed foods (of particular interest to Australia). The decisions on these matters remain to be taken.

Temperate Agriculture. The enlarged Community, as the most important food producer in the world, would take an early initiative to secure worldwide agreements covering the main agricultural products. These agreements would cover not only minimum and maximum quantities to enter into international trade and the price policy to be pursued by importing and exporting countries, but also production policy, stock-piling, and the special problems of trade with developing countries. Subject to revision every three years, the purpose of these agreements would be to work out the most suitable structure of international trade to ensure an agreed balance between the interests of consumers and producers. The Community formally recognized that its own price policy would be of particular importance to exporting countries, and that the Community must pursue a reasonable price policy, balancing the interests of European agriculture (wanting a high price and production level) with the harmonious development of world trade (which could be disrupted by too high a price and production level in Europe). "Confrontations" with the policies of other producers (including, notably, Commonwealth countries) would help keep this balance, and the Community would explicitly pledge itself to offer reasonable opportunities for overseas exporters in the Community market; quantitative restrictions would, of course, be imposed only in the event of grave disturbance.

For some time, the fate of the negotiations seemed to hinge on the "missing link" of what might happen between 1970, when the transition period for the Community's agriculture is over, and the conclusion of world agreements, should these not have been concluded earlier. Then the Community, while maintaining in form its nondiscrimination between third countries, made a concession in the procedural substance: Failing the conclusion of such world agreements, "the Community reaffirmed their readiness to conclude agreements for the same purpose with those countries who wished to do so, and, in particular, with Commonwealth countries." The Community recognized that New

Zealand might well face special difficulties, and expressed its readiness to consider granting special provisions to deal with them.

For the transition period, until these worldwide agreements (or failing them these Community-Commonwealth agreements) are concluded, a framework has been agreed upon for dealing with those commodities for which the common agricultural policy entails intra-Community preference; on cereals, this preference might not be applied in full by Britain, and if sudden and considerable alterations in trade patterns were to occur, its working would be reviewed.

Where the problems of the United Kingdom's own farming community are concerned, the Six have agreed to an "annual review" and a general assurance to farmers of fair standards of living in addition to the common agricultural policy. The details of how the British system of farm support is to be adapted to the common farm policy of the Six remain to be worked out—particularly on those aspects where the common policy of the Six has not yet taken final shape. How the decision of January, 1962—on the financing of the common farm policy (see p. 35 above)—is to be interpreted, is a subject still under dispute among the Six: France claims that all the proceeds of the common levy should go to finance the Community's agricultural policy, while Germany and Belgium, as big food importers, are on the British side. In fact, before the negotiations adjourned on August 5, the French made their agreement to the provisions on temperate agriculture, subject to the others adopting their view on the financing of the Community farm policy.

Further Problems

What has been agreed so far, then, is part of an "outline package." A good deal of the agreement consists simply in an agreement to try to agree with third parties hereafter. Even where outline agreement has been reached on substance, the broad phrases must still be translated into detailed legal drafting. Again, the "outline package" as such is incomplete: Even on the purely economic side, a number of important questions remain unsolved—be it certain items in the common external tariff, the opportunity for certain countries to be associated, or the finance of agricultural policy. And beyond the questions that are tabled, and on which there is as yet no agreement, there are others, which have not even been discussed—some of which, indeed, may never be discussed at all until a final decision has been taken. In some cases it is perhaps wise that they have not been raised explicitly at the negotiating table: These are matters which, by their nature, can no more be settled in advance than some of those which have been the subject of negotiations. The monetary issue—the consequences on the Community and on the Sterling Area of Britain's role in both—may be the most important of the economic problems on which there has been some thinking outside the negotiations, but little or no talk at the conference table.

But beyond straight economics, there are other important issues. Britain has formally made her entry into the Community dependent on the participation of her EFTA partners in an integrated market with the Community from the same date as herself. This might mean holding up British membership not only until Denmark and Norway have become members, and until the Community has decided whether Ireland should become a member, or be offered only Associate status, but also until the three neutrals have settled their relationship with the EEC. Austria will pose no particular problems, for everyone knows that she would wish to be a member if only the interpretation placed by the Soviet Union on the State Treaty would allow it. Sweden pleads a nonalignment maintained partly for the sake of Finland, which is thought to be compatible with Associate status, though membership is said to violate it. And Switzerland regards membership as incompatible both with her traditional neutrality (important in the days of Franco-German rivalry, but rather different in function today) and also with her system of direct democracy by referendum on economic matters. Whether Association under Article 238 is really the answer for states which do not intend to join eventually, and whether Association is preferable to comprehensive trade agreements on a most-favored nation basis is thus one of the main problems that will have to be solved before Britain's EFTA mortgage is finally liquidated.

Until the number of countries that will join the Community with Britain is settled, it will be difficult to determine finally the institutional adaptations required by Britain's own entry into the Community: And these adaptations in turn will be vital for the future development of the enlarged Community as a whole. Numbers in the Assembly and in the Economic and Social Council are a straightforward problem. An increase in the size of the Commission to twelve, for instance, might be tolerable without diluting the collegiate solidarity of the chief motor in the institutional machinery, or else a reshuffle of Commissioners could avoid even that. It is the voting rules in an enlarged Council of Ministers that would pose the really crucial problems.

Wherever the unanimity rule applies, the larger the number of states, the greater is the likelihood of a veto, whatever the political character of the new members may be. Will the Six in the future allow their progress in all the matters that call for unanimity to be held up by Ireland or by Norway? Or will the unanimity rule have to be replaced by a very rigorous near-unanimity rule that would deprive Luxembourg, Ireland, Norway, and Denmark (or any other country of less than, say, nine million inhabitants) of the power of unilateral veto? Or will the Six, to avoid this possible dilution of their dynamism, refuse to accept some of the smaller countries as members at all?

Where the qualified majority rule obtains, while Britain must be given equivalence with the three big founder-members, EFTA must obviously be prevented from having a joint veto. If three other States (Ireland, Denmark, and Norway) were to join simultaneously with the United Kingdom, one solution might be to give the three smaller new members one vote each—after all, none of them has more than half the population of Holland, which has only two votes. Then a qualified majority of 16 out of 24 would leave the new members, even in alliance with Luxembourg, unable to thwart the other five founder-members—though any other founder-member if agreed with the new EFTA members could exercise a veto. But all these are problems that have not yet been broached.

It is when we turn from these institutional questions to a yet wider one, that of political union, that there arises a further query—one that was indeed posed in no uncertain terms at the end of August, 1962, by Dr. Adenauer. In a much publicized television interview, he welcomed Britain's entry into the Common Market, but stated that her entry into the proposed political union was a separate issue: And he quoted no less an authority than Mr. Macmillan on this point. The resulting storm was instructive from more than one point of view.

There is, in fact, a very general problem to be faced (which is likely to get worse before it gets any better) when politicians speak in one country and forget that other countries are listening, and when people listen to what is being said in another country before they fully understand the context and the political idiom in which it is being said. Dr. Adenauer might well accuse the British Government of double-talk; in June, in reply to a question in the House of Commons asking the Prime Minister if he would make it perfectly clear that, whatever the outcome of negotiations on the Common Market, Britain would never go into a European political union, Mr. Macmillan had replied: "No. I think that is perfectly correct. We are discussing the question of entering the Common Market." Yet, in April, Mr. Heath had specifically stated that Britain would want to enter the political union at the same time as she entered the Common Market, and it was after this declaration that the Belgians and Dutch put a stop to the talks on political union. The suspicion that Britain had meant this declaration as a torpedo of the talks and had lost interest now that it had served its purpose was unfounded, but Dr. Adenauer could be forgiven if it crossed his mind, given the Prime Minister's categorical statement in the House.

There followed, immediately, a misunderstanding in the opposite direction—with even some British newspapers whose reporting is normally reliable suggesting that Dr. Adenauer had asked for Britain not to join the Economic Community, but to become only an Associate Member. But what seems more significant was the protest, which was heard in Britain even after the confusion between the existing Community and the plans for political union discussed in the Fouchet-Cattani Committee had been cleared up. A year before, the general climate of opinion had been that British entry into the Community was purely on the economic plane, and that of course she would take no part in any political union: her foreign policy was her own, and the distinction between the Economic Community and political schemes was vital. By August, 1962, Dr. Adenauer's statement that these were two distinct issues was regarded as an insult, not least by those uncommitted to Britain's entry into the Community.

One may well ask if such a sudden doctrine of inseparability is not in fact premature. It may help, in some respects, to demonstrate the political will to join the Six, but it raises other complications. Dr. Adenauer, preoccupied with the Berlin crisis and with the little time he has left to lay the foundations for a political union, cannot be expected to hold up everything until Britain has taken her decision—particularly if lengthy further negotiations and a general election are envisaged here. The Europeans in general, believing that a common foreign policy can be based only on a community of outlook, may well wonder if Britain is yet ready for joint foreign policies; and there may be no particular need to transfer more than one function to the same supranational institution at the same time.

The Commonwealth Conference

In accordance with its undertaking to consult the Commonwealth countries before a final decision is taken, the government summoned a Commonwealth Prime Ministers' Conference to meet at Marlborough House, in London, from September 10, 1962. The Conference was opened by the Prime Minister, with a speech couched in highly political terms, justifying Britain's entry into the Community not least for the sake of the Commonwealth's economic development. It was a notable departure from precedent that each national delegation held its own briefing of the press, so that the proceedings might almost as well have taken place in public: From a discreet club of gentlemen, the Conference turned almost into a miniature United Nations, with governments addressing much of their comment not only at each other, but also at their national electorates at home: And so, in some respects, the fact that several of the Prime Ministers were in a shaky domestic situation did not help the progress of the Conference.

The British Government came in for heavy fire from Canada,

less from Australia, and least of the three from New Zealand—a reversal of the order of magnitude of what each of these three Dominions has to lose. All three maintained that the terms so far agreed were too vague and did not guarantee them outlets comparable to those they at present enjoy. Nothing had been agreed with the Six on sugar or meat—though New Zealand seemed quite prepared to pay a 20 per cent tariff on mutton and lamb, provided there were no quantitative restrictions, and that Britain now did away with her subsidies protecting British farmers against New Zealand. Mr. Holyoake also wanted quantitative assurances on butter and cheese, where he felt higher prices would not compensate for any marked fall in quantities sold.

Of the three big Asian Commonwealth countries, Ceylon (whose main exports are rubber and tea) was largely unaffected by the Community's external tariff under the provisional package deal, but expressed solidarity with the criticism voiced by Mr. Nehru and President Ayub Khan. They suggested that negotiation of the comprehensive trade agreements must begin immediately, and that the common external tariff should not be applied by Britain on Asian exports until the comprehensive agreements were in force. The agreements themselves must provide reasonable outlets for Asian manufactures—with Pakistan objecting to quota restrictions on cotton textiles, while India was prepared to see agreement upon something like the present voluntary quota system, with the United Kingdom applied to the enlarged Community as a whole. They asked for the abolition of the external tariff on certain items important for Asian economies, but of little significance to the European importing countries, and in general expressed their fears that domestic pressures might lead the enlarged Community to maintain a protectionism that would hamper their industrialization and make it difficult for them to service their debts—thus hamstringing their Five-Year Plans.

The African and Caribbean countries, on the other hand, were sharply divided. The Prime Minister of Trinidad and Tobago repeatedly declared that an economically weak Britain was of no use to his country, and that after the Conference, he would fly to Brussels to see if Trinidad could become an associate even if Britain failed to join the Community. The Federation of Rhodesia and Nyasaland (to which, for political reasons, association has not yet been offered by the Six) asked to become an associate. As had been expected, Ghana, a country which already sends more of her exports to the Community than to the United Kingdom, declared that she would have no truck with the Community. The fact that Nigeria and Tanganyika took up the same attitude was a source of considerable disappointment, though Sierra Leone, like Jamaica, reserved her position. It seems that the Nigerians, at least, conceded the economic generosity of association, but feared that it implied an unacceptable political link with former colonial powers, and that it discriminated between associated and non-associated underdeveloped countries. Mr. Goka, representing Ghana in Dr. Nkrumah's absence, also claimed that association perpetuated a division of labor between Europe and Africa that would keep Africa an extension of Europe.

Among the other Commonwealth countries, the Malayan delegate proved particularly friendly to the Government, stressing that if entry were required for Britain's economic and political strength, then the Commonwealth should not challenge her decision; Archbishop Makarios neither accepted nor rejected the notion of association, but pointed out the importance of the Community market for Cyprus; and the Prime Minister of Malta declared that he would probably seek association whether Britain entered the Community or not.

After several days of plenary sessions, the Conference broke up into specialized committees to examine different problems, and then, after some tense negotiations at the end, issued an agreed *communiqué*. This squarely declared that "the responsibility for the final decision would rest with the British Government"—in other words that the mother country, too, could exercise self-determination, and then listed the main preoccupations of the overseas Commonwealth countries. These proved to be in no sense a common alternative plan, but a series of purely unilateral shopping lists. No mention was made of another Prime Ministers' Conference after the final terms for British entry into the Community had become known, and no promises were made by the British Government that would tie its hands in future negotiations, let alone involve the reopening of such parts of the "package" as had already been agreed upon.

But the most significant part of the *communiqué* lay in its acceptance of the four aims outlined by the British Government to the Conference: to expand world trade, to improve the organization of world markets for agricultural produce, to secure better trade opportunities for developing countries, and to regulate food-surplus disposal to help people in need. These four aims are a far cry from the parochial preoccupations with British horticulture of a year before and evidence of the mutually educative nature of the Brussels negotiations, which, from the Community's agricultural thesis and the British and Commonwealth antithesis, had led to concepts on a world scale. And the adoption of these ideas by the Prime Ministers' Conference, implying unambiguously, as they do, the submergence of the Commonwealth's preferential system in worldwide nondiscrimination, demonstrates the repercussions that the "ferment of change," introduced into the world with the Community concept, seems capable of producing well beyond the confines of Europe itself. Whether Britain joins the Common Market or not, we shall never be able to think of the Commonwealth in the same discriminatory Ottawa terms again: The very logic Britain has used to defend it before the Community has forced her into the nondiscriminatory defense of non-Commonwealth countries faced with analogous problems. It is thus not only the trading policy of the Six, but also those of the Commonwealth, that have taken a knock in the intellectual collision between the two—yet another example of the tendency that once change begins, once vested interests clash and are forced to face general reappraisal, the result of such a challenge is likely to be a less irrational state of affairs than the original one.

That is where the story of negotiations must for the moment be left. Clearly, the agreement—as it stands at the moment of writing—is not precise enough for anyone to say in detail what the effects on the rest of the world will be if Britain joins the Community. The package is naturally at its most precise where it concerns the African and Caribbean countries that wish to take advantage of the offer of association: Community relations with Africa constitute a problem which the Six have faced since 1957, and with which they now have five years' experience. But if Nigeria and East Africa maintain their rejection of the offer, then, indeed, the future is uncertain. If, as a result, the preferential aspects of association are attenuated, and if world-wide arrangements for tropical produce are entered into more speedily than would otherwise have been the case, then the upshot could even be a not unwelcome one from a world point of view.

In the case of India, Pakistan, and Ceylon, the agreement consists, in effect, in a guarantee of at least present export earnings, coupled with a resolve to agree with these countries on more far-reaching arrangements within the next four years. Since here the objectives are well defined, the issues relatively straightforward, and the partners to the agreements known, there is no reason why negotiations to fill in these details should not begin as soon as possible. It may be argued that the later the agreements are concluded, the more generous will they be, both for economic and for political reasons, in particular because the Community's commercial policy can be decided by qualified majority as of the beginning of 1966, so that any particularly protectionist country can then be overruled. This certainly was what the Indians had in mind in asking for grants to be made by 1967. But revision clauses, inserted in an agreement reached before then, could leave the way open for increasing liberality in both trade and aid, as the Six and Britain gain confidence and their sense of responsibility grows. The sooner these countries can feel assured of the intentions and the performance of an enlarged Community toward them, the better.

Inevitably, most vague of the three is the provisional agreement to deal with Australia's and Canada's main problem—temperate foodstuffs. For New Zealand, special arrangements are to be worked out in Brussels as part of the package deal before the provisional agreement is considered complete. Fortunately, Canada and Australia, like New Zealand, are rich countries, with standards of living higher than those in the United Kingdom or in the Six, and neither is at all heavily dependent on the United Kingdom market. (That is no argument for not safeguarding their interests, but it is an argument for their nerve not giving way if their demands for guarantees of a kind they have never been given by the United Kingdom are not immediately met by the Six.) In any case, their long-run interests lie in world agreements, which can provide far greater stability than the United Kingdom market. They may face a period of uncertainty while the promised world (or, failing them, the promised Community-Commonwealth) agreements are worked out. No world agreements can be made without bringing in the United States, the Argentine, and other South American producers, and at least several of the leading Asian countries. Certainly this work should be begun as soon as possible—indeed some of the preparative studies are already under way in various places. But in this field, the complexities are such that, however hard the officials work, and however boldly the politicians act, no agreements—signed, sealed, and delivered—can be expected for at least another three or four years.

One may of course be tempted to say: "Why not wait until all the details are spelled out? Why not wait until the world commodity agreements for temperate foodstuffs are concluded?" In a world in which time stood still, this would be the obvious solution. But that is not the world we live in. If British entry into the Common Market is to have significance for the power structure of the world, if it is to have significance for the rate of growth of her own and of developing countries overseas, she cannot stop the clock in Communist China, or in the undernourished parts of Asia until she has finished negotiations. In external policy, it may be that a sophisticated game of hovering on the brink of the club will give Britain equal weight with its members for a time. Thrusting problems of external relations at the Community before the Six were really ready to face them, Britain has undoubtedly had an influence on their thinking in foreign trade policy in the last few months. But that has been while Britain has had a government which gave the impression even to the Commonwealth prime ministers that it was "hell-bent" on entry, and the foreign-trade decisions she has affected have been provisional decisions conditional on her entry. How long the Six and the Commission would keep the door open, let Britain play this kind of game, and allow her to help define their commercial policy if she is plainly undecided as to whether to go in or not, is a totally different matter.

Moreover, it must be remembered that Britain's entry into the

Community is itself most likely to be a very transitional measure —transitional in the sense that in a few years, the bulk of problems that we are negotiating at the moment will have been transcended. We have seen this time and again in the process of European integration—that negotiations in great detail have taken place, massive diplomatic exercises have been deployed on the basis of a given context, and then—largely because of these negotiations, which seemed politically and psychologically so vital before the crisis—the context has shifted and the whole problem on which so much energy was spent came to look academic and irrelevant. This happened in one way in the case of EDC and EPC, it happened more pertinently in the case of the Saar, and of the escape clauses built into the Rome Treaty to safeguard the French. It is right that this kind of negotiations should be taking place now, and they will have their political and psychological significance. But the historian will see them largely as an exercise in the meeting of minds, an essential exploration together of the implications of a Community including Britain. This is not an argument for taking them less seriously. On the contrary, it is vital that nothing negotiated now should place obstacles in the way of wider and more generous solutions in the future, and that there should be sufficient sign that both the Community and Britain are keeping eyes fixed on these ultimate objectives. But Britain cannot hope to solve all the world's problems in one annex to the Treaty of Rome; and it would be putting the cart before the horse—she wants to enter the Community precisely to help use it as an instrument for resolving world problems—to demand that it solve these problems before she consents to enter it.

The Breakdown of the Negotiations

The foregoing sections of this chapter were written in September, 1962. There followed an intensification of the debate in Britain. At the Brighton Conference of the Labour Party Mr. Hugh Gaitskell, who had clashed violently in the summer with M. Paul-Henri Spaak at a meeting of European Socialists but who had found himself in large agreement with Commonwealth Socialist leaders in September, formally introduced the Labour Party's policy statement, which was opposed to British entry into the Community unless not only the interests of the Commonwealth, of EFTA, and of British agriculture, but also British independence in foreign policy and the right to national planning were safeguarded. But the whole tenor of his speech, which was acclaimed as the greatest triumph of his all too short career, was against British entry on principle: his warnings against reducing Britain to the status of Texas or California and against abandoning "a thousand years of British history" were plainly independent of the particular safeguards subject to negotiation. At the Conservative Conference, on the other hand, Mr. Macmillan and Mr. Heath stated more clearly than ever before that it was essential for Britain to enter the Community. And if, on the Labour side, the deputy leader, Mr. George Brown, gave a very different interpretation of the party's policy statement, and if a few rather ineffectual voices were raised among the Conservatives in defense of British sovereignty, the debate appeared to be becoming more of a straight party one than at any earlier time.

In Brussels, during this period, valuable time was lost. Tense negotiating battles were fought over issues like the common external tariff on tinned kangeroo meat while the greatest outstanding problem, the transitional arrangements for British agriculture, was put off. It was not until January that the British delegation felt able to abandon some of its negotiating positions and to agree that the price mechanism was to begin to help determine farmers' incomes immediately on Britain's entry, so that Britain's transition to the Community system was to be completed by the end of the Community's own transitional period. When Mr. Heath outlined these concessions to M. Couve de Murville on January 11, the latter is said to have replied that now no power on earth could prevent Britain's entry into the Community: Three days later, after President de Gaulle's press conference, the British negotiators remembered rather wryly that qualification of the power now requiring to stop Britain going in.

For the breakup of the negotiations, when it came on January 29, 1963, was the result of factors external to the Brussels negotiations. What passed between Mr. Macmillan and President de Gaulle at their two meetings at Champs early in June and at Rambouillet in the middle of December, 1962 has never been stated clearly in public. It seems, however, that not for the first time at such private "summit meetings" within the Western alliance the two gentlemen chiefly concerned misunderstood each other to the point where both afterwards felt deceived. Mr. Macmillan seems to have gathered that there was no overriding political objection to Britain's entry into the Community provided the economic conditions could be settled; and he also appears to have felt satisfied that he warned President de Gaulle that he was in difficulties with the British independent deterrent. President de Gaulle for his part seems to have gathered at Champs that Mr. Macmillan really accepted the Community in the spirit in which President de Gaulle chose to interpret it, and even that the difficulties over Skybolt would lead to a reappraisal of the Anglo-American special relationship—a reappraisal whose logic would lead to British participation in a purely European (perhaps Franco-British) policy of nuclear defense. But by the time of Rambouillet matters looked different: Mr. Macmillan was sent out shooting on his own all morning, and the most the two leaders could agree on was a repetition of the communiqué of Champs.

There is a good deal of evidence that as late as September, 1962, President de Gaulle, though averse to British entry into the Community, was prepared to resign himself to it. It was not until the late autumn, when the Labour Party seemed to swing decisively against the Common Market and the public opinion polls seemed to justify its stand, when the Brussels negotiations bogged down in details, and when (somewhat to his own surprise) the referendum on the direct election of the French President was followed by the general election landslide that gave President de Gaulle's supporters an absolute majority in the National Assembly, that President de Gaulle's hopes of excluding Britain rose. What perhaps finally made it seem essential to keep Britain out was the agreement between President Kennedy and Mr. Macmillan, concluded on December 21, at Nassau in the Bahamas.

British defense policy had ever since 1957 progressed from failure to failure. That was the year in which the Defense White Paper set out the policy of abolishing conscription (a change popular within Britain), maintaining a mobile specialist force (of the kind that could deal with situations of the Suez type), and laying special emphasis on an independent British deterrent (which should make Britain less vulnerable to nuclear blackmail in Suez-type situations, and maintain British status in the world by a share in the targeting and the world responsibility of Western nuclear power). The amendment of the MacMahon Act allowing nuclear secrets to be shared by the United States with Britain seemed to revive the special wartime relationship between the two Anglo-Saxon powers, and if the Continent felt cheated of British promises on the side of conventional arms and left behind in status by Britain's nuclear efforts, this seemed a minor price to pay.

Unfortunately for British policy there were technical and financial difficulties in pursuing the quest for an independent deterrent. The real technical problem today lies not in producing a bomb, but in producing the means of delivering it onto enemy territory: And the real financial problem today lies in keeping the means of delivery up-to-date, that is in producing successive generations of weapon systems each sufficiently ahead of successive generations of anti-missile weapons to retain a reasonable chance of reaching their target. (There is of course a third, political problem: concerned, not with the way, but the will and the decision actually to launch nuclear weapons in an emergency. Densely populated countries such as those of Europe are bound to look unconvincing in that respect, though of course even a strong possibility may be enough to deter.) By 1960 it was clear that Britain would not be able to afford to develop the Blue Streak missile which was already obsolescent, and so—in the year in which the Labour Party switched into opposing an independent British deterrent—the United States promised that the American Skybolt air-to-ground missile would be provided to maintain a "British" independent deterrent.

During all this period the French were developing their own nuclear bombs, in accordance with a decision taken by the French Socialist Prime Minister, M. Guy Mollet, under the Fourth Republic and maintained by President de Gaulle under the Fifth. For the moment the only means of delivery anywhere near the operational stage are manned bombers: But if the possession of nuclear capability has had no other effect, it has strengthened President de Gaulle's hand vis-à-vis his NATO allies and given him considerable nuisance value in international politics: No disarmament agreement can look convincing without France; no agreement even to ban nuclear tests can be complete without her participation. No wonder, then, if De Gaulle's refusal to cooperate in these fields has drawn irritation from both Britain and the United States.

In May, 1962, President Kennedy in fact came out clearly against the French independent deterrent; and—what is equally interesting in the present context—he did so with arguments which in reality also applied against the British independent deterrent, so long, at least, as it was genuinely independent. In the Cuban crisis, whereas France gave immediate support to the United States, the United Kingdom felt unconsulted and helpless. Just afterwards, Mr. Dean Acheson made a speech that raised hackles in Britain when he declared the obvious truths that Britain had lost an empire and not yet found a new role in the world. And then, on top of these straws in the wind, came the sudden technical discovery that the Skybolt program had to be abandoned, so that the future of the British "independent" deterrent was eliminated as the by-product of an American technical and financial decision. (Matters were not improved when it was found that the President had forbidden Skybolt to be tested again until the new agreement was complete, after which the first successful test of Skybolt took place.)

Mr. Macmillan and President Kennedy met in the Bahamas for four days in December. Mr. Macmillan rejected the President's offer that Skybolt might be developed further, with the United States paying only half the cost, the United Kingdom paying the other half. Instead, he suggested that the international missile, Polaris, which is best launched from submarines, might be made available to Britain. And the two leaders agreed, in the words of their communiqué, that

> a decision on Polaris must be considered in the widest context both of the future defense of the Atlantic Alliance and of the safety of the whole free world. They reached the conclusion that this issue created an opportunity for the development of new and closer arrangements for the organization and control of strategic Western defense and that such arrangements in turn could make a major contribution to political cohesion among the nations of the Alliance.
>
> 6. The Prime Minister suggested, and the President agreed, that for the immediate future a start could be made by subscribing to

NATO some part of the force already in existence. This could include allocations from United States strategic forces, from United Kingdom Bomber Command, and from tactical nuclear forces now held in Europe. Such forces would be assigned as part of a NATO nuclear force and targeted in accordance with NATO plans.

7. Returning to Polaris, the President and the Prime Minister agreed that the purpose of their two governments with respect to the provision of the Polaris missiles must be the development of a multilateral NATO nuclear force in the closest consultation with other NATO allies. They will use their best endeavors to this end.

8. Accordingly, the President and the Prime Minister agreed that the United States will make available on a continuing basis Polaris missiles (less warheads) for British submarines. The United States will also study the feasibility of making available certain support facilities for such submarines. The United Kingdom Government will construct the submarines in which these weapons will be placed and they will also provide the nuclear warheads for the Polaris missiles. British forces developed under this plan will be assigned and targeted in the same way as the forces described in paragraph 6. These forces, and at least equal United States forces, would be made available for inclusion in a NATO multilateral nuclear force. The Prime Minister made it clear that, except where Her Majesty's Government may decide that supreme national interests are at stake, these British forces will be used for the purposes of international defense of the Western alliance in all circumstances.

9. The President and the Prime Minister are convinced that this new plan will strengthen the nuclear defense of the Western alliance. In strategic terms this defense is indivisible and it is their conviction that in all ordinary circumstances of crisis or danger it is this very unity which is the best protection of the West.

10. The President and the Prime Minister agreed that in addition to having a nuclear shield it is important to have a non-nuclear sword. For this purpose they agreed on the importance of increasing the effectiveness of their conventional forces on a world-wide basis.

One can image the effect of this agreement on President de Gaulle. He could hardly believe that such a vital agreement had not been carefully prepared for months in advance—in which case Mr. Macmillan must have been deceiving him deliberately. If on the other hand such an agreement on national self-defense had been reached with the Americans in four days, why had the British been arguing about tariffs and similarly minor matters for eighteen months in Brussels? This was not the European spirit he had hoped for, but a reassertion of the Anglo-American special relationship in a new guise. And if the British had now sold their right to ultimate nuclear self-defense to the Americans, there could be no place for them in a Europe that was to become the equal of the United States, and at the very least their independent partner. He for his part would have none of the Polaris missiles President Kennedy offered him, though it might have looked as if this way his demands for a tripartite leadership of NATO could have been met. Indeed he was barely polite on the offer in the reply he gave in his press conference of January 14.

President de Gaulle, then and since, has been quite unequivocal:

> I repeat what I have often said:—that France intends to have her own national defense. . . . The American nuclear presence does not necessarily and immediately respond to all the eventualities of concern to Europe and France. And so considerations of principle and of circumstances have made us determined to equip ourselves with an atomic force that shall be our own. . . . We have begun, alone and by our own means, to invent, test, and produce atomic bombs and the vehicles to launch them. . . . The French atomic force, from the beginning of its organization, will have the dark and terrible capacity to destroy in a few moments millions and millions of men . . . I do not believe that anyone thinks we could subscribe to the Bahamas agreement. It would really not be of use to buy Polaris missiles when we have neither the submarines to launch them nor the thermonuclear heads to arm them. . . . When, one day, we shall have these submarines and these heads, what will the Polaris be worth then? And at that time anyway we shall probably have rockets of our own invention. So this affair is of no apparent interest to us. What is more, it just does not comply with the principle of which I have just been speaking, which consists in our having at our disposal our own atomic force.

It was at the same press conference that President de Gaulle—with sublime disregard for all that the British negotiators in Brussels had accepted—while ornamenting his rejection of the British candidature to EEC with economic considerations, squarely rejected it on grounds derived from the nature of Britain and the nature of the Common Market itself:

> The Treaty of Rome was concluded between six Continental states, states that are, economically speaking, one may say, of the same nature. Indeed, whether it be a matter of their industrial or

agricultural production, their external exchanges, their habits, or their commercial clientele, their living or working conditions, there is between them much more resemblance than difference. Moreover, they are adjacent, they interpenetrate, they prolong each other through their communications.

It is therefore a fact to group them and to link them in such a way that what they have to produce, to buy, to sell, to consume—well they do produce, buy, sell, consume, in preference in their own ensemble. Doing that is conforming to realities. Moreover, it must be added that from the point of view of their economic development, their social progress, their technical capacity, they are, in short, keeping pace. They are marching in similar fashion.

It so happens, too, that there is between them no kind of political grievance, no frontier question, no rivalry in domination or power. On the contrary, they are joined in solidarity, especially and primarily from the consciousness they have of defining together an important part of the sources of our civilization; and also as concerns their security, because they are Continentals and have before them one and the same menace from one extremity to the other of their territorial whole. Then, finally, they are in solidarity through the fact that not one among them is bound abroad by any particular political or military accord. . . .

Britain posed her candidature to the Common Market after having earlier refused to participate in the Communities we are now building, as well as after creating a free trade area with six other states, and, finally, after having—I may well say it (the negotiations held at such length on this subject will be recalled)—after having put some pressure on the Six to prevent a real beginning being made in the application of the Common Market.

If England asks in turn to enter, but on her own conditions, this poses without doubt to each of the six states, and poses to England problems of a very great dimension. England in effect is insular, she is maritime, she is linked through her exchanges, her markets, her supply lines to the most diverse and often the most distant countries; she pursues essentially industrial and commercial activities and only slight agricultural ones. She has in all her doings very marked and very original habits and traditions.

In short, the nature, the structure, the very situation that are England's differ profoundly from those of the Continentals. What is to be done in order that England, as she lives, produces, and trades, can be incorporated into the Common Market, as it has been conceived and as it functions? The question, to know whether Great Britain can now place herself like the Continent and with it inside a tariff which is genuinely common, to renounce all Commonwealth preferences, to cease any pretense that her agriculture be privileged, and, more than that, to treat her engagements with other countries of the free trade area as null and void—that question is the whole question.

It cannot be said that it is yet resolved. Will it be so one day? Obviously only England can answer. The question is even further posed since after England other states which are, I repeat, linked to her through the free trade area, for the same reasons as Britain, would like or wish to enter the Common Market.

It must be agreed that first the entry of Great Britain, and then these states, will completely change the whole of the actions, the agreements, the compensation, the rules that have already been established between the Six, because all these states, like Britain, have very important peculiarities. Then it will be another Common Market whose construction ought to be envisaged: But one which would be taken to eleven and then thirteen and then perhaps eighteen would no longer resemble, without any doubt, the one which the Six built.

Further, this Community, increasing in such fashion, would see itself faced with problems of economic relations with all kinds of other states, and first with the United States. It is to be foreseen that the cohesion of its members, who would be very numerous and diverse, would not endure for long, and that ultimately it would appear as a colossal Atlantic Community under American dependence and direction, and which would quickly have absorbed the Community of Europe.

It is a hypothesis which in the eyes of some can be perfectly justified, but it is not at all what France is doing or wanted to do—and which is a strictly European construction.

The other five governments of the Community attempted, in the negotiations at Brussels that opened next morning, to ignore the French President's press conference and to carry on with the negotiations. The Franco-German Treaty of friendship was signed as planned on January 22, and Dr. Adenauer went through the motions at least of trying to modify the French President's stand. But feverish diplomatic activity failed to find anything but a face-saving formula: And on January 29, 1963, the negotiations begun on October 10, 1961, ended when the seventeenth ministerial meeting of these negotiations was declared closed with a statement from the Belgian Chairman simply that "the member states of the EEC are prevented from continuing the negotiations on the accession of the United Kingdom."

VIII

Patterns of the Future

The failure of the Brussels negotiations marks the end of a phase. Neither Britain nor the European Community will ever be the same again; President Kennedy's "Grand Design" lies shattered, and the Western alliance has never been in such grave disarray. For many, this is a moment of deep pessimism and confusion. But need it really be?

Perhaps indeed we have been here before. Eight years ago, when the French National Assembly rejected the European Defense Community, all hopes of seeing the ancient enemies in Europe reconciled and working together as an integrated team seemed dashed to the ground. But less than a year afterward, the Six met at Messina and resolved to set up the Common Market—and until early 1963 this new, far more radical plan that is far more rooted in material interest and in popular imagination—this Economic Community progressed from success to success. In fact, let no one be under any illusion: In spite of any little local difficulty, in spite of any recent setback, there is a groundswell of revolution at work in the Western world today. It may be less dramatic than the Communist Revolution of 1917, less spectacular than the process of decolonization in Asia and Africa—but it is at least equally profound.

A hundred and seventy-four years ago the French Revolution spread the germ of nationalism first into Europe and then, in this century, out into the rest of the world. The nation-state was well adapted to progress in the nineteenth century. But when we failed to transcend it in the first half of the twentieth, two world wars resulted; the West was tarred with Auschwitz and Hiroshima; the world was split into at least a Communist and a Western bloc; and nationalism has come to condition the emotional responses of most of the economically underdeveloped parts of the world. But today, this new European revolution is eroding nationalism in Europe—and can, I believe, spread out from Europe to counter nationalism with a new ideal—with the Community concept.

We have seen how, at the end of the Second World War, progressive opinion all over the world looked for a new world order to abolish war and to harness world resources to the works of peace. Measured by these high hopes, the United Nations, for all its value, proved a sad disappointment; by 1947 it was clear that greater cooperation would be possible only on a smaller scale, and the federalists in Europe embarked on a pilot project for wider institutions.

Now some of them began this task with the same misconceptions, the same false hopes with which the world federalists had been cursed: the illusion that by creating common institutions you could somehow permanently paper over real clashes of interest and real divergences of outlook. Calling as they did for a United States of Europe to be set up more or less at one stroke they, just like the world federalists, were in for speedy disillusion. Federalism had its virtues in the eighteenth century and there may be parts of the world for which it is eminently suitable even today. But the people who are building the new Europe—even though some of them have called themselves federalists—are in fact tackling the problem in a totally different way.

These new "Europeans" are being far more practical, far more empirical, far more gradual in their approach. They recognize the reality of the nation-state and they do not believe that common institutions set up in a vacuum, can somehow create a common interest: They believe that common institutions must be developed concurrently with common interests and must interact with them, intensify them and thereby make further common institutions both necessary and practicable. So they use a pragmatic, functional technique, exploiting particular tactical situations in order to set up new institutions, which have helped solve other problems but have also in their turn themselves raised new problems that can be resolved only by further snowball progress along this same road.

This movement of European integration has in fact taken the form of a dialectic, of thesis and antithesis that can be reconciled only by a new imaginative step forward onto a higher level of integration each time. It started from the bottom upwards with the problem of the Ruhr. After the Second World War the Allies were determined that Germany must never regain control of her coal and steel resources. But one can not discriminate against any one country forever; any attempt to do that would breed precisely the sort of resentment, precisely the sort of new explosion it was designed to prevent. And to this antithesis was only one synthesis: that other nations should abdicate the same measure of control over their coal and steel resources that they intended the Germans never to regain. This precisely was the achievement of the Schuman Plan.

The institution of the Coal and Steel Community really had two main effects. The only territorial dispute between France and Germany at the conclusion of the Second World War was over the Saar—a territory that only matters because of the coal and steel it produces. Once coal and steel were pooled anyway between France, Germany, and other Community partners, this bitter dispute suddenly became not so much solved as dissolved: The shift in the whole context of Franco-German relations made the quarrel over coal and steel meaningless, and so the path lay open for further agreement between these two historic enemies.

The other effect of the Coal and Steel Community consisted not in the problems the Community solved, but in the new problems it raised—consisted in fact in the planned anomaly of this partial economic integration itself. How could there be a common policy for coal when there was none for oil or for natural gas or for atomic energy, when there was no harmonization of transport and no harmonization of labor policy? And if transport rates and labor policy are harmonized for coal and for steel, how can the rest of transport and labor policy continue to diverge? Again it was progress by a dialectical process; and from integration in two sectors of the economy the Six went forward to their general Economic Community.

At this point one must look for a moment at the institutional technique of this Community method of integration. It has, I think, three features remarkable above all.

First, each Treaty setting up one of the three existing Communities contains a rigid backbone of precise commitments—in the case of EEC a detailed twelve-year plan agreed on in advance, signed, sealed, and delivered come what may. (It was laid down for example that the common external tariff for dead poultry and edible offals thereof [except livers] fresh, chilled, or frozen would, as from January 1, 1960, be 18 per cent.)

But then joined to this rigid backbone of precise commitments there are what I would like to call the muscles: agreements, not on matters of substance, but simply agreements-to-agree on common policies hereafter by certain procedures and by certain deadlines. If all the problems that might be encountered in circumstances as yet unforeseen had been debated in 1956 in the detailed way attempted in the recent Brussels negotiations, the drafting of the Rome Treaty would still be going on today. As it is the agreed backbone of precise obligations does two things. On the one side it forces the pace for further mutual commitments as time goes on; it steps up the need to agree on joint policies. On the other hand it also facilitates such further agreements through the sheer passage of time, through consolidating mutual confidence between the countries working together within the Community, and through increasing the congruence of their substantial interests.

Then, thirdly, the Treaty sets up Community institutions independent of the member governments. It is these institutions that propose the policies, it is they that act, if one may continue the metaphor, as the brain that directs the muscles within the limits set by the skeleton Treaty. Such Community policies can and must be framed, not to reconcile the different national policies that are designed to solve partial problems or even to deflect them on to the next country, but to deal with the problem itself as it presents itself at Community level and to deal with it from a Community point of view, in the interests of all the Community's citizens regardless of nationality. But the final decisions on these major policies are not taken by the Commission of the Community itself, but by the national governments in the Council of Ministers.

In the Council, at the beginning, any one government could veto the Commission's proposals. But as time goes on votes on a vast range of subjects need not be taken unanimously any more: A qualified majority is sufficient, so that it takes at least two governments to veto a proposal, not counting Luxembourg, and even all three Benelux states can be overruled. The date from which a qualified majority of governments is sufficient to decide on the Commission's proposals varies with the field of action concerned: On cartels it was January, 1961; on foreign trade it will be 1966; on a whole range of other matters, 1970. The Treaty thus commits the governments to what we have called not simply a scale, but an escalator of supranationality. Here again this is not a federal structure but a Community system *sui generis,* in which the Community organs propose but the national governments dispose according to voting rules drawn up with a time dimension, rules that progressively limit the veto power of any one state alone.

So far then, one may draw two main conclusions: first, that the Community method of integration with its permanent dialogue between national governments and Community organs is quite different in its constitutional ideas and objectives from the notion of federation; and second, that in its method, so far from setting up once and for all a definitive constitution of any kind, the Community technique has shown and is still showing a continuing dynamic of its own, and has advanced in intensity over the past. But one can also ask how far this Community technique differs from federalism not only in tending to increase in intensity with time, but also in its capacity, or even its tendency, to expand in space: And it looks as if the Community dialectic is in fact already beginning to operate outward from Europe, involving wider circles of the rest of the world in the process of recognizing common responsibilities that can be met only by joint action.

Indeed it is noteworthy that—regardless of its recent failure—it seems that Britain's application has triggered off vitally important irreversible processes here. I argued earlier that the negotiations for Britain's entry into the Community, beginning as they did as negotiations to fit Britain into the Community of Europe turned very quickly, thanks to Britain's overseas commitments, into negotiations on how to fit the European Community into the world economy at large. From the antithesis between intra-Commonwealth preferential arrangements and extra-Community non-discrimination there could be only one logical way out in Brussels: to submerge Britain's demands for preferential trade and commodity guarantees into world-wide solutions to world-wide trade and commodity problems.

Now one may say that all the agreements that were reached in Brussels were provisional, or rather they were conditional on Britain's entering the European Community. So, formally, they were. And now that that old opponent of the European Community, President de Gaulle, is attempting to usurp and bend the Community to his own purposes, to make it a *masse de manoeuvre* untrammelled by links with what he calls "the Anglo-Saxons" and a third force in the world, now that he is claiming the right to a foreign policy independent of the Community, which Britain always claimed, and is using the national veto still allowed in the Rome Treaty on the admission of new members, surely, one might say, the whole exercise of Britain's application to join has been in vain. Are we not right back where we started from?

Certainly not. And that simply because, the British, after a decade of never having had it so good, have suddenly acquired a new superego, an image of themselves as "outward-looking" which might help them shortly to become that; but also because on the Continent too there is no turning the clock back. The British application has served as a catalyst—and five of the Six are now coming to realize that you cannot apply the Community spirit inside one half of Western Europe and still continue to bargain in the old balance-of-power terms with the rest of the world. Britain's exclusion by a political veto has thus become the symbol for an attitude toward Europe's place in world politics, particularly also in the sphere of defense.

Moreover, whatever the state of public opinion in Britain, as a result of efforts by those on the Continent who hoped that Britain would bring to the Community her own conceptions of parliamentary democracy, Britain's application has also become symbolic of an attitude toward the internal structure of the new Europe, while President de Gaulle's political veto—both in its form and in its foreign policy content—has hit at the heart of the whole give-and-take style of Community politics, has in fact ranged France over against the whole spirit of the European Community. Those who built the European Community regarded it always—and they said so quite clearly in the preambles to their Treaties and in all their speeches—as bound to lead to a Political Community, a Community in which in the last resort a European parliament would be directly elected and a European executive would be directly responsible to it. Now, today, over against that democratic concept of a Political Community, President de Gaulle has set up the concept of a Political Union, a misleading word if ever there was one, a Union in which in fact the heads of state or heads of government would make the decisions, in which the fundamental relationships are not those between the peoples, the citizens of the Community, but between the sovereign national governments. Each of these national governments may be individually controlled in greater or lesser degree by its national parliament, but in distinction to this several control, no attempt even is made at a common parliamentary control over decisions that in the last resort have to be taken in common. This is a system in which the Franco-German Treaty of January, 1963, could be an adequate substitute for multilateral relationships, in which in fact the old concept of alliances (which in the last resort, as Bismarck told us, always have a horse and a rider) is perhaps multilateralized, but the ultimate right of the nation-state to make its own decisions and the veto right for a minority to block the will of a majority is never compromised at all.

So while this clash between the concept of Political Community on the one side and the concept of Political Union on the other has been starkly revealed over the past year or so in Europe—even more bluntly, even more harshly has the British application laid bare the rival conceptions of Europe's external role in the world, Europe's role in economics, Europe's role in foreign policy and Europe's role in defense. On the one side again there is the Atlantic concept that men like Jean Monnet have always held, the concept of a Europe which, as a second pillar within the

Atlantic alliance, helps the United States to bear the responsibilities that fall on the industrial non-Communist countries of the world *vis-à-vis* both the Communist and the underdeveloped parts of the world. And on the other side there is the Gaullist concept which perhaps is stated often in oracular fashion by President de Gaulle but which is certainly very different from the concept of a Europe that seeks not only to integrate itself but that also seeks to integrate itself into the wider tasks of the world around us.

There are perhaps four possible interpretations of what President de Gaulle is after. A minimalist interpretation would be that President de Gaulle is really, with all his grand gestures, still today trying above all not to wreck NATO but on the contrary to build it on a more equitable, a more rational basis, to achieve that directorate of three—the United States, Britain, and France—that he asked for the moment he came into power and that seeks simply to give the Europeans a greater share in the running of the Western alliance. Then there is an intermediate interpretation of what President de Gaulle is thinking, what in fact he said in his press conference on January 14, 1962. What was worrying him there was the inevitability (or the high probability) of a United States withdrawal from Europe: Now that the United States can hit the Soviet Union with atomic weapons without using Europe as an airfield, Europe seems to have become expendable; and now that in return the Soviet Union can hit the United States, any guarantees to Europe, President de Gaulle believes, must seem to lack credibility. Where, twelve years ago, Europeans feared that the United States might be too trigger-happy, today some of them—like President de Gaulle—fear that the Americans might be thought too slow on the draw. Behind that, though not so clearly expressed of course for diplomatic reasons, there is a third preoccupation—the fear that the United States may one day make a deal with the Russians behind Europe's back, that Kennedy and Khruschev are bound in the long run to get together at the expense of their respective satellite allies. And then, as the maximal interpretation of what De Gaulle is after, there is the obverse of his fear of an American deal with the Russians behind the backs of the Europeans—the vision of a European understanding with the Russians independent of America, his old concept of a Europe from the Atlantic to the Urals, from Cadiz to Vladivostock.

We need not really ask which one of these four interpretations is correct and which three are wrong. In the short run all four might be compatible lines of thinking and compatible aims to pursue; and it would be like President de Gaulle, it would be like any politician or any good chess player, to be thinking of all four alternative later policies simultaneously, to threaten all four at a time and to make sure that he debars himself from none of them through any move he makes now. But none of them—certainly not the last three, which rest in the last analysis on mutual suspicion between America and Europe—none of these is a policy that France's partners in the Community really at present want to share. That is why Britain's application and her insistence in economics that the Community cannot do what President de Gaulle in his press conference asked it to do—to produce and sell and buy and consume all within one tight little area, to pursue its own independent foreign policy and its own independent defense policy—that is why Britain's stance toward the European Continent will remain of vital significance in the years to come.

In fact this is the point where we have to think back to what it was that made Britain want to link up with Europe in the first place. It was after all meant as the first step in an openly declared political strategy to meet the real challenge of this seventh decade of the twentieth century. The really big issues facing Britain now would seem to be three: defense and disarmament and Britain's whole relationship with Communist China and the Soviet Union; secondly, trade and aid and her relations with the underdeveloped two-thirds of the world; and thirdly, her economic growth and stability within the West as a whole, by which her capacity and her manner of dealing with the other two problems will largely be conditioned. On some of these problems she can go far on a European basis, but beyond that European unity can only be a step on the road. Basically, however, Britain must remember that it is not any institution that she has set up to meet these problems—it is the sheer scale of the problems themselves that has made her interdependent; and the common institutions are simply an attempt to catch up with these hard realities, to recognize the political nature of these problems, and to give the British the chance to formulate joint policies democratically and effectively in order to solve them.

So, while obviously there is scope for pressing on with smaller specific projects—such as building a supersonic airliner with France, collaborating on the peaceful uses of atomic energy with Euratom, perhaps digging a channel tunnel—the next real new initiative toward the European Six will have to be along political, along institutional lines.

Simply to have another series of treaties like the Franco-German Treaty of January between the Six and Britain might be a start, but it would not solve the problem: Not only would it suggest that all European school children should learn four second languages, but a whirl of bilateral consultations with foreign ministers chasing each other around Europe would soon have to lead to a central multilateral forum of just the kind that the old proposals for Political Union amounted to.

But what Britain can do is this: President de Gaulle says Britain is not mature enough for the Community. Surely she can show herself far more ready to adopt a Community approach than De Gaulle. The Political Community planned by the Six cannot be realized while President de Gaulle maintains his present stand. But is it too fanciful to suggest that Britain prepare the ground at least for a Political Union along the lines that President de Gaulle himself has been putting forward over the past two years and propose similar or even more far-reaching consultation on foreign affairs and cooperation in culture and education with any European countries willing to take part? And could Britain not, for good measure, also lay far more stress than De Gaulle on the role, in all this, of parliamentary institutions? Perhaps Britain should invite all European countries willing to join, or perhaps she should get the Italians or the Germans to act as the sponsors. But what matters is that she should rally her friends on the Continent by proving that her application to Europe is not just commercial bargain-hunting but is a political act, and that she is genuinely concerned with furthering the political unity of Europe.

Now I fear that this kind of initiative may embarrass President de Gaulle. But if someone is pursuing a policy that is the opposite of one's own, and by methods incompatible with what one believes should become accepted international style, then—while embarrassment is certainly not one's object, it may be an unavoidable by-product of doing what one considers to be right. That does not mean that one would fall into a policy of diplomatic pin-pricks against France; but there is every reason for Britain to stand by the Community concept that largely initiated from France and which many of the most influential men on the Continent are still—in spite of President de Gaulle—striving to realize. If Britain stands on Community principles and then finds that President de Gaulle has isolated himself, it certainly will not be her fault.

The other subject on which the other five and Britain hold closely allied views that are rather different from President de Gaulle's is defense. Could Britain not try then to think through the possibility of applying the Community method in Europe to conventional defense—of which Europe will have to provide far more in the future? Britain seems after all to have begun in the process of negotiation to apply a similar technique within NATO to the Western deterrent. More and more this terrible subject will prove the key to Britain's relations with Europe as with America, and clearly this is a field in which the real debate is still to come.

Now as far as Europe is concerned, both on the side of foreign policy and of defense, there is already one organization that links Britain with the Six: Western European Union, the old Brussels Treaty of 1948 that was revamped after the defeat of EDC. WEU has some substantial advantages: It exists, Britain is in it, and so are the French: So no great new treaties would have to be signed, and if things were to go wrong it would not be France rebuffing Britain from a new body, but France walking out and leaving an empty chair in an existing concern. WEU has an Assembly of Parliamentarians, it has a small independent secretariat—it has (on paper at any rate) economic objectives as well as political ones, and it also (again on paper) has majority voting on certain matters of defense. If you took it literally, in fact, Britain, Italy, Holland, and Luxembourg—those four—would be sufficient under the Treaty, to force President de Gaulle to remove his nuclear weapons from the Continent of Europe and station them in Guadeloupe or on the Ile du Levant. But the trouble is that WEU has always been used as a safety net of last resort in Europe; it has never had real life to it, and Britain herself has hardly taken it very seriously in the past. So the Continent would need a great deal of convincing, if Britain did try to revive this all but moribund body, that—this time—she did mean it.

Over and above foreign policy coordination in Europe and these rather more Community-type approaches to defense, there are three other points one could put forward in a five-point program—initiatives that all go beyond Europe itself. On trade between industrial countries Britain should give every support to the Kennedy round of tariff negotiations—and at least till 1966 they will be very difficult indeed. But why does Britain not make a start by offering to reciprocate any tariff cuts up to fifty per cent right across the board—provided EEC and the U.S.A. do the same? She would have to pair that probably with another attempt at establishing a more flexible world payments system. Then, fourthly, she should go on pressing for the comprehensive commodity and trade agreements that she was working her way toward in Brussels—particularly those on tropical produce and those meant to increase the export opportunities of the countries just starting to industrialize: maybe Britain should feel less cagey, too, about the proposals that would ease the lingering malnutrition in large parts of the world with the Western surplusses of temperate foodstuffs—even if it did cost Britain, as the largest food importer, a good deal of foreign exchange. And fifthly, following the Six, she should give fair representation to the developing countries in effective bodies to deal with world development strategy.

There is no space here to elaborate such notions in detail, and in a sense it would be self-contradictory when advocating a Community approach also to define the exact stages to be gone through or the precise shape of the final solution—indeed perhaps even to believe that there could be anything like a "final solution" in our lifetime. The whole point of the Community approach is its flexible step-by-step character, and as Dag Hammarskjöld once said: "Working at the edge of the development of human society is to work on the brink of the unknown." But what is clear is that the functional attack on all these problems—just like the Economic Community in Europe—will have political implications, this time on a far wider scale. Commodity arrangements and world development plans will require institutions to group together the interested industrial and developing countries on a basis of equality: And the more such important problems are dealt with by Community-type institutions, the more urgent will democratic supervision become. The existing Community institutions with their links to associated Africa, the Commonwealth consultative machinery, and other existing regional bodies could thus be reconstituted along Community lines, and could form, with revamped organs of the United Nations, a network of overlapping circles, untidy perhaps, but with an untidiness that reflects the functional character of each body, tailored in composition and structure precisely to fulfill a particular concrete task.

Here it seems to me lies the answer to President de Gaulle's trend of thinking, which tries to pervert the functional Economic Community and solidify a Continental regional bloc. He may well (as some people think) have a farsighted political strategy in mind: the conception of a Europe some day stretching from the Atlantic to the Urals, in which Soviet Russia would take her place in meeting the threat from Red China that De Gaulle—and perhaps now Khrushchev—see as a threat to Eastern and Western Europe alike. Such a conception of Europe as a third force between the United States and Communist China may well presuppose the exclusion of the Anglo-Saxons from the Continental unit. But the real problem is not even whether, in the short run, one half of Western Europe has the resources to pass through the intermediate phase of only loose links to the Anglo-Saxon world; the real problem is what sort of a partnership it could be, between Russia on the one hand and France, Germany, and their allies on the other: and even thereafter, in the long run, whther the ultimate problem of Communist China can really be best approached through building a third, larger European bloc inclusive of Russia. Surely, if we want to speculate that far ahead, the Soviet Union will find it far easier to work with non-Communist countries gradually on a functional basis in different wider organizations in which common interests are involved, than to join a European regional unit. And in the last resort surely it will be easier to work with Communist China on a similar functional basis organized on a world scale. Not the least object of this whole construction of interlocking frameworks is, after all, precisely to soften the crystallization of the world into sharply defined power blocs.

Perhaps we do not yet have to look quite that far ahead—though it is always worth leaving open the way for one's next move but one. But what is immediately relevant to our situation is this: Britain may not be able to join the Common Market, but that does not exhaust its challenge to her political creativity. The point of the Community is not that it has built a new bloc of its own in the old balance-of-power game, from which Britain is now excluded, but that it has pioneered a new approach designed to transcend power politics as such. What matters is not so much its regional, as its functional character, not the unit it has built, but the process it has set rolling. This process must not be hemmed in and confined to one half of Western Europe, nor must it exhaust itself in a purely Atlantic framework.

The Community dialectic has never worked by historic inevitability but has at each stage required hard effort of intellectual planning and political will. It could be Britain's greatest task today to work with all those who reject the formation of a new, larger, sovereign Continental unit, and who work on the contrary—and far more corrosively—for the dissolution of uniquely independent sovereign units and the substitution of functionally oriented, democratically controlled and geographically interlocking institutions as the basis—indeed in large measure also as the form—of a higher, more civilized, even perhaps a more democratically responsible world order.

All this, of course one may say, is very high-minded—but is it practical politics? Will public opinion ever wear iniatives of this kind? The answer depends on what one regards as the alternative to taking such action. So far as I can see, the chief alternative is taking no action at all. Surely the electorates would rather vote for a bold policy than for no policy: And particularly in foreign affairs Commonwealth countries are looking for leadership. Nor should our timetable today be set by the more timid interpreters of domestic politics: We should worry far more about the precipitate speed of events in Africa, Latin America, Southeast Asia, and in Communist China. It is on these external factors that our survival depends—and we may not have much time to lose.

INDEX